RESEARCH IN ACCOUNTING REGULATION

Volume 11 • 1997

RESEARCH IN ACCOUNTING REGULATION

Editor: GARY JOHN PREVITS
Weatherhead School of Management
Department of Accountancy
Case Western Reserve University

Associate Editor: LARRY M. PARKER
Weatherhead School of Management
Case Western Reserve University

Assistant Editor: THOMAS R. ROBINSON
School of Business Administration
University of Miami, Coral Gables

VOLUME 11 • 1997

JAI PRESS INC.

Greenwich, Connecticut *London, England*

55 Old Post Road, No. 2
Greenwich, Connecticut 06830

JAI PRESS LTD.
38 Tavistock Street
Covent Garden
London WC2E 7PB
England

ISBN: 0-7623-0168-6
ISSN: 1052-0457

Manufactured in the United States of America

CONTENTS

LIST OF CONTRIBUTORS

Jerry Arnold	Leventhal School of Accounting University of Southern California
Dennis R. Beresford	Financial Accounting Standards Board
Debra Burke	College of Business Western Carolina University
E. James Burton	Middle Tennessee State University
Ronald L. Campbell	Department of Accounting North Carolina A&T
Anthony Catanach	University of Virginia McIntire School
Barbara Clemenson	Department of Accounting Case Western Reserve University
Mark DeFond	Leventhal School of Accounting University of Southern California
Michael Ettredge	School of Business University of Kansas
Ross D. Fuerman	Department of Accounting Suffolk University
Steven L. Harris	KPMG Peat Marwick Chicago
William H. Holder	Leventhal School of Accounting University of Southern California
Philip Little	College of Business Western Carolina University

Michael W. Maher Graduate School of Management
University of California—Davis

Dale E. Marxen Accounting Department
Mankato State University

Keith A. Moreland School of Management
University of Michigan—Flint

Obeua S. Persons College of Business Administration
Rider University

Thomas R. Robinson Department of Accounting
University of Miami, Coral Gables

Georgia Saemann School of Business Administration
University of Wisconsin—Milwaukee

Mark A. Segal Department of Accounting
University of South Alabama

David B. Smith Department of Accounting
University of Dayton

Research in Accounting Regulation, Volume 11

INVITED REFEREES

Michael Barrett, Esq.
Private practice, Washington, D.C.

John Brozovsky
Virginia Polytechnical Institute and State College

Robert Cohen, Esq.
Ernst & Young

Donald Chapin
United States General Accounting Office, retired

Jeanne Calderon
New York University

Ray Dever
Coopers & Lybrand

Michael Dugan
University of Alabama

Dale Flesher
University of Mississippi

Thomas Frecka
University of Notre Dame

Julia Grant
Case Westeren Reserve University

Larry Handler
Remington Products Co.

Thomas A. Lee
University of Alabama

Carl D. Liggio
Dickinson, Wright, Moon, Van Dusen & Freeman

Stephen E. Loeb
University of Maryland at College Park

Timothy Lucas
Financial Accounting Standards Board

Frank Nekracz
Michigan Technological University

Terrence O'Keefe
University of Oregon

Karen Pincus
University of Arkansas

Marilyn Pendergast
Urbach, Kahn & Werlin

Arnold Schneider
Georgia Institute of Technology

Mark Segal
University of South Alabama

Jerry Strawser
University of Houston

Doyle Z. Williams
University of Arkansas

Stephen Young
Arthur Andersen & Co.

PART I

MAIN PAPERS

THE POLICY IMPLICATIONS OF LEGISLATING ACCOUNTING CHANGE:

THE CASE OF S&L GOODWILL AND TAX NOLs

Anthony H. Catanach, Jr.

ABSTRACT

The Supreme Court recently ruled that the U.S. government breached its contracts with several acquirers of insolvent savings and loans (S&Ls, thrifts) when it mandated goodwill write-offs in 1989. This study shows that investors recorded tax attributes (net operating losses and built-in losses) received in these regulatory-assisted mergers as goodwill. Consequently, goodwill write-offs were overstated by the value of tax attributes and regulatory enforcement actions against many S&Ls may have been premature. This study's results will interest regulators, thrift owners, and lawyers who currently are litigating "breach of contract" suits. The study also provides insights into the interaction of legislative policy with accounting, the regulatory process, and the general conduct of business.

Research in Accounting Regulation, Volume 11, pages 3-23.

ISBN: 0-7623-0168-6

INTRODUCTION

During the 1980s, the Federal Savings and Loan Insurance Corporation (FSLIC) promoted mergers of financially troubled savings and loans (S&Ls, thrifts) in which institution liabilities exceeded assets. For accounting purposes, the acquiring entity recorded the excess of liabilities assumed over assets acquired (excess purchase price) as goodwill. Acquirers often paid this excess purchase price to receive tax attributes such as net operating loss carryovers and built-in losses (NOLs).[1] However, accounting standards at that time generally precluded these tax benefits from being recorded as tax assets unless their realization was assured beyond any reasonable doubt.[2] Consequently, NOLs also were recorded as goodwill.

In 1989 Congress enacted the Financial Institutions Reform and Recovery Act (FIRREA). FIRREA required S&Ls to delete from their books any recorded goodwill from failing thrift acquisitions during the 1980s. The resulting goodwill write-offs forced hundreds of S&Ls into insolvency. If tax benefits were recorded as goodwill, then the write-offs were overstated by the value of the NOLs. Thus, regulators may have taken enforcement action prematurely based on understated equity measures that did not consider the NOLs as assets.

In recent years, the owners of these "insolvent" S&Ls filed over 100 claims against the federal government alleging that the 1989 regulatory goodwill accounting change represented a "breach" of their original acquisition agreements.[3] In August 1995, the U.S. Court of Appeals for the Federal Circuit found the government liable, and ordered the U.S. Court of Federal Claims to hold a trial to set damages. In July 1996, the U.S. Supreme Court endorsed the appellate court's decision.

This study argues that tax benefits recorded as goodwill be considered in the estimation of future damage awards. To support this argument, this investigation uses an ordinary least squares (OLS) model to examine the association between recorded S&L goodwill and net operating loss tax benefits. Research results indicate that recorded goodwill is significantly and positively associated with the acquisition of net operating losses and deposit liabilities. Since none of the sample's thrifts reported deferred tax assets related to acquired tax losses, the findings support the argument that tax assets were recorded as goodwill in thrift balance sheets.

Accountants, investors, lawyers, legislators, and regulators will appreciate this study for the insights it provides into the interaction of legislation with accounting and the regulatory process. It will be particularly useful to parties involved in litigating damages related to goodwill write-off claims. The paper also suggests that the Supreme Court's recent ruling may be applicable to other industries including utilities, telecommunications, health care, and defense.

The remainder of this paper is organized as follows: (1) the government's contract with thrift acquirers, (2) assessing damages in goodwill write-off claims, (3) testing the goodwill/tax loss relation, (4) policy implications of legislating accounting change, and (5) a summary.

THE GOVERNMENT'S CONTRACT WITH THRIFT ACQUIRERS

Background

During the 1980s, the FSLIC faced the enormous task of resolving hundreds of bankrupt thrifts.[4] Since the agency itself was facing insolvency, liquidating all of the failed S&Ls was not possible. Unfortunately, the FSLIC found few willing "buyers" for these institutions since their value was frequently less than nothing. The deposit insurer was forced to offer financial assistance and regulatory forbearances to induce investors to take these S&Ls off the government's hands. Frequently, the FSLIC provided acquirers limited amounts of cash and callable FSLIC notes to bring an institution's net worth to zero. The agency also gave acquirers "capital loss coverage" or "yield maintenance payments" on problem assets. However, as the FSLIC's available cash resources dwindled, it relied increasingly on tax incentives to market insolvent S&Ls.

Despite these incentives, the fair value of liabilities assumed by acquirers in these assisted combinations usually exceeded the fair value of the tangible and identified intangible assets acquired.[5] For accounting purposes, this excess constitutes goodwill (supervisory goodwill in assisted S&L transactions).[6] Under most agreements, investors also could elect to amortize the intangible over periods up to 40 years. In short, if a healthy S&L was willing to absorb a distressed thrift, regulators allowed the acquirer to record goodwill to meet capital standards. By the middle of 1989, 749 S&Ls carried $19.7 billion in goodwill on their books. This intangible represented nearly 35% of the industry's capital (Wyatt 1989).

With the FSLIC's insolvency, Congress enacted FIRREA in 1989. In addition to increasing capital requirements, limiting investment powers, and strengthening enforcement in thrifts, this legislation reduced the total amount of goodwill that thrifts could include in capital and accelerated its amortization. This accounting change was prompted by warnings that the billions of dollars in goodwill carried on thrift books was simply an "accounting gimmick being used to hide losses" (Knight 1996). FIRREA also directed the Office of Thrift Supervision (OTS) to define the level and type of goodwill to be allowed as assets, and required institutions to eliminate all supervisory goodwill by 1994 (White 1991). Following FIRREA's enactment, the OTS and the Federal Deposit Insurance Corporation (FDIC), the FSLIC's successor, quickly enforced the new rules.

Breach of Contract

FIRREA's goodwill write-offs reduced net worth below required capital minimums in many institutions forcing the closure of hundreds of thrifts. Benjamin Franklin Federal Savings and Loan of Portland, Oregon eliminated $287.7 million in goodwill from its balance sheet in 1989, contributing to a net loss of $377.1 million (*Wall Street Journal*, April 17, 1990). Shortly after the write-off, the institution was subjected to regulatory enforcement action.

Glendale Federal Bank of California recorded more than $700 million in goodwill in its acquisition of a failing Florida thrift in 1981. FIRREA's required write-offs substantially eroded Glendale's capital levels. The institution shrunk its asset size to meet its minimum capital-to-assets ratio. To reduce its size, Glendale sold assets at a loss creating additional earnings pressures for the thrift (Barrett 1996a).

These thrifts and many others believed that they had an agreement with the government concerning the accounting treatments accorded to goodwill. They perceived FIRREA and its subsequent enforcement as a breach of that contract. As a result, they sued the OTS, FDIC, and the U.S. government, asking that their original acquisition assistance agreements be enforced or that they be provided some other form of damages or restitution (Nielsen 1992).[7]

Lower Court Decisions

By the middle of 1992, only a few of the goodwill cases had been resolved. In February 1992, the U.S. Claims Court ruled that the government must pay damages to Winstar Corporation. The court found that the government abrogated the right of Winstar's subsidiary, United Federal Savings Bank, to include its goodwill in capital (McNamee 1992). One month later, a Federal District Court in Oregon held that investors in Far West Federal Bank were entitled to have their agreement with the government rescinded and receive restitution of their $27 million investment (Nielsen 1992).[8] Then, in August 1995, the U.S. Court of Appeals for the Federal Circuit ruled in favor of Glendale Federal Bank of California and two failed thrifts. This decision freed Glendale to pursue its $1.9 billion damage claim in the U.S. Court of Federal Claims (Seiberg 1995a).

Although the assistance agreements in these cases differ significantly, the decisions reached are consistent on several points. First, the government contracted with investors when it allowed them to record goodwill as assets and include it in capital. While FIRREA may have rendered performance impossible, it did not excuse the government from providing damages or restitution to injured investors. The courts also rejected the government's argument that goodwill agreements were not enforceable contracts. The government countered by arguing that investor claims were barred by the "sovereign acts doctrine," which states that the government's authority to act in a sovereign capacity cannot be restricted by contract. However, the courts rejected this argument also indicating that goodwill contracts do not restrict the government's regulatory authority. They noted that the government has a dual capacity in contract cases: that of a sovereign entity and that of a contractor subject to the same obligations as any private contractor.

Other Interested Parties

By the middle of 1995, over 100 more thrifts filed claims against the government on the goodwill issue. The Glendale ruling made it likely that the $130 billion S&L cleanup cost would rise by as much as $20 billion since many of these thrifts would collect judgments (Lowenstein 1995). However, banks, shareholders of failed thrifts, and venture capitalists also have interests in this litigation (Seiberg 1995b). Large banks like First Union Corporation, NationsBank Corporation, and Shawmut National Corporation expanded by acquiring thrifts. By purchasing the entire S&L, these banks retained the acquiree's goodwill claims against the government.[9]

If the Resolution Trust Corporation (RTC) sold assets and liabilities of failed thrifts piecemeal to interested parties, the shareholders of the failed S&Ls hold the goodwill claims. Several shareholder groups are filing derivative actions to pursue claims that would entitle them to a least a portion of any damages awarded.[10]

Several venture capitalists also are attempting to purchase goodwill claims. Their hope is to obtain the claims inexpensively and profit if the courts issue large damage awards. While the Assignment of Claims Act would appear to preclude this strategy, these investors could circumvent the law by obtaining the government's agreement to the claims purchase.

Given the potential damages and variety of litigants and interested parties, the government asked the U.S. Supreme Court to review lower court decisions in the Glendale Federal Bank, Winstar Corporation, and American Life Group Incorporated cases. In January 1996, the Supreme Court agreed to hear the Justice Department's appeal.

The Supreme Court's Decision

In July 1996 the high court ruled that Congress violated contracts with S&Ls when it changed the goodwill accounting rules. It ordered the Court of Federal Claims to decide damages owed to the three thrifts that brought the lawsuit. The court endorsed an earlier ruling by the U.S. Court of Appeals for the Federal Circuit which stated that the government had a contractual obligation to allow the institutions that acquired failed thrifts to use goodwill accounting. Writing for the majority, Justice Souter rejected Justice Department arguments that Congress has the right to change decisions of regulatory agencies and that the courts should interpret contracts in a way that protects the government's sovereign authority. The ruling's broad language in discussing the government's defenses suggests that it also would apply to other public contracting cases (Barrett 1996b).

The Supreme Court's decision clearly opens the door for hundreds of S&Ls and interested parties to collect damages resulting from required goodwill write-offs. In an unusual twist, the FDIC filed twin motions in the U.S. Court of Federal Claims seeking to be a plaintiff in two pending cases filed by failed thrifts against the government. By joining the suits, the agency is acting in its role as successor to the RTC, the previous receiver for failed S&Ls. As guardian of the insurance funds, the agency is entitled to monies paid to close an institution. Any funds remaining would then be paid to other creditors and finally stockholders. It is possible that the FDIC could join as many as 45 cases currently pending and up to 250 more cases which have yet to file suit. Prior to these filings, the FDIC assisted the Justice Department in defending government goodwill claims. The agency's recent decision places it on both sides of the goodwill issue (*Wall Street Journal*, July 25, 1996).

ASSESSING DAMAGES IN GOODWILL WRITE-OFF CLAIMS

General Considerations

Determining the government's damage liability will not be easy. The job is complicated by the different types of FSLIC assistance agreements, as well as the public's general perception of accounting goodwill. Jake Lewis, a researcher at Public Citizen, exemplifies this attitude when he states:

> It (goodwill) was a sham. The empty bag of air labeled 'goodwill,' in the end, was just another gimmick that delayed the inevitable. Everyone would have been better off—certainly the taxpayers—if the Congress and the executive branch had faced up to the problem (Segal 1996).

If goodwill is indeed perceived as "air," then translating its write-off into damages becomes a perplexing problem. Some thrifts are asking for damages equal to the goodwill amounts written off. Others claim that the government should compensate thrifts for the money they could have made if goodwill had not been eliminated. Finally, some plaintiffs assert the "wounded bank" theory. In this approach, the government repays all the costs (including opportunity costs) that the institution incurred because of the goodwill loss. For example, many thrifts (e.g., Glendale) reduced their size and/or raised new capital to comply with capital requirements. S&Ls also maintain that they should be compensated for the "lost income stream" resulting from the smaller asset bases, as well as the legal and accounting expenses incurred in reacting to the legislative change. However, the government is likely to argue that many acquirers eventually would have been closed even if Congress had not enacted FIRREA.[11]

The Role of Tax Benefits in Assessing Damages

In estimating damages the courts also should consider the acquirer's incentives in agreeing to record so much goodwill in these assisted combinations. A major incentive was the desire to obtain tax benefits. It is recognized widely that tax considerations played a major role in the FSLIC's strategy to dispose of insolvent institutions. Resource constraints forced the FSLIC to use tax incentives to market insolvent S&Ls. Examples of these tax benefits included tax-free FSLIC assistance (interest on FSLIC notes, capital loss coverage, and yield maintenance) and net operating loss carryovers and built-in losses. The FSLIC viewed the potential NOL tax benefits as an extra "asset" that would reduce the FSLIC's financial contribution. Consequently, it frequently assigned either all or part of the insolvent institution's tax benefits to acquirers as part of federally assisted merger transactions. By "selling" these tax attributes, the FSLIC substituted forgone Treasury tax collections for FSLIC funds, permitting it to stretch its resources farther.[12]

Financial accounting standards during the 1980s generally precluded acquirers from recognizing purchased tax attributes as assets. Until the release of *Statement of Financial Accounting Standards No. 109* (*SFAS No. 109*) in 1992, *Accounting Principles Board Opinion No. 11* (*APB No. 11*) outlined the accounting for purchased NOLs. *APB No. 11* indicated that tax loss carryforwards could not be recognized until actually realized, unless their realization was assured beyond any reasonable doubt at the time the loss carryforwards arose. Even though the tax attributes provided an incentive to acquire troubled S&Ls, acquired NOLs generally were not recorded as deferred tax assets because acquirers could not overcome the "reasonable doubt" criteria of *APB No. 11*.[13] Therefore, when excess purchase prices were paid, the value of the acquired NOLs was recorded as goodwill, rather than as a separately identifiable tax asset. The case of Pinnacle Bancorp Inc. supports this assertion. In 1990 Deloitte and Touche allowed Pinnacle to reduce the impact of goodwill write-offs by recognizing the tax benefits associated with operating loss carryforwards it obtained in acquiring Citizens Federal in 1983 (Shingler 1990).

If tax benefits were recorded as goodwill, then goodwill was not all "air" as many believe and courts should consider the value of these tax attributes when calculating damages. Furthermore, the classification of these tax benefits as goodwill suggests that goodwill write-offs were overstated by the value of the NOLs. This suggests that regulators took enforcement actions prematurely based on understated net worth levels that did not consider NOLs as deferred tax assets.

AN ASSOCIATION TEST OF THE GOODWILL/NOL RELATION

Pinnacle's goodwill experience must be supplemented with empirical evidence if the courts are to be convinced that NOLs are important in damage assessment. Kormendi, Bernard, Pirrong, and Snyder (1989) confirm that tax benefits play a role in federally assisted S&L mergers. They also find that the FSLIC received no compensation for the tax benefits it granted to acquirers, suggesting that acquirers did not pay for the tax attributes received. However, they do not address the goodwill/NOL question directly. This study specifically examines whether an association exists between goodwill and NOLs. The investigation is unique in that it uses financial information rather than survey data (Bruno and Waller 1985; Falk and Gordon 1977) to provide evidence on the factors comprising goodwill.

Sample Description

Acquiring thrift institutions with reported goodwill were identified on the 1989 Compustat file. The 1989 tape provided the largest number of surviving S&Ls with available Compustat information.[14] The year 1982 was the earliest for which combination information was available. Years subsequent to 1989 were not considered because FIRREA's required goodwill write-offs made the identification of thrifts with pre-FIRREA goodwill more difficult if not impossible. Furthermore, the special tax benefits that regulators included in assisted merger agreements were reduced by 50% as of January 1, 1989 and were eliminated altogether by FIRREA (Kormendi, et al. 1989). The final data set consists of 39 thrift acquisitions by 26 S&Ls during the period 1982 through 1989. Table 1 describes the sample's acquisition activity.

Once the goodwill thrifts were identified, corporate annual reports and NAARS were used to determine the source of the recorded intangibles. Information on the potential determinants of goodwill was then collected including data on the purchase of net operating loss carryforwards, built-in losses, and several control variables. None of the sam-

Table 1. Sample Description

Panel A. Reconciliation of Compustat S&Ls to Sample Thrifts with Goodwill	
Total S&Ls on 1989 Compustat Tape	40
S&Ls without recorded goodwill	(12)
S&Ls with negative goodwill	(1)
S&Ls with incomplete or missing data	(1)
Total sample S&L's with positive goodwill	26
Panel B. Enumeration of S&L Combinations in Sample that Generate Positive Goodwill	
S&Ls with one acquisition	16
S&Ls with two acquisitions	5
S&Ls with three acquisitions	4
S&Ls with eight acquisitions	1
Total sample S&Ls with positive goodwill	26
Total business combinations in sample	46[a]
Panel C. Reconciliation of Sample Combinations to Combinations used in Model Estimation	
Total business combinations in sample	46
Combinations with incomplete data:	
S&Ls with one acquisition	(3)
S&Ls with three acquisitions	(1)
S&Ls with eight acquisitions	(3)
Total usable combinations	39

Note: [a]Total calculated by multiplying each group of S&Ls in panel B by its respective number of acquisitions.

ple's thrifts reported deferred tax assets related to any of the NOLs acquired through merger. Descriptive statistics for the sample are shown in Table 2. Ten of the 26 sample institutions engaged in multiple acquisitions which increased their size relative to the single merger thrifts.

Model Development

OLS is used to test whether goodwill is associated with NOLs. Other variables have been included in the model to control for factors cited by survey research and the professional literature as contributing to the payment of an excess purchase price. These other factors include corporate goals for diversified business lines, non-NOL regulatory financial assistance, new market access, and the acquisition of deposits. Strong assumptions have been made in selecting proxies for these control variables which may bias against the study finding results for these factors. The following model is estimated:

Table 2. Descriptive Statistics[a]

	Mean	Median	Standard Deviation	Skewness	Minimum	Maximum
Goodwill (000,000s)[b]	65.87	21.00	129.14	3.55	.009	693.54
Goodwill/Assets	.01	.01	.03	2.86	2.4E-05	.12
Log((Goodwill/Assets) * 10 million)[c]	10.41	10.100	1.80	-.06	5.511	14.010
Acquired Deposits (000,000s)[d]	776.98	424.21	1009.94	2.47	1.000	5193.32
Acquired Deposits/Assets	.16	.05	.22	1.89	5.9E-07	.82
(Deposits/Assets)$^{.25}$	.51	.48	.24	-.03	.028	.95
Acquirer Assets (000,000s)[e]	10571	5090	11076	1.08	363.8	40258
NOLDUM	.41	0.0	.49	NA	0	1
ASSIST	.59	1.0	.49	NA	0	1
STATE	.44	0.0	.50	NA	0	1
NEWBUS	.13	0.0	.34	NA	0	1

Notes: [a]Except for acquirer assets and goodwill, descriptive statistics relate to each acquired institution.

[b]Goodwill is the excess purchase price recorded by the acquirer for each acquisition that is disclosed in the thrift's annual report.

[c]Before taking the natural log, the fraction goodwill divided by assets, is multiplied by 10 million to normalize the dependent variable to a positive value. This transformation does not affect the magnitude, sign, or significance of the model's coefficients, or the significance of the variables.

[d]Deposits are the deposit liabilities of the acquiree purchased or assumed by the acquirer in the merger.

[e]Assets are the total assets of the acquiring thrift at the beginning of the fiscal year in which the combination occurred.

NA = Not applicable.

NOLDUM = +1 if a thrift acquired NOLs in a business combination, 0 otherwise;

NEWBUS = +1 if the acquired entity operated in a non-thrift industry, 0 otherwise;

ASSIST = +1 if the combination was not federally assisted, 0 otherwise;

STATE = +1 if a thrift acquisition resulted in interstate banking, 0 otherwise.

$$\text{GDWILL} = b_0 + b_1\text{NOLDUM} + b_2\text{NEWBUS} + b_3\text{ASSIST} + b_4\text{STATE} + b_5\text{DEP} + e$$

where:

GDWILL	=	Positive goodwill recorded by an acquiring thrift;
NOLDUM	=	+1 if a thrift acquired NOLs in a business combination, 0 otherwise;
NEWBUS	=	+1 if the acquired entity operated in a non-thrift industry, 0 otherwise;
ASSIST	=	+1 if the combination was not federally assisted, 0 otherwise;
STATE	=	+1 if a thrift acquisition resulted in interstate banking, 0 otherwise;
DEP	=	Deposit liabilities acquired in a business combination; and
e	=	Normally distributed error term.

GDWILL represents total financial accounting goodwill recorded by the acquirer at the business combination date for each individual acquisition. This study argues that the purchaser was willing to pay an excess purchase price to obtain NOLs and other favorable institution attributes. Consequently, NOLs are expected to be positively associated with goodwill. The variable NOLDUM identifies those thrifts in which NOLs were acquired in business combinations.

Diversification into new business lines also is cited as a reason for paying a purchase premium (Falk and Gordon 1977, Bruno and Waller 1985). The control variable NEWBUS is used to identify those thrift acquisitions that represented new ventures into non-thrift business lines, such as mortgage banking, insurance, and real estate development. A positive relation is expected between GDWILL and NEWBUS.

Professional accounting guidelines for banks and savings institutions (AICPA 1996) suggest that non-NOL financial assistance also may influence recorded goodwill in regulator-assisted business combinations. Other types of regulatory assistance may include: (1) options to return certain acquired assets, (2) rights to acquire certain assets at specified terms, (3) cash or notes if liabilities exceed assets acquired, (4) yield maintenance assistance on specified assets, (5) purchase of equity securities, and (6) indemnification against certain loss contingencies. *SFAS No. 72* indicates that non-NOL financial assistance should be considered in calculating goodwill (a reduction) if receipt of the assistance is probable and the amount is reasonably estimable. If not, any future receipts of assistance should be reported as a goodwill reduction when collected. For example, if a solvent regulatory authority promises to pay an acquirer a specific sum, this amount would be recorded as a receivable by the acquirer, thus reducing any recorded goodwill at the transaction date. However, if the amount of the assistance cannot be measured objectively, no separate receivable asset is recorded to reflect the regulator's promise. Instead, goodwill is reduced when the regulatory assistance is subsequently collected. The control variable ASSIST tests the assertion that non-NOL financial assistance is associated with goodwill. ASSIST identifies those acquisitions that were not federally assisted transactions. No prediction is made for the direction of the goodwill/financial assistance relation given the variety of assisted transactions negotiated by the FSLIC with acquirers of troubled thrifts during the period examined.

The accounting literature indicates that investors often pay extra for market access or entry. This study uses access to new out-of-state markets as a proxy for market entry. The control variable STATE identifies those acquisitions that provided the acquirer new interstate banking opportunities. A positive association between GDWILL and STATE is anticipated.

Finally, branch networks, escrow deposits, and market share have been cited as possible determinants of goodwill.[15] Well developed branch networks, mortgage servicing escrow accounts, and market share are likely correlated with deposit size in most financial institutions. Therefore, this study uses the variable DEP as a proxy for these factors, where DEP is total acquiree deposit liabilities recorded by the acquirer at the date of combination.[16] A positive relation between GDWILL and DEP is expected.

Results

Table 3 shows that recorded goodwill is associated with the acquisition of NOLs and deposit liabilities in thrift combinations. These findings confirm previous *non-thrift* survey research concerning goodwill determinants. Results for NOLDUM are significant at the 5% level and the sign is in the predicted direction. The control variable DEP is significant at the 1% level and the sign also is consistent with expectations. Neither NEWBUS, ASSIST, nor STATE is significantly associated with goodwill for sample thrifts. The lack of significance in these control

Table 3. Regression Results for NOL Model ($N = 39$)

$$GDWILL = b_0 + b_1 NOLDUM + b_2 NEWBUS + b_3 ASSIST + b_4 STATE + b_5 DEP + e$$

Variable	*Prediction*	*Estimated Coefficient*	*t-Statistic*	*p-Value*[a]
Intercept	NA	7.650	10.214	.0001
NOLDUM	+	1.601	2.379	.0239
NEWBUS	+	-.685	-1.021	.3146
ASSIST	NP	.405	.691	.4946
STATE	+	.532	1.081	.2874
DEP	+	3.421	3.201	.0030
F-Value		8.122[b]		
Adjusted R^2		.484		

Notes: [a] *p*-values are for one-tailed tests.
[b] Significant at the .0001 level.
NA = Not applicable
NP = No prediction
GDWILL = Positive goodwill recorded by a sample thrift;
NOLDUM = +1 if a thrift acquired NOLs in a business combination, 0 otherwise;
NEWBUS = +1 if the acquired entity operated in a non-thrift industry, 0 otherwise;
ASSIST = +1 if the combination was not federally assisted, 0 otherwise;
STATE = +1 if a thrift acquisition resulted in interstate banking, 0 otherwise;
DEP = Deposit liabilities acquired in a business combination

variables may be due to the strength of the assumptions made in selecting proxies for these factors.

These results suggest that sample S&Ls paid excess purchase prices for thrifts to obtain NOLs and deposit liabilities. These findings are particularly noteworthy because none of the sample thrifts reported deferred tax assets related to acquired NOLs. These results also suggest that the FSLIC was compensated for the NOLs and deposit liabilities through the payment of an excess purchase price, a finding contrary to that of Kormendi et al. (1989). However, the evidence does not support the payment of an excess purchase price for diversification or market access.[17]

POLICY IMPLICATIONS OF LEGISLATING ACCOUNTING CHANGE

Industry Effects

The Supreme Court's decision in *U.S.* v. *Winstar* will have a significant impact on the conduct of future business between private parties and the federal government. The case is particularly important to those considering acquiring a troubled bank or thrift that are worried the government may be an unreliable counterparty. It is now clear that if the government induces investors to acquire troubled financial institutions with promises of forbearances or other incentives, the courts will uphold the basic contract rights of investors in assistance agreements. Without this decision, the FDIC may have had a difficult time finding buyers for failed institutions in the future.

Not-for-profit health care providers and defense businesses with government contracts also are likely to benefit from the Winstar case (Felsenthal 1996). The ruling means that government must be as responsible in meeting its contractual obligations as any other party. For those firms providing health care and social services to the needy, the decision may protect against governmental cutbacks that result from changing political climates. The Winstar opinion also provides defense contractors with the basis to challenge proposed legislation that would repeal contractor rights to government reimbursement for downsizing and restructuring costs.

Some lawyers believe that the case might be applicable to the utilities and telecommunications industries as well (Felsenthal 1996). Electric power companies might rely on the ruling to challenge a law ordering them to pay for the cleanup of government nuclear facilities.[18] It also might assist utilities and telecommunications companies in recovering amounts spent on capital improvements when regulations made them essentially monopolies. With deregulation, these industries became more competitive and service prices declined. These companies argue that they should be reimbursed by state governments because they relied on assurances that they would be able to charge high enough prices to recover their costs.

Regulatory Impact

Controversy now surrounds the issue of what the FDIC should do with its estimated $8 billion share of damages, once it has been deposited in the FSLIC Resolution Fund (Seiberg 1996). Regulators believe the agency should transfer the monies to the U.S. Treasury to compensate taxpayers for the billions spent on the S&L crisis. However, those in the banking industry argue that the FDIC must use the funds to pay off the Financing Corporation bonds that were issued in the 1980s to initiate the S&L cleanup. The bankers note that 1987 legislation requires that the bonds be paid off using the FSLIC Resolution Fund. Paying off the bonds would preclude the banking industry from having to bear the costs of their eventual retirement.

Finance Considerations

The goodwill issue also is having an unforeseen effect on current and future merger transactions (Bronstein 1996). The expected government payments are becoming a major negotiating point in many S&L mergers, since they frequently are the most valuable assets at many thrifts. Investors disagree on how damages should be split given that only one party incurred the costs of the goodwill claim. Recently, Hinsdale Financial Corporation revealed that it plans to share its $48 million goodwill claim with its intended merger partner, Liberty Bancorp. Shareholders are furious about the money that Hinsdale is giving away, contending that it amounts to $17.70 per share, and that a take-over would have been better. Clearly, resolving the goodwill recovery issue requires careful merger planning and creative deal-making.

Financial Accounting Implications

Misclassifying tax attributes as goodwill also can effect the usefulness of financial statements. For example, users may regard unidentifiable goodwill differently from deferred tax assets. Therefore, recording the value of tax attributes as goodwill may distort financial analyses. Additionally, goodwill and deferred tax assets likely will have different amortization periods. There is no reason to assume that thrift goodwill amortization periods, which are tied to the estimated remaining life of interest-bearing assets, are identical to those for NOL-related deferred tax assets. Therefore, misclassifying tax attributes as goodwill can lead to a misstatement of net income since tax attributes are being amortized over the goodwill period.[19]

SUMMARY AND CONCLUSION

This study illustrates the complex set of interrelationships that exist between accounting, legislative change, and regulatory oversight. The paper finds that acquirers of failing thrifts during the 1980s recorded certain tax attributes as goodwill. However, these "tax assets" were erased from acquirer books when Congress enacted FIRREA. As the Court of Federal Claims determines damages owed by the government to investors and other interested parties resulting from the recent goodwill claims litigation, it should carefully evaluate the nature of goodwill and investor incentives to record it. Specifically, the court should consider assessing damages to compensate acquirers for the value of tax attributes that they could not realize because of enforcement actions prompted by goodwill write-offs. This paper also details the potential effects that the Supreme Court's recent decision in the goodwill claim cases will have on the banking, health care, defense, utilities, and telecommunication industries.

ACKNOWLEDGMENT

The author wishes to thank Charles Christian, Sanjay Gupta, Sally Jones, David Maloney, Mark McNabb, Gary Previts, Shelley Rhoades, John Robinson, tax seminar participants at Arizona State University, and participants at the 1993 American Tax Association Mid-Year Meeting for their comments and suggestions on earlier versions of this paper. The author is particularly grateful to Bruce Behn for his technical assistance and to the McIntire School of Commerce for its financial support.

NOTES

1. Net operating losses are the amounts by which a corporation's adjusted deductions exceed its gross income. Such losses can be carried over to future periods under certain conditions. Built-in losses are unrealized losses related to assets that have a tax basis greater than market value. Net operating loss carryovers and built-in losses are collectively referred to as NOLs in this study.
2. *Accounting Principles Board Opinion No. 11* addressed the financial accounting and reporting of acquired NOLs until it was superseded by *Statement of Financial Accounting Standards No. 109* in February 1992.
3. Owners argue that since regulators approved their combinations, any subsequent legislation that required the write-off of goodwill and that resulted in closure constitutes a breach of the original agreement between the government and the acquirer.
4. Margavio (1993) and White (1991) provide a historical perspective of the savings and loan crisis of the 1980s. They discuss the causes, outcomes, and implications of the crisis and suggest a tradition of accounting measurement problems in this industry.
5. During the 1980s, S&Ls invested in long-term, fixed-rate mortgages funded by passbook or other short-term deposits. When interest rates rose sharply, the fair market value of fixed-rate loan investments dropped below that of deposit liabilities.

6. *Statement of Financial Accounting Standards No. 72* (*SFAS No. 72*) addresses the recording and amortization of goodwill when the fair value of liabilities assumed exceeds the fair value of assets acquired. The FSLIC often permitted its contributions of cash and notes to be treated as contributed capital by the acquiring entity which further increased recorded goodwill on the acquirer's regulatory set of books.

7. The goodwill claims filed by major thrifts are Dime Bancorp for $693 million, H.F. Ahmanson for $600 million, Glendale Federal for $557 million, Long Island Bancorp for $500 million, California Federal for $485 million, Coast Savings for $299 million, and Astoria Financial for $180 million (Kleege 1996).

8. Lower courts reached similar decisions in cases involving Security Federal Savings and Loan Association of Albuquerque, New Mexico, and Charter Federal Savings Bank of Bristol, Virginia.

9. The Assignment of Claims Act generally prohibits an institution from selling its stake in a lawsuit against the government. These banks used a loophole that allows a company to retain a claim if it purchases the *entire* company. For example, Shawmut National Corporation received its goodwill claim when it purchased Northeast Savings. However, banks that bought the assets and liabilities of a failed thrift from the Resolution Trust Corporation cannot assert a goodwill claim, because the thrift charter was not purchased.

10. These shareholders are acting on the failed thrift's behalf since the RTC, the appointed receiver, never filed a claim. Soon after the Federal Circuit Court of Appeals decision in the Glendale case, the stock of Meritor Savings Bank which failed in 1992 began to trade at five cents per share and soared to two dollars, principally on the hopes of its goodwill lawsuit.

11. Perpetual Savings Bank of Alexandria provides such an example. Although goodwill write-offs negatively impacted Perpetual's expenses and net worth, it was a stagnant real estate market, declining thrift charter values, and the inability to raise new capital that eventually prompted its closure in January 1992.

12. The tax attributes of acquired institutions in these transactions frequently were passed on to acquirers through the use of a type G, tax-free reorganization. "G" reorganizations are tax-free mergers involving the transfer of assets in Bankruptcy Act cases and receiverships, foreclosures, or similar cases under federal or state law (IRC Sec. 368(a)(1)(G) and (3)).

13. A review of the financial statements of the 40 thrifts examined in this study did not reveal deferred tax assets related to any of the acquired NOLs.

14. By using 1989 to construct a list of acquirers with recorded intangibles, survivorship bias may be introduced into the study. However, the authors believe that its effect does not diminish the findings for several reasons. First, federally assisted acquisitions required the approval of the regulatory authorities. Such approval required assurance that the post merger entity would be a viable operation for at least five years subsequent to the acquisition. Through this requirement, the government attempted to ensure that the post merger institution would be a "survivor." Consequently, the likelihood that a significant number of acquiring thrifts (those with goodwill) dropped off the Compustat tapes prior to 1989 is considered low.

Second, acquirers are considered more likely to value NOLs into their purchase price if they expect a high probability of survival. Only if they survive and generate future profits will they be able to utilize the benefits associated with acquired tax attributes.

Consequently, it is the "surviving" thrifts that are of interest in this study, since it is these institutions that expect to use the benefits of acquired NOLs.

15. *Financial Accounting Standards Board (FASB) Interpretation No. 9, Staff Accounting Bulletin (SAB) 42,* and *Accounting Standards Executive Committee (AcSEC) Guidance for Mutual Combinations* were issued by the FASB, Securities and Exchange Commission, and American Institute of CPAs, respectively. These statements, in addition to *APB No. 16* and *SFAS No. 72*, discuss factors affecting the recognition and valuation of goodwill in financial institutions.

16. This study assumes that all deposits of the acquired entity are core or retail deposits. It is possible that some of the deposit liabilities purchased were broker-originated deposits. Inclusion of these brokered funds in total deposits likely biases against finding a relationship between deposits and goodwill, since purchasers would not pay premium purchase prices for brokered deposits.

17. Ten firms had multiple acquisitions which accounted for 26 observations out of a possible 39. These multiple acquisitions may violate the independent and identically distributed assumption of OLS regression. To ascertain whether the results are biased and inconsistent, two additional tests were performed. First, using a bootstrapping procedure, one acquisition was randomly selected from each firm that had multiple acquisitions and individual regressions were rerun using 23 observations (13 from firms with one original acquisition and one acquisition each from the 10 firms with multiple acquisitions). For bootstrapped samples of 1000 and 5000, the average *t*-statistics on NOLDUM and DEP were (2.98, 2.87) and (2.63, 2.55) respectively. Next, using the original model, a dummy variable (MULT) was added to control for the effects of multiple acquisitions, and the OLS regression was rerun. MULT was coded 1 if the observation was an acquisition from a firm that had multiple acquisitions, and 0 otherwise. The coefficient on MULT was insignificant, while the coefficients on NOLDUM and DEP were still significant with t-statistics of 2.09 and 2.36 respectively. Although not all combinations of acquisitions were tested, these additional results suggest that the original findings are not confounded by the multiple acquisitions included in the sample.

18. Utilities purchased enriched uranium from the Energy Department during the 1960s and 1970s. Then, in 1992, Congress enacted legislation requiring these companies to pay a "special assessment" for radiation cleanup costs. In the case of Yankee Atomic Electric Company, a federal claims court has ruled that the company should not have to pay the assessment. The government has appealed.

19. *SFAS No. 109* did not change substantially the accounting for acquired NOLs as outlined by *APB No. 11*. Under *SFAS No. 109*, deferred tax assets can now be recognized for differences between assigned values and the tax bases of assets and liabilities, as well as for future benefits attributable to NOLs. However, *SFAS No. 109* indicates that a valuation allowance may be necessary if it is "more likely than not" that some portion of the deferred tax asset will not be realized. Such a provision is similar to the "reasonable doubt" criteria of *APB No. 11*. Consequently, to the extent that a valuation allowance is still considered necessary for acquired tax attributes, acquirers will allocate an excess purchase price entirely to goodwill.

SFAS No. 109 now requires that subsequent recognition of the tax benefits related to the tax attributes be recognized by first reducing goodwill and then other intangibles related to the acquisition. This treatment is consistent with the arguments made in this study that acquired tax attributes (NOLs) have been misclassified as goodwill.

REFERENCES

Accounting Principles Board. 1967. *APB Opinion No. 11*, Accounting for Income Taxes. New York: AICPA.

______. 1967. *APB Opinion No. 16*, Business Combinations. New York: AICPA.

American Institute of Certified Public Accountants. 1996. *AICPA Audit and Accounting Guide: Banks and Savings Institutions*. New York: AICPA.

Barrett, P. 1996a. High court backs S&Ls on accounting, declines to hear affirmative action case. *The Wall Street Journal*, July 2, p. A3.

______. 1996b. S&L cleanup bill could rise $10 billion if U.S. loses appeal at supreme court. *The Wall Street Journal*, January 22, p. B3.

Bronstein, B. 1996. Knotty problem for thrift deals: Sharing the goodwill windfall. *American Banker*, August 9, p. 1.

Bruno, J.D., and T.C. Waller. 1985. SFAS No. 72: Has it addressed the real issues? *The Woman CPA* (October): 12-15.

Falk, H., and L.A. Gordon. 1977. Imperfect markets and the nature of goodwill. *Journal of Business Finance & Accounting* (Winter): 443-462.

Felsenthal, E. 1996. Lawyers try to apply S&L ruling in a wide variety of other suits. *The Wall Street Journal*, July 15, p. B6.

Financial Accounting Standards Board. 1976. *FASB Interpretation No. 9*, Applying APB Opinions 16 and 17 When a Savings and Loan Association or Similar Institution Is Acquired in a Business Combination Accounted for by the Purchase Method. Stamford, CT: FASB.

______. 1983. *Statement of Financial Accounting Standards No. 72*, Accounting for Certain Acquisitions of Banking or Thrift Institutions. Stamford, CT: FASB.

______. 1992. *Statement of Financial Accounting Standards No. 109*, Accounting for Income Taxes. Norwalk, CT: FASB.

Kleege, S. 1996. High court's goodwill ruling expected to move thrift stocks. *American Banker*, June 24, p. 21.

Knight, J. 1996. "Goodwill" rule had huge impact. *The Washington Post*, July 2, p. A9.

Kormendi, R., V. Bernard, S. Pirrong, and E. Snyder. 1989. The origins and resolution of the thrift crisis. *Journal of Applied Corporate Finance* 2: 85-99.

Lowenstein, R. 1995. New life is breathed into the S&L crisis. *The Wall Street Journal*, September 21, p. C1.

Margavio, G. 1993. The savings and loan debacle: The culmination of three decades of conflicting regulation, deregulation, and re-regulation. *The Accounting Historians Journal* (June): 1-32.

McNamee, M. 1992. Nobody is laughing about this funny money now. *Business Week*, May 4, p. 168.

Nielsen, C.H. 1992. Government must ante up: Courts favor investors in goodwill dispute. *Bank Management* (April): 12-14.

Securities and Exchange Commission. 1981. *Staff Accounting Bulletin No. 42*, Application of Existing Accounting Standards to Business Combinations Accounted for by the Purchase Method Involving Financial Institutions. Washington, D.C.: Office of the Chief Accountant.

Segal, D. 1996. Lawyers get to feast on another slice of the S&L pie. *The Washington Post*, July 8, p. C1.

Seiberg, J. 1995a. Appeals court hands a win to Glenfed on goodwill. *American Banker*, August 31, p. 1.

______. 1995b. Banks also have stake in goodwill litigation. *American Banker*, November 8, p. 2.

______. 1996. FDIC to sue U.S. for goodwill billions; victory could end thrift fund crisis. *American Banker*, July 26, p. 2.

Shingler, D. 1990. Pinnacle sees positives from negative balance. *Cincinnati Business Courier*, January 29, p. 3(1).

White, L.J. 1991. *The S&L Debacle: Public Policy Lessons For Bank and Thrift Regulation*. New York, NY: Oxford University Press.

Wyatt, E.A. 1989. No savings grace: Goodwill is bad news for S&Ls. *Barron's*, July 10, p. 40.

AN INVESTIGATION OF AUDITOR RESIGNATIONS

Mark DeFond, Michael Ettredge, and David B. Smith

ABSTRACT

In *Financial Reporting Release No. 31* of 1988, the SEC required clients whose auditors resign to disclose the resignations in their form 8-K filings. This implies resignations differ from dismissals, and that the existence of an auditor resignation is useful information for investors. We examine these claims by comparing characteristics of a sample of companies whose auditors resigned with those of sample companies that dismissed their auditors. We also compare stock market reaction to resignations versus dismissals. A logit analysis indicates that auditor resignations are more likely to be associated with auditor-client disagreements and with declines in client firm cash flows. These results suggest a scenario in which resignations are triggered by auditor distrust of client management coupled with declining client financial health. Excess returns of resignation clients are found to be significantly worse than for dismissal clients, lending some support to the SEC's assertion that resignations differ from dismissals.

Research in Accounting Regulation, Volume 11, pages 25-45.

ISBN: 0-7623-0168-6

INTRODUCTION

The business press reports a recent increase in resignations motivated by auditors' desires to shed risky clients.[1] Client companies whose auditors resign must specifically mention the resignations in their Form 8-K filings. This Securities and Exchange Commission (SEC) requirement, imposed in *Financial Reporting Release* (*FRR*) *No. 31* of 1988, implies that resignations differ from dismissals, and that the existence of an auditor resignation is useful information for investors.[2] We examine these claims by comparing characteristics of companies whose auditors resign with those of companies that dismiss their auditors. We also compare stock market reaction to resignations versus dismissals.

We argue that resignations are driven by litigation risk and hypothesize that the clients involved are predictably different from companies that dismiss their auditors.[3] We test these hypotheses by comparing 62 companies reporting auditor resignations to a randomly chosen control sample of 61 companies disclosing an auditor change without a reported resignation. Our sample is drawn from the pre-*FRR No. 31* era, 1982-1987, so that this study provides evidence useful for concluding whether the SEC's implied assertions about auditor resignations are consistent with data available to the SEC at the time *FRR No. 31* was promulgated. A logit analysis indicates that auditor resignations are more likely to be associated with auditor-client disagreements and with declines in client firm cash flows. These results are somewhat consistent with a scenario in which resignations are triggered by auditor distrust of client management coupled with declining client financial health.

One implication of our scenario is that resignations convey worse news than dismissals about the client companies involved, and so we investigate stock market reaction to these auditor changes. Excess returns of resignation clients were found to be significantly worse than for dismissal clients during the pre-filing period from the date of auditor change through the day before 8-K filing. One possible explanation is that insiders "leaked" information about the resignations during this period. Additional investigation indicated that, among the resignation sample, market reaction was most negative in the pre-filing period among those firms that took the longest time to file. This lends some credence to the leakage scenario and suggests the need for additional research.

The remainder of the paper is divided into six parts. The second section discusses why an auditor might resign. Testable hypotheses about client-auditor characteristics associated with resignations are presented in the third section. We discuss the sample selection procedure and the logit variables in the fourth section. The fifth section presents the logit results. Market reaction results are presented in the sixth section, and conclusions are discussed in the final section.

WHY DO AUDITORS RESIGN?

Over time, the auditor's costs and benefits of continued association can be altered due to changes in the client company's risk.[4] If the client becomes riskier, several resolutions are possible. First, the risk-reward balance could be restored through a fee increase. Second, the risks of association could be reduced through increasing the quality of audit work performed. This solution also would involve increasing the fee. Finally, the auditor can resign. Each alternative has been discussed in the business press, in auditing texts, and in professional standards.[5]

The above arguments suggest that an increase in the risk of continued association with the client is a prime cause of auditor resignations. Litigation is likely to be a major source of such risk.[6] St. Pierre and Anderson (1984) find client bankruptcy, significant client losses, and drops in client stock price to be the most common events precipitating litigation against auditors. Palmrose (1987) finds that litigation against auditors arising from business failures is typically dismissed (with no auditor payments) unless management fraud is also present. Stice (1991) presents evidence that poor financial performance, among other attributes, characterizes clients whose auditors subsequently are sued. Lys and Watts (1994) find that financial difficulties, poor stock price performance, and qualified opinions typify such clients. Taken together, these studies suggest that increased litigation risk is more likely to motivate auditor resignation when the client's financial condition is deteriorating and management integrity has come under suspicion.[7]

Our test sample consists of resignations voluntarily reported by companies in the pre-*FRR No. 31* era. Prior to promulgation of *FRR No. 31* in 1988, Form 8-K requirements for reporting auditor changes (both dismissals and resignations) are those revised by *ASR No. 165* in 1974, and by *ASR No. 247* in 1978, and include the following. The client must:

a. state the date of the auditor's termination;
b. state whether a disagreement with the former auditor existed at the time of termination or within the two prior years;

c. state whether the former auditor's opinions of the past two years were adverse, disclaimed, or qualified;
d. request the former auditor to provide a letter addressed to the SEC, to be appended to the 8-K, confirming or dis-confirming the client's statements (a), (b), and (c) and, if dis-confirming, providing details;
e. state whether the decision to change independent accountants was approved by the client's Board of Directors or its audit committee (if any).

In *ASR No. 247*, issued in 1978, the SEC declined to require 8-K disclosure of the reasons for a change in accountant, but encouraged client disclosure of these reasons on a voluntary basis. This pronouncement encourages terminated auditors to provide additional information beyond the minimum required in letter (d) above. This suggestion is consistent with the SEC's ongoing emphasis, previously stated in *ASR No.165*, that independent accountants should exercise their initiative in bringing significant information to the attention of investors, even when not literally required to do so.[8] Given the SEC's enforcement powers, reviewed in Feroz, Park, and Pastena (1991), and the long-term nature of the relation between SEC Practice Section accounting firms and the SEC, it should not be surprising if accountants encouraged clients to disclose resignations in the pre-*FRR No. 31* era.[9]

Since both the auditor and client are required to provide statements for inclusion in an auditor change 8-K, the contents of the 8-K are potentially the product of a joint decision process. In conversations with auditors we learned that clients and auditors usually informally coordinate their individual contributions to the auditor change 8-K. Both client and auditor are interested in seeing that the 8-K does not contain contradictory statements, since such contradictions would not be in the interest of investors and can draw unfavorable attention from the SEC (see, for example, *ASR No. 247*). One explanation for the appearance in Form 8-K of "voluntary" client statements that potentially cause adverse market reactions is that the statements are not really voluntary. In both the pre- and post-*FRR No. 31* periods, auditors can influence the content of Form 8-K by threatening to write letters that contradict the clients' statements and that present the auditors' versions of the termination.[10]

In summary, an auditor is expected to resign an engagement if changes in the client are perceived to result in unacceptable risk, given the fee that can be charged. These risk changes are likely to involve deterioration in the client's financial position, and decreased trust in the client's control environment. A negative market reaction will occur if the resignation conveys adverse, value-relevant information not previously known to the market. Information about a client's poor financial condition and management's low credibility would seem to be value-relevant. Whether this information is news when disclosed in the context of a resignation is an empirical question. The SEC, in *FRR No. 31*, implies that it is news.

In the next section we develop several hypotheses, consistent with this scenario, about the reasons for and effects of auditor resignations.

HYPOTHESIS DEVELOPMENT

Our hypotheses are stated relative to a control group of clients that changed auditors but did not report a resignation.

When management is perceived to lack integrity, the auditor may believe that it cannot trust management's representations. This adversarial role makes it more difficult and costly to design audit procedures that give reasonable assurance that the financial statements are free of material error. Rather than risk litigation, the auditor will resign.

While management integrity is difficult to publicly observe, the SEC often censures managers by issuing Accounting and Auditing Enforcement Releases (AAER's). AAER's result from SEC investigations of suspected wrong-doing with respect to financial reporting matters where the SEC has determined that a breach of the Securities Acts have occurred. This yields our first hypothesis:

H_1. Companies reporting auditor resignations are more likely to have been subjects of prior AAERs that criticized management's behavior.

Conflicts between the auditor and management over financial reporting and disclosure issues are expected to increase the auditor's distrust of management. One indication of such conflicts is the disclosure of an auditor-client disagreement in the 8-K reporting the auditor change. When a company reports an auditor change, the SEC requires disclosure of any significant disagreements between management and the auditor during the previous two fiscal years and any recent interim period. These disagreements indicate that the auditor-management relationship has become adversarial. This leads to our next hypothesis:

H_2. Companies reporting auditor resignations are more likely to report an auditor-client disagreement.

Auditors recognize that managers have greater incentives to manipulate reported accounting numbers during times of declining client financial health (Arens and Loebbecke 1988). Since we expect auditor resignations to occur when the auditor suspects that management is intentionally attempting to misstate the financial reports, we also expect resignations to be more likely during times of declining financial health.

While there are several financial variables that may indicate a decline in client health, many of them are highly correlated. Therefore, we restrict our analysis to changes in three commonly used measures of financial health—return on assets, cash flow from operations and leverage. Our next three hypotheses are:

H_3. Companies reporting auditor resignations are more likely to have smaller increases, or larger declines, in return on total assets.

H_4. Companies reporting auditor resignations are more likely to have smaller increases, or larger declines, in cash flows divided by total assets.

H_5. Companies reporting auditor resignations are more likely to have larger increases, or smaller declines, in total liabilities divided by total assets.

The requirement to explicitly disclose auditor resignations indicates that the SEC views such disclosure as important information to the capital markets. The preceding discussion explains why this information may indeed be useful. A resignation signals a more adversarial relationship between the auditor and the client.[11] Further, the resignation suggests that management is less concerned with fair presentation of the financial statements than investors had previously thought. Thus, the disclosure of an auditor resignation is expected to have a negative effect on client firm value. This provides our last hypothesis:

H_6. Companies reporting auditor resignations are likely to have more negative, or less positive, excess stock returns surrounding announcement of the auditor change.

Numerous studies have examined stock market reaction to auditor changes (Smith and Nichols 1982; Nichols and Smith 1983; Smith 1988; Eichenseher, Hagigi, and Shields 1989; Johnson and Lys 1990; Teoh 1990; Albrecht and Lamy 1992; Klock 1994). Results have been mixed. Among the more recent studies, for example, Eichenseher et al. (1989) cumulated excess returns for 87 OTC firms over five weeks surrounding the auditor change dates in 1980-1982. They observed negative mean CARs, but their event window is quite wide. Johnson and Lys (1990) examined daily excess returns around 8-K filing dates for 194 firms in 1973-1982. Excess returns did not differ from zero. Albrecht and Lamy (1992) computed excess returns around 8-K filing dates for 144 firms in 1980-1986. They found significant excess returns over a six-day period surrounding the filing date. Klock (1994) investigated daily excess returns around 8-K filing dates for 50 firms in 1986-1987. Excess returns did not differ from zero. To our knowledge, no prior study has specifically examined auditor resignations, although the SEC identified these events as an important subset of auditor changes in *FRR No. 31*.

SAMPLE SELECTION AND LOGIT MODEL VARIABLES

Our control and resignation samples are both chosen from the population of companies that changed auditors, as reported in the *Public Accounting Report* (PAR), between 1982 (inception of the report disclosing resignations) and 1987. This is the period prior to issuance of *FRR No. 31*, so disclosure of resignations is voluntary during this period. The PAR notes whether an auditor change resulted from an auditor-initiated resignation based upon management disclosures included in the 8-K's and, when possible, telephone conversations with company management. Of the 3,443 auditor changes reported in the PAR during this time period, the PAR identified 219 (or 6.4%) as originating from an auditor resignation.

Table 1 reconciles our final sample with the PAR identified resignations. Major causes of sample attrition included unavailable 8-Ks (33 firms) or unavailable financial statements (24 firms). Numerous auditor

Table 1. Sample Selection Information for Auditor Resignation Treatment Sample and Non-resignation Control Sample

	Auditor Resignations	*Non-resignation Control Group*
Total Auditor resignations listed in the 1982-1987 P.A.R.	219	
Random sample of non-resignation auditor changes from the 1982-1987 P.A.R.		100
Initial Sample Attrition:		
8-K's unavailable	(33)	(15)
No indication of resignation based on examination of 8-K	(41)	
Subsidiary of another sample firm	(6)	—
Sub-total	139	85
Resignations due to changing auditor circumstances:		
Independence issues	(26)	
CPA no longer qualified	(11)	
CPA practice disolved	(10)	
Health, geographical & other	(6)	
Remaining resignations	86	
Financial statement information unavailable	(24)	(24)
Final logit analysis samples	62	61

changes designated as resignations by PAR were eliminated because no resignation was mentioned by management in the 8-K filed with the SEC (41 firms). This discrepancy occurs when PAR's telephone conversation with management reveals that the predecessor auditor resigned even though it was not disclosed in the 8-K.[12] Finally, 53 firms were deleted because the 8-K indicated the resignation was required by a change in the auditor's circumstances. The final resignation sample contains 62 auditor resignations presumably motivated by changes in the client's circumstances or behavior.[13] A control sample of 100 non-resignation auditor changes was randomly drawn from the PAR for the same period. Thirty-nine of these changes were eliminated due to lack of data. The final control sample contains 61 auditor changes.[14]

Table 2 gives a profile of the two samples' primary SIC codes. With the exception of the services industry grouping the table indicates little difference between the samples.

Explanatory variables used to test Hypotheses 1-5 using logit are explained in Table 3. Two variables proxy for auditor distrust of man-

Table 2. Industry Distribution of Resignation and Control Samples

Industry		Resignation		Control	
		Logit	*Market*	*Logit*	*Market*
SIC code	*Name*	*tests*	*tests*	*tests*	*tests*
0-1000	Agriculture Forestry and Fisheries	0	0	1	1
1000-1499	Mining	8	5	11	6
1500-1999	Contract Construction	1	0	0	0
2000-3999	Manufacturing 22	11	19	9	
4000-4999	Transportation 1	1	5	1	
5000-5999	Wholesale & Retail	8	4	6	3
6000-6799	Finance, Insurance & Real Estate	10	6	16	1
7000-8999	Services	12	10	3	2
		62	37	61	23

Table 3. Description of Explanatory Variables Used in Logit Analysis

SECREL	Dummy variable indicating a prior SEC enforcement action was filed (AAER) criticizing management behavior.
DISAGREE	Dummy variable indicating an auditor-client disagreement was reported in the auditor-change 8-K.
ROACHG	Change in net income divided by total assets (ROA), scaled by the absolute value of net income divided by total assets in the last year with the predecessor auditor.
CASHCHG	Change in cash flows from operations divided by total assets, scaled by the absolute value of operating cash flows divided by total assets in the last year with the predecessor auditor.
LEVCHG	Change in total liabilities divided by total assets, scaled by total liabilities divided by total assets in the last year with the predecessor auditor.

Note: The change variables are measured from the last year with the predecessor auditor to the first year with the successor auditor.

agement's control environment. First, a dichotomous variable SECREL indicates the prior issuance of an SEC enforcement action (AAER) against company management.[15] This information is derived from a search of the Lexis/Nexis database. Second, a dichotomous variable DISAGREE represents the presence of auditor-client disagreements reported in the 8-K. Three measures of the client's changing financial health are employed: scaled change in return on assets, ROACHG, scaled change in cash flow from operations, CASHCHG, and scaled change in total debt to assets, LEVCHG. All three changes are measured from the client's last year with the former auditor to the first year with the new auditor. Data for the three financial measures are obtained from comparative financial statements found in Form 10-K for the first year with the successor auditor.

Table 4. Descriptive Statistics and Univariate Tests of Resignation and Non-resignation Auditor Change Companies

Panel A. Logit Variables		*Resignations = R (n = 62)*	*Controls = C (n = 61)*	*One-tailed prob.*[a]
Expectation	*Variable*	*mean/median/(Std. Dev.)*		
R > C	SECREL	0.113 0 (.319)	0.066 0 (.250)	0.274
R > C	DISAGREE	0.274 0 (.450)	0.033 0 (.180)	0.001
R < C	ROACHG	−2.077 0.018 (6.044)	−0.693 −0.047 (7.285)	0.467
R < C	CASHCHG	−15.056 −0.121 (107.296)	6.014 −0.145 (42.97)	0.066
R > C	LEVCHG	0.660 0.040 (3.005)	0.174 0.037 (0.752)	0.152

Panel B. Auditor-related Data	*Resignations (n = 62)*	*Controls (n = 61)*	*Two-tailed prob.*[a]
% of firms with Big Eight predecessor auditor	58.1%	65.6%	.459
% changing from Non-Big Eight to Big Eight auditor	19.4%	18.0%	.999
% changing from Big Eight to Non-Big Eight auditor	21.0%	23.0%	.830
% disclosing prior qualified opinion from predecessor auditor in Form 8-K	48.4%	18.0%	.001

Note: [a]Resignation and control samples are compared using Wilcoxon 2-sample tests for continuous variables and Fisher's exact tests for categorical variables.

Descriptive statistics for the variables used in the logit analysis are presented in Panel A of Table 4. Fisher's exact tests are used to compare the frequencies of dichotomous variables, and Wilcoxon two-sample tests are used to compare the continuous variables.[16] The existence of prior SEC enforcement actions against company management, SECREL, does not differ significantly across the two groups even though the resignation group contained almost twice as many of these actions. Auditor-client disagreements reported in the auditor change 8K, DISAGREE, are significantly more frequent among the resignation sample ($p = .001$).

Among the financial health variables, only the change in cash flow from operations divided by assets, CASHCHG, is significantly different at conventional levels ($p = .066$). Lastly, the increase in leverage for the resignation sample is not significantly different than the control sample.

Panel B of Table 4 presents statistics on auditor-related data not included in the logit model. There is no difference between the resignation and control samples on the frequency of Big Eight predecessor auditors (58.1% and 65.6%, respectively) or on the frequency of changes to or from Big Eight auditors. There is, however, a greater frequency of qualified opinions given by the predecessor auditors during the previous two fiscal years among the resignation sample (48.4% versus 18.0%). This difference is significant at $p = .001$. Of the 30 qualified opinions given to clients whose auditors later resigned, 26 were "going concern" qualifications, three were asset realization qualifications, and one was a disclaimer of opinion. Thus the higher frequency of qualified opinions is consistent with the deteriorating financial health of the resignation firms.

LOGIT ANALYSIS TEST RESULTS

A logit analysis is used to test Hypotheses 1-5 simultaneously. In addition to the standard logit tests of significance, approximate randomization tests (Noreen 1989) are also performed. Randomization provides an alternative approach to specifying the null distribution of logit test statistics. In the approximate randomization approach the dependent variable is randomly reordered (shuffled) and the logit model is re-estimated many times (999 in this study). For each dependent variable, this yields a distribution of coefficients under the null hypothesis of no association with the dependent variable. The 999 observations of each coefficient are compared to the estimate of the coefficient obtained from the logit model estimated without random reordering. The significance level of a coefficient is determined to be:

$$(NGE + 1)/(NS + 1)$$

where:

NGE = number of coefficients greater than or equal to the nonrandom estimate of the coefficient;

NS = number of random shuffles of the dependent variable observations.

Table 5. Logit Analysis
62 Resignation and 61 Control (Non-resignation)
Auditor Change Companies

Explanatory Variables	*Predicted Sign*	*Coefficient*	*T-Statistic*	*Prob.*[a]	*Prob. (Random)*[b]
intercept	n/a	−0.370	−1.705	0.044	0.002
SECREL	+	0.469	0.669	0.252	0.335
DISAGREE	+	2.411	2.982	0.001	0.001
ROACHG	−	−0.016	−0.518	0.302	0.308
CASHCHG	−	−0.105	−1.867	0.031	0.005
LEVCHG	+	0.058	0.313	0.372	0.423
Model chi-square	23.52				
($p < 0$)	.000				
Correctly classified	65.9%				

Note: [a]one-tailed probability except for intercept
[b]one-tailed probability except for intercept. Probability assessed using an approximate randomization procedure.

Definition of variables:

Dependent variable: Coded 1 if the auditor resigned and 0 otherwise. Based on 8-K.

SECREL = Dummy variable indicating a prior SEC enforcement action was filed (AAER) criticizing management behavior.

DISAGREE = Dummy variable indicating an auditor-client disagreement was reported in the auditor-change 8-K.

ROACHG = Change in return on assets (ROA), from the last year with the predecessor auditor to the first year with the successor auditor, scaled by the absolute value of ROA in the last year with the predecessor auditor.

CASHCHG = Change in cash flows from operations divided by assets, from the last year with the predecessor auditor to the first year with the successor auditor.

LEVCHG = Change in total liabilities divided by total assets, scaled by total liabilities divided by total assets in the last year with the predecessor auditor.

If the hypothesis predicts a negative sign, the number of coefficients less than or equal to the nonrandom estimate replaces NGE in the formula above.

The logit results are presented in Table 5 and are consistent with the uni-variate results.[17] The coefficient associated with auditor-client disagreements, DISAGREE, is significant at $p = .001$ and the coefficient associated with the change in cash flows, CASHCHG, is significant at $p < .05$. These results suggest that management-auditor conflicts and deteriorating financial health are factors leading to auditor-initiated resignations.[18] As with the uni-variate tests, the accrual-based measure of return on assets is not significant at conventional levels. The finding that cash flows decline for the resignation sample as compared to the control sample while accrual income changes (reflected in ROA) are not significantly different for both samples is consistent with the auditor relying primarily on cash flow information in shaping the decision to resign.[19]

The results obtained using the randomization procedure are also presented in Table 5 and the significance levels are consistent with those obtained using standard logit tests. Thus, the results do not appear to be sensitive to violations of the assumptions underlying standard logit test statistics.

MARKET REACTION TO AUDITOR CHANGES

We investigate whether resignations differ from other auditor changes from an investor perspective by comparing the excess return behavior of the two samples. A market adjusted residual is calculated for three periods: (1) from the day of the auditor change through the day before the filing of the Form 8-K (the "pre-filing" period); (2) for five business days beginning from the day the Form 8-K is received by the SEC (the "post-filing" period); and (3) the combination of the first two periods (the "combined" period). Period (1) is chosen because it allows us to examine possible information "leakage" prior to the Form 8-K filing. The mean (median) pre-filing periods for the resignation and control firms are 18.6 (16) and 25.8 (16), respectively.[20] Period (2) is chosen because we can determine the date the SEC received the Form 8-K disclosing the change (by the SEC stamp on the form 8-K) but not the precise date the SEC publicly disclosed what was in the Form 8-K by sending it to its public library. Our discussions with employees at the SEC indicates that the Form 8-K's are reasonably assured of being submitted to the library within four trading days of the stamp date.

The market adjusted residual equals each sample company's common stock return over the respective measurement period, adjusted for the general market conditions over the same time period. Closing stock prices were obtained from the Dow Jones News Retrieval Service Tradeline data base and from Standard & Poor's Daily Stock Price Record, as were cash dividends and stock split information. The numerator of the common stock return is the closing bid price for the last day of the measurement period minus the closing bid price for the day prior to the beginning of the measurement period plus any dividends. The denominator is the closing bid price for the day prior to the beginning of the measurement period.

We use the adjustment method found in Kinney and McDaniel (1989) to adjust common stock returns for the general market conditions. The market index, found on the Center for Research in Security Prices

Table 6. Cumulative Excess Returns Surrounding the Auditor-Change 8-K Filing Date

	Pre-filing Period[a]	*Post-filing Period*[b]	*Combined Period*[c]
a. Resignation companies (*n* = 37)			
Mean excess returns	−.102	−.023	−.125
Median excess returns	−.053	−.017	−.093
Percent negative	73%	62%	78%
Significance level for Wilcoxon sign-rank test (null = 0, two-tailed)	.001	.036	.000
b. Non-resignation companies (*n* = 23)			
Mean excess returns	.072	−.029	.042
Median excess returns	.010	−.013	.015
Percent negative	39%	70%	44%
Significance level for Wilcoxon sign-rank test (null = 0, two-tailed)	.323	.030	.681
c. Comparison of resignation and non-resignation companies			
Significance of Wilcoxon two-sample test that a < b (one-tailed)	.003	.602	.004

Notes: [a]The pre-filing period is measured from the day of the resignation or termination through the day prior to receipt of the 8-K by the SEC.
[b]The post-filing period is measured from the day of receipt of the 8-K by the SEC through the following four business days.
[c]The combined period is the sum of the pre and post-filing periods.

(CRSP) tape is accumulated over the same period used to calculate the common stock return and then subtracted from the company return to compute the excess return. The return measure was not adjusted for systematic risk due to the predominance of over-the counter firms in the samples and the resultant difficulty in obtaining risk estimates. Companies were deleted from the sample if common stock price information was not available. The resignation sample for market tests contained 37 companies and the control sample contained 23 companies.

Table 6 compares the cumulative market adjusted returns for the three periods. Wilcoxon signed-rank tests are used to assess whether the returns of the resignation and control samples are significantly different from zero, and Wilcoxon two-sample tests are used to compare returns across the samples. Excess returns for the resignation sample are significantly less than zero at $p < .05$ in each of the three periods, while returns for the control sample are significantly less than zero only in the post-filing period. Excess returns for the resignation sample are significantly less than those of the control sample in the pre-filing period and in the combined period. The returns are statistically indistinguishable across the two samples during the post-filing period.[21]

The post-filing period results indicate that the stock market views both resignations and dismissals as bad news and that there is no difference in the central tendency of excess returns between the two samples. A significant difference in excess returns is observable for the combined period, but this is driven by the difference in pre-filing excess returns. During the period from the date of the auditor change to the date of the 8-K filing, the resignation sample experiences a mean (median) excess return of −10.2% (−5.3%), significantly different from zero. During this period the mean and median excess returns of control firms do not differ significantly from zero and are significantly greater than for the resignation firms. Taken together, the pre-filing and post-filing excess returns provide limited support for the SEC's implied assertion that public disclosure of resignations conveys different information to investors relative to other auditor changes. Although dismissals and resignations generate similar market reactions in the post-filing period, resignations appear to generate significantly more negative excess returns in the pre-filing period. If this phenomenon is due to insider leakage of the upcoming resignation disclosures, then resignations do have differential information content, although that information may not be reaching the market in the way that the SEC intended.

An alternative explanation for the post-filing negative excess returns exhibited by both samples is that the market is reacting to other "bad news" events contemporaneously disclosed in the 8-K announcing the auditor change, or in the business press. To investigate the impact of contemporaneous disclosures, an ordinary least squares regression of the cumulative excess returns on a set of dummy variables was conducted. Dummy variables indicated whether the auditor resigned, and whether other bad news accompanied the auditor change disclosure. Along with auditor changes, the SEC mandates that 8-K's be used to disclose changes in control of the registrant, major asset acquisitions, bankruptcy filings, resignation of a registrant's director and any other events that the registrant deems to be of interest to security holders. In addition the existence of disagreements with the predecessor auditor must also be disclosed in the 8-K announcing the auditor change.

We consider bankruptcy, the resignation of a director and the existence of an auditor-client disagreement as bad news events. Analysis of the 8-K's turned up 13 auditor-client disagreement disclosures (twelve resignation and one control company), one disclosure that a resignation company was filing bankruptcy, and one disclosure that a board member resigned from a resignation company. Three dummy variables were created to capture this information: one for disagreements, one for the board member resignation, and one for the bankruptcy announcement. Because 8-K disclosures not in a bad news category might also impact returns, they were also coded using one dummy variable. In addition, a search was performed of financial press news releases and articles that came out during the post-filing period. A dummy variable was created to indicate whether a news article or release appeared pertaining to any of the companies in the samples (other than information already disclosed in the 8-K). We preferred this approach to reducing sample size by deleting firms subject to news reports.

When the explanatory variables described above were regressed against excess returns for the post-filing period, the regression model was not significant at conventional levels. This result indicates that the Table 6 results for the post-filing period are unaffected by other kinds of contemporaneous bad news. When the model was estimated with pre-filing excess returns as dependent variable, the auditor resignation and bankruptcy variable coefficients had negative signs and differed significantly from zero. The remaining variables were not significant at conventional levels.[22] These results suggest that the negative excess returns to resignation clients in the pre-filing period are not due to confounding news events.[23]

One additional investigation was conducted concerning the negative market reaction to resignations in the pre-filing period. We suggest above that this market reaction could be due to insider leakage of the upcoming resignation disclosure. If so, it seems more likely that leakage will occur when the pre-filing delay is lengthy rather than short.[24] We divided the sample of 37 resignations into two groups as nearly equal in size as possible. One group contained the 17 firms with the longest filing delays (greater than 16 days). The second group of 20 firms had the shortest filing delays (less than or equal to 16 days). We then computed mean CAR within each group for the pre-filing period. The mean CAR for the slowest (fastest) filers was –0.153 (–0.059). The difference in means was marginally significant at the .08 level using a one-tailed *T*-test. Although this evidence appears consistent with a leakage scenario, we prefer to reserve judgment pending further research.[25]

CONCLUSIONS

By issuing *Financial Reporting Release* (*FRR*) *No. 31* in 1988, the SEC implicitly asserted that resignations differ from other auditor changes, and that this difference is meaningful to investors. We examine these claims by testing whether companies whose auditors resign differ predictably from those that dismiss their auditors, and whether market reaction to disclosure differs between resignations and other auditor changes. Because the sample of auditor changes is drawn from the pre-*FRR No. 31* era, 1982-1987, this study provides evidence whether the SEC's implied assertions are consistent with data available to the SEC at the time that regulation was promulgated.

We hypothesize that voluntary auditor resignations are motivated by perceived increased litigation risk arising from distrust of client management and from deteriorating client financial health. Our logistic regression results are consistent with this scenario and provide limited support for the SEC's view that resignations differ from dismissals. The resignation sample companies tend to have more auditor-management disagreements and more adverse changes in the ratio of operating cash flow to total assets compared to the control sample. In addition, a majority of these companies received "going concern" audit opinion qualifications prior to the resignations.

We also examine the excess stock returns surrounding the 8-K disclosure of auditor resignations and compare these to the excess returns experienced by companies reporting other auditor changes. Resignation companies have significant, negative abnormal returns from the time of the resignation to the date of Form 8-K filing, and from the filing date through four additional days. The excess returns of the control sample firms do not differ from zero on average in the earlier period, and are significant and negative in the latter period. When excess returns are compared across samples by accumulation period, the returns for the resignation companies are significantly lower in the pre-filing period but do not differ from the control sample in the post-filing period. The significant difference between samples in the pre-filing period suggests that the distinction between resignations and dismissals is meaningful, but that news of resignations frequently reaches the market before Form 8-K is filed. Additional research into the stock market reaction to resignations appears to be warranted.

ACKNOWLEDGMENTS

The authors appreciate helpful comments on earlier versions of this paper from Pat Hughes, Jim Jiambalvo, Marilyn Johnson, Jim Manegold and workshop participants at Claremont McKenna, Texas Christian University and Washington State. The authors also thank Bill Altman of Ernst and Young and Ed Lamb, formerly of Arthur Young, for their first-hand insights; John Riley of the Chief Accountants Office of the SEC, Barbara Rew of the SEC Public Reference Library and Harry Fay of Disclosure, Inc. for their helpful assistance; Jung Jeon and Mike Staheli for their excellent research assistance; and the Accounting Circle at USC for their generous financial support.

NOTES

1. See, for example, "Big Accounting Firms Weed Out Risky Clients" in the June 26, 1995 *Wall Street Journal*, p. B1.

2. FRR No. 31 was prompted in part by Congressional pressure arising from the highly publicized resignation of Ernst and Whinney from ZZZZBest. The House Energy and Commerce Oversight and Investigations Subcommittee (Dingell Committee) felt that the Form 8-K disclosure requirements then in effect were insufficient to assure adequate disclosure of the events surrounding Ernst and Whinney's resignation (see, "Congress May Require CPAs to Notify the SEC when they Resign" in *SEC Accounting Report*, June 1988, p. 2). These actions by Congress and the SEC indicate auditor resignations are an important subset of auditor changes.

3. Some resignations arise from changes in the auditor's circumstances rather than in the client's risk. These include resignations due to lack of independence, auditor retirement, or similar causes. In contrast, *FRR No. 31* appears intended to ensure disclosure of resignations motivated by client characteristics or behavior (see note 2). We focus on such cases and exclude from our sample resignations due to changes in the auditor's circumstances.

4. See Audit Risk Alert (AICPA, 1992) for a discussion of risk arising from audit engagements. The client's business risk is related to the client's survival and profitability. Audit risk is the risk that the auditor may unknowingly fail to modify his or her opinion on financial statements that are materially misstated. The auditor's business risk is the risk of loss of money or reputation arising from association with the client (via, for example, unrecoverable fees or payments to settle litigation).

5. We do not list rendering a qualified opinion as an appropriate response to increased risk based on the findings in Carcello and Palmrose (1994). In multivariate tests, they find that the presence of a qualified opinion does not protect auditors who subsequently end up in court.

6. Bockus and Gigler (1995) present an analytical model in which an auditor perceiving increased liability risk resigns rather than increasing the audit fee. They show that a high bid will only be accepted by clients who have committed fraud.

7. Title III of Public Law No. 104-67, passed in 1995 and popularly referred to as the Tort Reform Bill, requires auditors who discover "consequential" fraud to report it

to management. If management fails to act, and if the fraud has a material effect on the financial statements, the accountant must report to the board of directors. If the board does not notify the SEC within one day, the auditor must do so. We speculate that some auditors who distrust client management may resign before firm evidence of fraud is discovered to avoid being placed in this watchdog role.

8. In *ASR No. 165* the SEC notes with approval an instance in which an auditor reports that its client's reporting procedures, while in accordance with generally accepted accounting principles, are not optimal given the client's circumstances.

9. We attempted to contact several managers of companies whose auditors resigned (pre-*FRR No. 31*) to ask why they disclosed the resignations. After considerable effort, we were able to track down the current location of three such managers. One, through his secretary, refused to speak with us about the resignation. The other two indicated that the disclosure was made at the request of the auditor.

10. See, for example, "Deloitte Disputes IDB's Explanation of It's Resignation" in the June 15, 1994 *Wall Street Journal* (p. A5).

11. As stated in note 3, we do not investigate resignations that are due to changes in the auditor's circumstances.

12. Since we did not feel it was prudent to rely on PAR's verbal data collection process, we exclude the 41 changes that did not explicitly report a resignation in the 8-K filed with the SEC.

13. This sample includes resignations that were disclosed without explanation.

14. Because resignation disclosure was not mandatory during the 1982-1987 time period, some undisclosed resignations could be included in our control sample. This would bias against finding statistical significance in our hypotheses tests. Resignations remain rare events even post-*FRR No. 31*, so we do not think unreported resignations in the control sample are a serious problem in this study.

15. The prior existence of an AAER criticizing management's behavior should not be news to the auditor at the date of resignation. We assume that the auditor reinterprets any prior AAER in the context of recent adverse client developments such as declining financial condition.

16. Comparisons of means with medians in panel A of table 4 indicate highly skewed data and suggest the use of non-parametric tests.

17. The largest correlation observed among explanatory variables was 0.225, a level that does not suggest serious multi-collinearity problems. The scaled change in cash flows to assets variable (CASHCHG) has two very large outliers—a ratio of –844.58 in the treatment group and a ratio of +335.95 in the control group—due to very small cash flows in the denominator (i.e., the last year with the predecessor auditor). These extreme values caused the logit model to estimate an infinite beta coefficient on this variable. Therefore, we Windsorized this variable at a value just beyond the next largest (absolute) value contained in the distribution (see Foster 1986, 101). Specifically, we set the outliers for the treatment and control groups equal to –45 and +45, respectively, since the next largest absolute value after the outliers was –43.94. To test sensitivity to this transformation we also estimated the logit regression with the variables truncated at –90/90 and with the entire distribution truncated at –20/+20 (which only affected one additional variable). Each transformation yielded qualitatively identical results with respect to the significance levels of the estimated coefficients.

18. However, we do not wish to overstate the strength of these results. Several variables hypothesized to play a role in the resignation decision had insignificant coefficients. On balance we view our logit results as offering modest support for the role of conflict and financial health. The importance of financial health in the auditor's decision is strengthened by the prevalence of prior "going concern" qualifications among clients whose auditors resigned.

19. The regression was also estimated with the log of total assets (in the last year with the predecessor auditor) and with growth in assets as independent variables. While the coefficient on the log of total assets variable was significantly negative at $p < .05$, the significance levels on the other coefficient estimates were essentially unchanged.

20. It is notable that the mean and median filing times of both samples exceed the statutory requirement, in the SEC's *Accounting Series Release No. 165*, of 15 calendar days. Overall, 33 of the 60 companies took 16 or more days to file.

21. As with Kinney and McDaniel (1989) the excess return analysis, as presented in Table 6, is performed without adjusting for unequal accumulation periods. The analysis was rerun after scaling by the number of days in the accumulation periods, with results essentially the same as those obtained without adjustment.

22. Our results are inconsistent with Smith and Nichols (1982) who found a negative reaction to disagreements. Possible explanations for the differing results include the following. First, Smith and Nichols performed a pairwise comparison and did not specifically control for other 8K disclosures. Second, the disagreement firms in our study are almost exclusively resignation firms (12 out of 13). This hinders our ability to distinguish empirically between excess returns due to disagreements versus resignations.

23. When excess returns for the pre-filing period were used as dependent variable, a dummy was coded one if a news article appeared in the financial press *during that period.* The OLS analysis also was run including the natural logarithm of assets (in the last year with the predecessor auditor) as an independent variable. The results were essentially the same as those obtained without the inclusion of size.

24. Many investors and managers believe that delay in public disclosure of information increases leakage and insider information. See Ettredge et al. (1996) for a discussion.

25. *Financial Reporting Release* (*FRR*) *No. 34*, issued in 1989, accelerated the allowable 8-K filing lag for auditor changes from 15 calendar days to five business days. Future research could determine whether this action reduced the amount of information apparently reaching the market during the pre-filing period.

REFERENCES

AICPA, Auditing Standards Division. 1992. *Audit Risk Alert—1992*. New York: AICPA.

Albrecht, W., and R. Lamy. 1992. The determinants of the market reaction to an announcement of a change in auditor. Unpublished manuscript, Bowling Green State University.

Arens, A., and J. Loebbecke. 1988. *Auditing: An Integrated Approach, 4th ed. Englewood Cliffs, NJ: Prentice-Hall.*

Bockus, K., and F. Gigler. 1995. Audit pricing, fraud, and resignation. Unpublished manuscript, University of Chicago.

Carcello, J., and Z. Palmrose. 1994. Auditor litigation and modified reporting on bankrupt clients. *Journal of Accounting Research* 32(Suppl.): 1-30.

Eichenseher, J., M. Hagigi, and D. Shields. 1989. Market reaction to auditor changes by OTC companies. *Auditing: A Journal of Practice & Theory* 9(Fall): 29-40.

Ettredge, M., D. Simon, D. Smith, and M. Stone. 1996. Do timely reviews delay the release of quarterly earnings? Unpublished manuscript, University of Alabama.

Feroz, E., K. Park, and V. Pastena. 1991. The financial and market effects of the SEC's accounting and auditing enforcement releases. *Journal of Accounting Research* 29(Suppl.): 107-142.

Foster, G. 1986. *Financial Statment Analysis*, 2nd ed. Englewood Cliffs, NJ: Prentice-Hall.

Johnson, W., and T. Lys. 1990. The market for audit services: Evidence from voluntary auditor changes. *Journal of Accounting and Economics* 12(January): 281-308.

Kinney, W.R., and L.S. McDaniel. 1989. Characteristics of firms correcting previously reported earnings. *Journal of Accounting and Economics* 11: 71-93.

Klock, M. 1994. The stock market reaction to a change in certifying accountant. *Journal of Accounting, Auditing & Finance* (Spring): 339-347.

Lys, T., and R.L. Watts. 1994. Lawsuits against auditors. *Journal of Accounting Research* 32(Suppl.): 65-93.

Nichols, D., and D. Smith. 1983. Auditor credibility and auditor changes. *Journal of Accounting Research* 21(Fall): 534-544.

Noreen, E. 1989. *Computer Intensive Methods for Testing Hypotheses*. New York: John Wiley.

Palmrose, Z. 1987. Litigation and independent auditors: The role of business failures and management fraud. *Auditing: A Journal of Practice & Theory* 6(Spring): 90-103.

St. Pierre, K., and J. Anderson. 1984. An analysis of factors associated with lawsuits against public accountants. *The Accounting Review* LIX(April): 242-263.

Securities and Exchange Commission. 1974. *Accounting Series Release No. 165*. Washington, DC: SEC.

______. 1978. *Accounting Series Release No. 247*. Washington, DC: SEC.

______. 1988. *Financial Reporting Release No. 31*. Washington, DC: SEC.

______. 1989. *Financial Reporting Release No. 34*. Washington, DC: SEC.

Smith, D.B. 1988. An investigation of securities and exchange commission regulation of auditor disclosures: The case of accounting series release #165. *Journal of Accounting Research* 26(Spring): 134-145.

Smith, D.B., and D.R. Nichols. 1982. A market test of investor reaction to disagreements. *Journal of Accounting and Economics* 4: 109-120.

Stice, J.D. 1991. Using financial and market information to identify pre-engagement factors associated with lawsuits against auditors. *The Accounting Review* 66(July): 516-533.

Teoh, S. 1992. Auditor independence, dismissal threats, and the market reaction to auditor switches. *Journal of Accounting Research* 30(Suppl.): 1-27.

REGULATING RESEARCH:
RELEVANCE VERSUS ELEGANCE?

Michael W. Maher

ABSTRACT

This paper examines the effect of the Ford Foundation's business school reform efforts on managerial accounting research. During the 1950s, a group of academics initiated a self-regulated reform of business schools using the resources and influence of the Ford Foundation to further their cause. This paper hypothesizes that those reformers had a significant impact on managerial accounting research. In particular, the reformers affected research methods used, reliance on outside disciplines such as economics and mathematics, and authorship by practitioners. In addition, the paper examines the influence of the *Journal of Accounting Research* in the reform effort.

The results support the hypotheses, and indicate that the reformers created a shift in the literature unparalleled in the history of managerial accounting research. These results provide insights into reasons for recent criticisms of managerial accounting research which argue that researchers focus on narrow, tractable problems instead of issues relevant to the practice of accounting.

Research in Accounting Regulation, Volume 11, pages 47-72.

ISBN: 0-7623-0168-6

INTRODUCTION

This paper examines the effect of the Ford Foundation's business school reform efforts on managerial accounting research. During the 1950s, a group of academics initiated a self-regulated reform of business schools using the resources and influence of the Ford Foundation to further their cause. Although not a legislative reform, these reformers intended their efforts to have an effect similar to legislation by permanently influencing the shape of managerial accounting research. This paper hypothesizes that these reformers had a significant impact on the nature of managerial accounting research; an impact that, in fact, may have resulted in considerable criticism of managerial accounting research in recent years.[1]

It is generally understood that the nature of managerial accounting research has changed over time from conceptual and descriptive work focusing on practical problems to research that is based on modeling and hypothesis testing with an emphasis on problems drawn from economics and psychology. What is not well known, however, are the causes and the process that led to the transformation of the literature. This paper examines the causes and process of that change in managerial accounting research by examining the effect of two key initiatives advanced by the business school reformers: (1) to advance the use of more sophisticated research methods in business school research; and (2) to increase reliance on external disciplines, particularly in the social and behavioral sciences. This paper examines the direct effects of these initiatives on managerial accounting research as well as two additional implications of the reformers' activities: (1) the reduction of the proportion of the research published by practitioners; and (2) the influence of the *Journal of Accounting Research* that started during the reform period at the University of Chicago, which was one of the universities targeted by the reformers to spearhead the reform movement.

The results reported later show that the reformers were largely successful in their efforts. An implication of these findings is that the business school reform effort resulted in greater academic respectability for managerial accounting research by emphasizing more sophisticated research methods and drawing on theories from outside disciplines. At the same time, the reform may in part be responsible for recent criticisms that managerial accounting research does not deal sufficiently with practical problems because researchers focus on narrow tractable problems instead of institutional issues. Thus, the new research literature may have given up relevance to practical problems in exchange for elegance in method and problem selection.

This paper is organized as follows. The second section discusses the four reform initiatives and the resulting hypotheses tested in this paper. The third section discusses the source of data and research methods. The fourth section presents the empirical results, and the fifth section presents the summary and concluding remarks.

REFORM INITIATIVES AND HYPOTHESES

Background

The Ford Foundation's reform efforts were spearheaded by an outside advisory committee comprised of two business school deans, nine university professors (two from business administration, five from economics and two that taught both business and economics), two representatives of nonprofit organizations and one member from business (Schlossman, Sedlack, and Wechsler 1987, 10). This advisory committee's intent to reform business schools meshed with the concerns of the Ford Foundation officials who, by 1953, were convinced of the importance of improving business education and research because of two post-war social and economic factors: a substantial increase in business school enrollments after World War II and the Cold War environment in which the difference between the economic systems of the Soviet Union and the United States was a key battleground element (Schlossman et al. 1987).

Such concerns about business school reform were consistent with general criticisms of the U.S. educational system for failing to keep up with scientific advances in the Soviet Union. According to Dopuch (1982), the U.S. response to Sputnik in 1957 led to a wave of reviews of the educational process, rapid developments in computer technology, and increased demands for statistics and mathematics training in many areas of research. "Reform of business education, along with many other educational causes in the 1950s, became nearly synonymous with patriotism, a stance which placed faculty opponents of reform, as well as foundation critics, on the defensive" (Schlossman et al. 1987, 55).

Business school critics expressed concern that business school research did not meet appropriate academic standards which they attributed largely to the practitioner background of faculty. They claimed that much of the best research in business came from other disciplines, such as economics, and there was little contact between social scientists and business professors. "Even such basic methodological innovations as quantitative modeling (derived from operations research) disseminated very slowly" (Schlossman et al. 1987, 7).

Reform Initiatives and Hypotheses

The four hypotheses tested in this paper are motivated by the two key reform initiatives plus two implications of those initiatives.

Increased Use of Sophisticated Research Methods

The first key reform initiative dealt with the lack of sophisticated research methods. According to a report sponsored by the Ford Foundation, "...research in the business schools needs to become more analytical, to develop a more solid theoretical underpinning, and to utilize a more sophisticated methodology" (Gordon and Howell 1959, 439). Therefore, Hypothesis 1 claims that a greater proportion of articles relied on modeling, empirical hypothesis testing and experimental studies after the reform movement.

H1. A significantly greater proportion of managerial accounting research articles were based on modeling, experimental or empirical research methods after the reform movement.

Increased Reliance on Mathematics, Social Sciences, and Other Outside Disciplines

The second key reform initiative dealt with the isolation of business school research from the fundamental disciplines such as economics. The reformers argued that business was a laboratory to which theories developed in social sciences should be applied, and business school professors were the natural bridge to test fundamental social science theory in business organizations (Schlossman et al. 1987). Gordon and Howell (1959) argued that the new research agenda required researchers to bring the underlying fundamental disciplines into the business school research agenda. Therefore, Hypothesis 2 maintains that managerial accounting research significantly increased its reliance on social sciences and other disciplines rooted outside of business schools after the reform movement.

H2. A significantly greater proportion of managerial accounting research articles relied on outside disciplines after the reform movement.

Reduction in Practitioner Authorship

An implication of the increased emphasis on sophisticated research methods and outside source disciplines is a reduction in the proportion of articles authored by practitioners. Practitioners presumably had a comparative advantage in selecting problems of interest and relevance to the practice of accounting, not in using sophisticated research methods or drawing on outside source disciplines. Therefore, Hypothesis 3 maintains that the proportion of articles authored by practitioners decreased after the reform movement.

H3. A significantly smaller proportion of managerial accounting research articles were authored by practitioners after the reform movement.

Influence of the Journal of Accounting Research

Another implication of the reform movement is the influence of the *Journal of Accounting Research* on the reform. The *Journal of Accounting Research* started in 1963 during the last years of the official Ford Foundation reform work. By locating at the University of Chicago, one of five research universities targeted by the Ford Foundation to spearhead the business school reform movement (Schlossman et al. 1987), it should have been influential in publishing the new reform-oriented literature. According to Davidson (1984), the *Journal of Accounting Research* was founded to "...serve as a vehicle for publication of the expected new wave of accounting research....the editors of *The Accounting Review* at that time seemed reluctant to accept articles with a heavy empirical or quantitative content" (Davidson 1984, 282).

Hypothesis 4 states that the *Journal of Accounting Research* published a significantly greater proportion of articles that complied with the intentions of the business school reformers compared to *The Accounting Review*. Hypothesis 4a proposes that the *Journal of Accounting Research* published significantly more articles using sophisticated research methods while Hypothesis 4b proposes that the

Journal of Accounting Research published significantly more articles that were based on outside source disciplines such as economics and psychology.

H4a. After the reform movement, a significantly greater proportion of managerial accounting research articles published by the *Journal of Accounting Research* used modeling, experimental or empirical research methods compared to *The Accounting Review.*

H4b. After the reform movement, a significantly greater proportion of managerial accounting research articles published by the *Journal of Accounting Research* were based on outside source disciplines compared to *The Accounting Review.*

The next section discusses the data and methods used to test these hypotheses.

DATA AND METHODS

Time Period

The study covers the period 1926 through 1980. The key dates for the analysis are as follows:

1926: Beginning of *The Accounting Review* and start of the pre-reform period for purposes of this study.
1953: Business school reformers initiate business school reform under the auspices of the Ford Foundation.
1959: The Ford Foundation sponsors a report that is highly critical of business schools (see Gordon and Howell 1959).[2]
1961: Beginning of post-reform period for purposes of this study.
1964: End of the Ford Foundation formal reform program.
1980: End of study.

The start of the analysis is 1926, which is the first year of publication for *The Accounting Review.* As the only academic accounting research journal having continuous publication before, during, and after the reform efforts, *The Accounting Review* provides a bounded set of academic accounting research articles to examine. Examining the literature back to the beginning of *The Accounting Review* indicates whether the changes prompted by the reformers were the result of the reform or were simply part of a trend in the literature that started before the reform.

The year 1959 was a watershed in the reform movement. That year, the Ford Foundation's study of business schools was published (Gordon and Howell 1959), as was a similar study financed by the Carnegie Corporation (Pierson 1959). These two studies criticized business schools for lack of rigor and excessive vocationalism. In his discussion of the rise of the accounting profession, Carey (1970) states that these reports stimulated colleges and universities to re-examine their business programs. According to Dyckman and Zeff (1984), "The two reports were everywhere the topic of discussion in business schools, and their impact seems to have been strong" (pp. 231-232).

The Ford Foundation stopped its official reform activities in 1964 but continued funding ongoing programs until 1968 (Schlossman et al. 1987).

Tests of the hypotheses, which will be discussed at length in the next section, compare the "post-reform period" to the "pre-reform period." These tests assume the period from 1926-60 is the pre-reform period. Cutting off the pre-reform period as 1960 may be conservative because the reformers started their work in 1953. However, it is not reasonable that researchers could have become trained to do the type of research envisioned by the reformers in a short time even if researchers believed that to be in their interest. Nor is it likely that the editorial policies of the primary journal at that time, *The Accounting Review*, would have changed immediately.[3] Consequently, it is necessary to allow a reasonable period for the reform movement to take effect.

For most hypotheses tests, the post-reform period starts in 1966, which allows time for doctoral programs to be revised, as recommended by the reformers, and for the newly trained researchers to publish their work. The data collection continues through 1980 to assess whether the effects of the reform movement were a short-term aberration or an ongoing phenomenon. As discussed further in the next section, the results are robust to virtually any reasonable cut-off or start dates for either the pre-reform or post-reform periods.

Data

The following journals were primarily oriented to publishing accounting research during the time period 1926-80: *The Accounting Review*,

Table 1. Managerial Accounting Articles by Journal: 1926-1980

*Journal**	*(1) 1926-50*	*(2) 1951-55*	*(3) 1956-60*	*(4) 1961-65*	*(5) 1966-70*	*(6) 1971-75*	*(7) 1976-80*	*Total Articles*
(1) The Accounting Review	82	26	33	56	67	55	36	355
(2) Journal of Accounting Research				11	20	29	26	86
(3) Accounting Organizations and Society							25	25
(4) Accounting Research	1	13	2					16
(5) Abacus					5	5	5	15
(6) Total	83	39	35	67	92	89	92	497

Note: **The Accounting Review* started in 1926; the *Journal of Accounting Research* started in 1963; *Accounting Organizations and Society* started in 1976; *Accounting Research* was published from 1948-1958; and *Abacus* started in 1965.

Journal of Accounting Research, Accounting Research, Abacus, Accounting, Organizations and Society, and the *Journal of Accounting and Economics*. These journals were not the only outlet for managerial accounting research, but they provide a bounded set for study of the development of the management accounting research literature.

Table 1 shows the number of managerial accounting articles published by these journals through 1980. *The Accounting Review* is the only accounting research journal spanning the entire period and therefore is an important indicator of the transformation of the research literature. Further, *The Accounting Review* published more than 70% of the total managerial accounting research articles from 1926-1980. The *Journal of Accounting Research* published the next largest number of managerial accounting research articles, approximately one-half the number published by *The Accounting Review* between 1963 and 1980.

Three non-U.S. research journals published about 11% of the total managerial accounting articles studied. These journals were *Accounting Research*, which was published between 1948 and 1958 in the U.K., *Accounting, Organizations and Society* (*AOS*) which started in 1976 and was published in the U.K., and *Abacus* which started in 1965 and was published in Australia. The *Journal of Accounting and Economics*, which started in 1979, contained no articles on managerial accounting in the period studied.

Because the Ford Foundation's efforts were directed at US schools, one might limit the analysis to just the U.S. journals. The non-U.S. journals (*Accounting Research, Abacus*, and *AOS*) are included to pick up the effect of U.S. authors, Ph.D.s from U.S. institutions, and researchers influenced by U.S. business schools who published in those journals. As it turns out, excluding any or all of those journals does not affect the results or conclusions of this paper.

Only articles publishing original research are included; therefore, main articles, notes, short articles, and research reports are included, but not comments, replies or rejoinders. The data set includes the *Journal of Accounting Research Supplement* because it contains research articles. The data set does not include the American Accounting Association Committee Reports on managerial accounting published in regular issues of *The Accounting Review* between 1952 and 1962 (n = 5), nor Committee Reports published in *Supplements to The Accounting Review* (n = 6) because these were reports on committee activities, not reports of research.

The following two definitions of managerial accounting were used to separate managerial accounting articles from other articles. Davidson, Stickney and Weil (1987), in *Accounting: The Language of Business*, define managerial accounting as "Reporting designed to enhance the ability of management to do its job of decision making, planning and control; contrast with *financial accounting*" (p. 50). In their review of managerial accounting, Demski and Kreps (1982) say, "Generally speaking, if the accounting numbers being discussed have substantial direct impact on the internal decisions of managers, whether that impact is explicitly considered in the model, we felt that the paper qualified [as managerial accounting]" (p. 119).

Based on these definitions, the following topics are included in the data set: decision making, cost-volume-profit, cost estimation, capital budgeting, behavioral decision making in a managerial context, planning and control, budgeting, variance analysis and investigation, transfer pricing, and agency problems in a managerial setting (superior-subordinate, but not owner-manager), and information economics in a managerial context. Cost allocation and product costing are included if the purpose of the allocation or product costing was managerial, but not where the purpose was inventory valuation for external reporting (thus excluding several articles on the direct versus absorption costing controversy).

RESULTS

This section presents the results from testing the four hypotheses set forth in the section titled "Reform Initiatives and Hypotheses."

Use of Research Methods

Basic Results

According to Hypothesis 1:

> A significantly greater proportion of managerial accounting research articles were based on modeling, experimental or empirical research methods after the reform movement.

To measure the change in use of research methods, articles were first assigned to one of the following five categories.

- *Modeling.* These are articles presenting and analyzing explicit mathematical models. (This category includes the six managerial accounting research articles that used simulation.)
- *Experimental.* These articles present the results of laboratory experiments.
- *Empirical.* These are articles reporting the results of field studies, including field experiments, or cross-section or time-series analyses of data. The distinction between these studies and descriptive studies, described next, is that empirical studies involved the testing of hypotheses subject to refutation whereas the descriptive papers did not.
- *Descriptive.* These articles describe phenomena either through survey of practices or case study, but do not manipulate data to test explicit or implicit hypotheses.
- *Conceptual development.* These articles report frameworks, hypotheses, and recommended accounting methods, but do not involve mathematical modeling, empirical, experimental or descriptive work.

Papers in the first three categories—modeling, empirical and experimental papers—employ the type of methods recommended by the business school reformers.

Table 2 presents the number and proportion of articles in each of the above five categories in five-year blocks from 1926 through 1980. The proportion of articles using modeling, empirical, or experimental research methods increased from 14.3% of the total in the 1956-60 period to 43.5% in the 1966-70 period, just 10 years later. Most of the change in research methods is explained by the increase in modeling papers. Between 1966-70, modeling papers made up 83% of the sum of modeling, experimental and empirical papers. By the period 1976-80, empirical and experimental papers had increased in number and proportion. Modeling articles still made up 56% of the sum of modeling, experimental and empirical papers, but the dominance of modeling papers that was apparent in the early post-reform years was declining.

Business school reformers were particularly critical of the lack of mathematical methods in business school curriculum and research (Schlossman et al. 1987). The emphasis on modeling in the early post-reform years addressed this particular criticism. Because of the mathematical background required to do modeling research, modeling articles

Table 2. Managerial Accounting Articles by Method of Analysis: 1926-1980

*Method of Analysis**	*(1) 1926-50*	*(2) 1951-55*	*(3) 1956-60*	*(4) 1961-65*	*(5) 1966-70*	*(6) 1971-75*	*(7) 1976-80*	*Total Articles*
Number of Articles Using Modeling, Experimental, or Empirical Methods:								
(1) Modeling	3	4	5	16	33	49	35	145
(2) Experimental	0	0	0	2	6	13	14	35
(3) Empirical	2	0	0	2	1	10	13	28
(4) Subtotal: Articles Using Modeling, Experimental or Empirical Methods	5	4	5	20	40	72	62	208
(5) Percent of total articles	6.0%	10.3%	14.3%	29.9%	43.5%	80.9%	67.4%	
Number of Articles Using Descriptive or Conceptual Development Methods:								
(6) Descriptive	21	5	4	3	4	2	2	41
(7) Conceptual Development	57	30	26	44	48	15	28	248
(8) Subtotal: Articles Using Descriptive or Conceptual Development Methods	78	35	30	47	52	17	30	289
(9) Percent of total articles	94.0%	89.7%	85.7%	70.1%	56.5%	19.1%	32.6%	
(10) Total Articles	83 100.0%	39 100.0%	35 100.0%	67 100.0%	92 100.0%	89 100.0%	92 100.0%	497

Notes: ***Modeling**: Articles presenting and analyzing explicit mathematical models. Includes simulation articles.

Experimental: Articles based on results of laboratory experiments.

Empirical: Articles that report the results of field studies or cross-sectional or time-series analyses of data. These studies involve testing explicit or implicit hypotheses subject to refutation. Excludes laboratory experiments, but includes field experiments.

Descriptive: Articles that describe phenomenon either through survey of practices or case study but do not manipulate data to test explicit or implicit hypotheses. Includes surveys of practice.

Conceptual Development: Articles that develop ideas, frameworks, hypotheses. Articles that recommend accounting methods. Excludes articles presenting explicit model manipulation, empirical data or experimental data. Excludes descriptive studies.

Table 3. Test of H1: Number of Articles Using Modeling, Experimental, and Empirical Methods Compared to Articles Using Descriptive and Conceptual Development Methods Before and After the Business School Reform Movement*

	Pre-Reform Period 1926-60	Post-Reform Period 1966-80
Modeling, Experimental and Empirical Methods	14 (8.9%)	174** (63.7%)
Descriptive and Conceptual Development Methods	143 (91.1%)	99 (36.3%)
TOTAL	157 (100%)	273 (100%)

Notes: * See note to Table 2 for definitions of modeling, experimental, empirical, descriptive and conceptual development methods.

** The proportion of articles using modeling, experimental or empirical methods was significantly higher in the post-reform period ($p < .01$, chi-square test).

provided a credible signal that the reformers' criticisms were being addressed, perhaps more so than empirical or experimental research.

Table 3 shows the results of the hypothesis test. As predicted, a significantly greater proportion of the articles used modeling, empirical or experimental methods in the post-reform period compared to the pre-reform period. The pre-reform cutoff year was 1960. The results are robust to any alternative pre-reform cutoff year from 1950 through 1965. The post-reform start date was set at 1966 and the cutoff was 1980. The results were robust for any post-reform start date from 1961 through 1970, and for any post-reform cutoff between 1971 and 1980.

Nature of the Transition

The reformers stated that new approaches to research would come from revamped doctoral programs, implying that current faculty would not make the transition to the new methods of research (Schlossman et al. 1987; Pierson 1959). Reviewing the authors who published during the pre- and post-reform periods shows that few authors made the transition from conceptual or descriptive methods to modeling, empirical or experimental methods, as predicted by the reformers. Of the 69 authors who published managerial accounting research articles using conceptual or descriptive methods between 1951 and 1960, only 4 authors sub-

Table 4. Managerial Accounting Articles by Source Discipline: 1926-1980

*SourceDiscipline**	*(1)* *1926-50*	*(2)* *1951-55*	*(3)* *1956-60*	*(4)* *1961-65*	*(5)* *1966-70*	*(6)* *1971-75*	*(7)* *1976-80*	*Total* *Articles*
(1) Number of Articles Based Primarily on Statistics, Math, or OR	1	2	4	24	24	19	9	83
(2) Number of Articles Based Primarily on Economics	11	7	6	6	13	13	20	76
(3) Number of Articles Based Primarily on Psychology or Sociology	0	0	0	2	4	11	34	51
(4) Number of Articles Based Primarily on Other Disciplines	0	0	1	1	1	1	4	8
(5) Subtotal: Articles Based on Outside Disciplines	12	9	11	33	42	44	67	218
(6) Percent of total articles	14.5%	23.1%	31.4%	49.3%	45.7%	49.4%	72.8%	
(7) Number of Articles Not Based on Outside Disciplines	71	30	24	34	50	45	25	279
(8) Percent of total articles	85.5%	76.9%	68.6%	50.7%	54.3%	50.6%	27.2%	
(9) Total Articles	83	39	35	67	92	89	92	497

Note: *Outside discipline refers to a discipline that is primarily based outside of the business school such as economics or psychology.

Table 5. Test of H2: Number of Articles Based on Outside Source Discipline Compared to Number of Articles Not Based on Outside Discipline*

	Pre-Reform Period 1926-60	Post-Reform Period 1965-80
Articles Based on Outside Source Discipline	32 (20.4%)	153** (56.0%)
Articles Not Based on Outside Source Discipline	125 (79.6%)	120 (44.0%)
Total	157 (100%)	273 (100%)

Notes: * See Table 4 for the list of outside disciplines.
** The proportion of articles based on outside disciplines was significantly higher in the post-reform period compared to the pre-reform period ($p < .01$, chi-square test).

sequently published managerial accounting research articles using modeling, empirical or experimental methods.

Reliance on Outside Disciplines

According to Hypothesis 2:

> A significantly greater proportion of managerial accounting research articles relied on outside disciplines after the reform movement.

Reliance on an outside discipline means the article drew its basic hypotheses, theory or concepts from a discipline outside of business schools.[4]

Table 4 shows an interesting trend in reliance on outside source disciplines. The most influential outside source discipline during the early post-reform years was the category "mathematics, operations research and statistics" (MORS for short). As with the use of modeling as a research method, articles based on MORS clearly addressed the reformers' requirements for more rigorous and analytical research. Papers based on MORS also fit the trend toward more scientific and mathematics based research that was part of the U.S. educational response to Sputnik.

Table 5 shows the results of the hypothesis test. As predicted, a significantly greater proportion of the articles relied on outside source disciplines after the post-reform period compared to the pre-reform period.

As with the test of Hypothesis 1, the pre-reform cutoff year was set at 1960. The results are robust to any alternative pre-reform cutoff year from 1950 through 1965. The post-reform start date was set at 1966 and the cutoff was 1980. The results were robust for any post-reform start date from 1961 through 1970, and for any post-reform cutoff between 1971 and 1980.

Practitioner Authorship

According to Hypothesis 3:

> A significantly smaller proportion of managerial accounting articles were authored by practitioners after the reform movement.

Authors were designated to be practitioners if their organizational affiliation was an organization other than a university or college. Practitioners included academics who were on leave from universities or colleges to work in (say) other organizations such as public accounting firms.

Table 6 shows the trend in practitioner authorship. In Panel A, each co-author counts as one full author. In Panel B, each co-author counts as a fraction of the total number of co-authors on an article; thus, if an article has three co-authors, each co-author counts as one-third of an author. The results in both panels show a substantial drop in practitioner authorship to zero in the 1976-80 period. Table 7 shows the results of the hypothesis test. As predicted, a significantly smaller proportion of the articles were authored by practitioners after the post-reform period compared to the pre-reform period. As with the tests of Hypotheses 1 and 2, the pre-reform cutoff year was set at 1960, but the results are robust to any alternative pre-reform cutoff year from 1950 through 1965. The post-reform start date was set at 1966 and the cutoff for the post-reform period was 1980. The results were robust for any post-reform start date from 1961 through 1970, and for any post-reform cutoff between 1971 and 1980.

Influence of the *Journal of Accounting Research*

According to Hypotheses 4a and 4b:

> H4a: After the reform movement, a significantly greater proportion of managerial accounting research articles published by the *Journal of Accounting Research* used modeling, experimental or empirical research methods compared to *The Accounting Review.*

Table 6. Number of Authors by Author Affiliation: 1926-1980

	*Author Affiliation**	*(1) 1926-50*	*(2) 1951-55*	*(3) 1956-60*	*(4) 1961-65*	*(5) 1966-70*	*(6) 1971-75*	*(7) 1976-80*	*Total*
Panel A:	**Number of authors counting each co-author as one author**								
(1)	Academic	55	21	31	68	121	132	128	556
(2)	Percent of total	65.5%	75.0%	88.6%	85.0%	97.6%	97.8%	100.0%	
(3)	Practitioner	29	7	4	12	3	3	0	58
(4)	Percent of total	34.5%	25.0%	11.4%	15.0%	2.4%	2.2%	0.0%	
(5)	Total Known Affiliations	84	28	35	80	124	135	128	614
(6)		100.0%	100.0%	100.0%	100.0%	100.0%	100.0%	100.0%	
(7)	Unknown Affiliations	2	12	4	0	0	0	0	18
(8)	Total Authors	86	40	39	80	124	135	128	632
Panel B:	**Equivalent number of authors counting each co-author as a fraction (e.g., if 3 co-authors on a paper, each counts as 1/3 author)**								
(9)	Academic	54.50	20.50	28.00	56.50	89.50	87.83	92.00	428.83
(10)	Percent of total	66.5%	75.9%	87.5%	84.3%	97.3%	98.7%	100.0%	
(11)	Practitioner	27.50	6.50	4.00	10.50	2.50	1.17	0.00	52.17
(12)	Percent of total	33.5%	24.1%	12.5%	15.7%	2.7%	1.3%	0.0%	
(13)	Total Known Affiliations	82.00	27.00	32.00	67.00	92.00	89.00	92.00	481.00
(14)		100.0%	100.0%	100.0%	100.0%	100.0%	100.0%	100.0%	
(15)	Unknown Affiliations	1.00	12.00	3.00	0.00	0.00	0.00	0.00	16.00
(16)	Total Authors	83.00	39.00	35.00	67.00	92.00	89.00	92.00	497.00

Notes: ***Academic**: Refers to affiliation with a college or university.

Practitioner: Refers to affiliation with organizations other than colleges or universities, such as public accounting firms, industry, and government agencies, including academics on leave from universities or colleges.

Table 7. Test of H3: Proportion of Articles Having Practitioners as Co-Authors*

	Pre-Reform Period 1926-60	*Post-Reform Period 1965-80*
Panel A: Each co-author counts as one author		
Academics	107 (72.8%)	381*** (98.4%)
Practitioners	40 (27.2%)	6 (1.6%)
Total	147 (100%)	387 (100%)
Panel B: Each co-author counts as a fraction of the total number of authors per article**		
Academics	103 (73%)	269.3*** (98.6%)
Practitioners	38 (27%)	3.7 (1.4%)
Total	141 (100%)	273 (100%)

Notes: * See note to Table 6 for definitions of academic and practitioner.
** For example, if an article has three co-authors, each co-author counts as 1/3 of an author.
*** The proportion of co-authors who were academics was significantly higher in the post-reform period compared to the pre-reform period ($p < .01$, chi-square test).

H4b: After the reform movement, a significantly greater proportion of managerial accounting research articles published by the *Journal of Accounting Research* were based on outside source disciplines compared to *The Accounting Review.*

Table 8 shows the trend in articles published by method of analysis for *The Accounting Review* (Panel A), the *Journal of Accounting Research* (Panel B), and the three non-U.S. journals (Panel C). Although both the *Journal of Accounting Research* and *The Accounting Review* published mostly articles relying on modeling, experimental and empirical research methods in the post-reform period, the non-U.S. journals published mostly articles using conceptual development and descriptive methods. It is possible that the editors of the non-U.S. journals felt they had more freedom not to comply with the wishes of the business school reformers.

Table 9 presents the test of Hypothesis 4a. As predicted, a significantly greater proportion of managerial accounting research articles published by the *Journal of Accounting Research* used modeling, experimental or empirical research methods compared to *The Accounting Review.*

Table 8. Managerial Articles by Journal and by Method of Analysis: 1926-1980

Journal and Method of Analysis	*(1) 1926-50*	*(2) 1951-55*	*(3) 1956-60*	*(4) 1961-65*	*(5) 1966-70*	*(6) 1971-75*	*(7) 1976-80*	*Total Articles*
Panel A: The Accounting Review (TAR)								
(1) Modeling	3	0	4	13	23	32	22	97
(2) Experimental	0	0	0	1	1	7	4	13
(3) Empirical	2	0	0	1	1	4	4	12
(4) Subtotal	5	0	4	15	25	43	30	122
(5) Percent of Total Articles	6.1%	0.0%	12.1%	26.8%	37.3%	78.2%	83.3%	
(6) Descriptive	20	3	4	2	3	1	0	33
(7) Conceptual Development	57	23	25	39	39	11	6	200
(8) Subtotal	77	26	29	41	42	12	6	233
(9) Percent of Total Articles	93.9%	100%	87.9%	73.2%	62.7%	21.8%	16.7%	
(10) Total Articles: TAR	82	26	33	56	67	55	36	355
(11)	100%	100%	100%	100%	100%	100%	100%	
Panel B: Journal of Accounting Research (JAR)								
(12) Modeling				3	10	16	12	41
(13) Experimental				1	5	6	7	19
(14) Empirical				1	0	6	6	13
(15) Subtotal				5	15	28	25	73
(16) Percent of Total Articles				45.5%	75.0%	96.6%	96.2%	
(17) Descriptive				1	0	0	0	1
(18) Conceptual Development				5	5	1	1	12
(19) Subtotal				6	5	1	1	13
(20) Percent of Total Articles				54.5%	25.0%	3.4%	3.8%	
(21) Total Articles: JAR				11	20	29	26	86
(22)				100%	100%	100%	100%	

(continued)

Table 8. (Continued)

	Journal and Method of Analysis	*(1) 1926-50*	*(2) 1951-55*	*(3) 1956-60*	*(4) 1961-65*	*(5) 1966-70*	*(6) 1971-75*	*(7) 1976-80*	*Total Articles*
Panel C:	**Other:***								
(23)	Modeling	0	4	1		0	1	1	7
(24)	Experimental	0	0	0		0	0	3	3
(25)	Empirical	0	0	0		0	0	3	3
(26)	Subtotal	0	4	1		0	1	7	13
(27)	Percent of Total Articles	0.0%	30.8%	50.0%		0.0%	20.0%	23.3%	
(28)	Descriptive	1	2	0		1	1	2	7
(29)	Conceptual Development	0	7	1		4	3	21	36
(30)	Subtotal	1	9	1		5	4	23	43
(31)	Percent of Total Articles	100%	69.2%	50.0%		100%	80.0%	76.7%	
(32)	Total Articles: Other	1	13	2		5	5	30	56
(33)		100%	100%	100%		100%	100%	100%	
(34)	Total all Articles	83	39	35	67	92	89	92	497

Note: **Abacus* (1965-), *Accounting Research* (1948-58), *Accounting, Organizations and Society* (1976-).

Table 9. Test of H4a: Proportion of Articles Using Modeling, Experimental, or Empirical Methods Published in the *Journal of Accounting Research* compared to *The Accounting Review* for the Post-Reform Period 1966-80.

	The Accounting Review	*Journal of Accounting Research*
Modeling, Experimental or Empirical Methods	98 (62.0%)	68* (90.1%)
Descriptive or Conceptual Framework	60 (38.0%)	7 (9.9%)
Total	158 (100%)	75 (100%)

Note: * Differences between the *Journal of Accounting Research* and *The Accounting Review* are significant at $p < .01$ (chi-square test).

Table 10 looks like Table 8 except that it presents the results for reliance on source discipline. Most of the articles in both *The Accounting Review* and the *Journal of Accounting Research* relied on outside source disciplines in the post-reform period. *The Accounting Review* articles relied slightly more on mathematics, statistics or operations research (MORS) while the *Journal of Accounting Research* articles relied about equally on MORS and economics from 1966-75. After that the *Journal of Accounting Research* articles relied more on economics.

Table 11 shows that, as predicted by Hypothesis 4b, a significantly greater proportion of managerial accounting research articles published in the *Journal of Accounting Research* were based on outside source disciplines compared to *The Accounting Review*. By the 1976-80 period, however, the proportion of articles relying on outside source discipline was about equal for the two journals.

A limitation of this analysis is that it does not take into account the direct effect of the reform movement on *The Accounting Review* without the influence of the *Journal of Accounting Research*.[5] One could argue that the reform movement might have had little or no effect on the literature without the pressure created by the *Journal of Accounting Research* on *The Accounting Review* to respond to the reform movement. Alternatively, without *The Journal of Accounting Research* to absorb the effects of the reform movement, *The Accounting Review* might have responded even more to the reform movement. We simply do not know what effects the reform movement would have had on *The*

Table 10. Managerial Accounting Articles by Journal and by Source Discipline: 1926-1980

Journal and Source Discipline	*(1) 1926-50*	*(2) 1951-55*	*(3) 1956-60*	*(4) 1961-65*	*(5) 1966-70*	*(6) 1971-75*	*(7) 1976-80*	*Total Articles*
The Accounting Review (TAR):								
(1) Articles: Statistics, Math, or OR	1	2	3	18	18	13	6	61
(2) Articles: Economics	11	3	6	5	7	5	8	45
(3) Articles: Psychology or Sociology	0	0	0	2	3	4	10	19
(4) Articles: Other Disciplines	0	0	1	1	1	0	2	5
(5) Subtotal: Articles Based on Outside Discipline	12	5	10	26	29	22	26	130
(6) Percent of total articles	14.6%	19.2%	30.3%	46.4%	43.3%	40.0%	72.2%	
(7) Articles: No Outside Discipline	70	21	23	30	38	33	10	225
(8) Percent of total articles	85.4%	80.8%	69.7%	53.6%	56.7%	60.0%	27.8%	
(9) Total Articles: TAR	82	26	33	56	67	55	36	355
(10)	100.0%	100.0%	100.0%	100.0%	100.0%	100.0%	100.0%	
Journal of Accounting Research (JAR):								
(11) Articles: Statistics, Math, or OR				6	6	5	2	19
(12) Articles: Economics				1	5	6	11	23
(13) Articles: Psychology or Sociology				0	1	6	7	14
(14) Articles: Other Disciplines				0	0	0	0	0
(15) Subtotal: Articles Based on Outside Discipline				7	12	17	20	56
(16) Percent of total articles				63.6%	60.0%	58.6%	76.9%	
(17) Articles: No Outside Discipline				4	8	12	6	30
(18) Percent of total articles				36.4%	40.0%	41.4%	23.1%	
(19) Total Articles: JAR				11	20	29	26	86
(20)				100.0%	100.0%	100.0%	100.0%	

Other:*

(21)	Articles: Statistics, Math, or OR	0	0	1		0	1	1	3
(22)	Articles: Economics	0	4	0		1	2	1	8
(23)	Articles: Psychology or Sociology	0	0	0		0	1	17	18
(24)	Articles: Other Disciplines	0	0	0		0	1	2	3
(25)	Subtotal: Articles Based on Outside Discipline	0	4	1		1	5	21	32
(26)	Percent of total articles	0.0%	30.8%	50.0%		20.0%	100.0%	70.0%	
(27)	Articles: No Outside Discipline	1	9	1		4	0	9	24
(28)	Percent of total articles	100.0%	69.2%	50.0%		80.0%	0.0%	30.0%	
(29)	Total Articles: Other	1	13	2		5	5	30	56
(30)		100.0%	100.0%	100.0%		100.0%	100.0%	100.0%	
(31)	Total all Articles	83	39	35	67	92	89	92	497

Note: **Abacus* (1965-), *Accounting Research* (1948-58), *Accounting, Organizations and Society* (1976-).

Table 11. Test of H4b: Proportion of Articles Based on Outside Discipline Published in the *Journal of Accounting Research* compared to *The Accounting Review* for the Post-Reform Period 1966-80.

	The Accounting Review	*Journal of Accounting Research*
Based on Outside Disciplines	77 (48.7%)	49* (65.3%)
Not Based on Outside Disciplines	81 (51.3%)	26 (34.7%)
Total	158 (100%)	75 (100%)

Note: *Differences between the *Journal of Accounting Research* and *The Accounting Review* are significant at $p < .05$.

Accounting Review absent the existence of the *Journal of Accounting Research* or a similar reform-oriented journal.

SUMMARY AND CONCLUSIONS

The results in this paper show support for two hypotheses that are key initiatives of the business school reformers—the significant change in research methods and reliance on outside discipline after the business school reform movement. The results also show support for two hypotheses that, although not part of the reform per se, are reasonable consequences of the reform movement—the significant reduction in practitioner authorship and the significant differences between the *Journal of Accounting Research* and *The Accounting Review* in publishing reform-oriented articles.

It is clear from the data that the shift in the literature following the business school reform movement was unparalleled in the history of published academic managerial accounting research. This shift marked the beginning of "modern" managerial accounting research. Some critics contend that this shift means managerial accounting research has sacrificed relevance for elegance over the past several decades. A consequence of the business school reform movement may have been managerial accounting researchers who are not well versed in institutional problems because that knowledge is not needed to publish in academic research journals. As a result of the reform movement, accounting academics may have increased their academic respectability and closed the gap between business school academics and their colleagues in other academic disciplines. But in doing so, they may have increased the gap between research and practice.

ACKNOWLEDGMENTS

I am grateful to Brad Barber, Harold Bierman, Jr., Germain Boer, William W. Cooper, Thomas R. Dyckman, Roger Hermanson, Charles Horngren, James Horrigan, Raffi Indejikian, Yuji Ijiri, Robert Kaplan, William Kinney, Ella Mae Matsumura, Don Palmer, Jacob Thomas, Gary Previts, Frank Selto, Joseph J. Schultz, Jr., Ross Watts, Miriam Wells, the two reviewers, participants at the American Accounting Association annual meeting August 1995, and participants at the American Accounting Association Managerial Accounting Research Conference, October 1995 for helpful comments, and to Kurt Heisinger and Charles Klemstine for their able assistance.

NOTES

1. Kaplan and Johnson (1987), Dyckman (1989), and Kaplan (1993) particularly criticize the applicability of managerial accounting research to real-world problems. According to Kaplan and Johnson, managerial accounting researchers have concentrated "...on increasingly elegant and sophisticated approaches to analyzing costs for single-product, single-process firms..." (p. 15) bearing little relation to actual organizations that have complex, multistage production processes. Lev and Ronen (1971) echo these sentiments in a broader criticism of accounting research.
2. That same year, the Carnegie Corporation also sponsored a report that was highly critical of business schools (Pierson 1959).
3. In fact, the quote from Davidson (1964) cited above indicated that *The Accounting Review* was slow to change its editorial policies.
4. Relying on an outside discipline is not the same as using research methods developed in an outside discipline. For example, some modeling papers relied on outside disciplines (e.g., economics) but other modeling papers did not.
5. I acknowledge the comments of a reviewer who made this point.

REFERENCES

Carey, J.L. 1970. *The Rise of the Accounting Profession: To Responsibility and Authority, 1937-1969.* New York: American Institute of Certified Public Accountants.

Davidson, S. 1984. The origins of the *Journal of Accounting Research.* Appendix to T.R. Dyckman and S.A. Zeff, "Two decades of the *Journal of Accounting Research.*" *Journal of Accounting Research* 22(Spring): 281-285.

Davidson, S., C.P. Stickney, and R.L. Weil. 1987. *Accounting: The Language of Business*, 7th ed. Sun Lakes, AZ: Horton and Daughters.

Demski, J.S., and D.M. Kreps. 1982. Models in managerial accounting. *Journal of Accounting Research* 20(Suppl.): 117-148.

Dopuch, N. 1982. The impact of technology on accounting research—Past, present, and future. In *Technological Change: Its Impact on Accounting*, ed. by E. Summers. Reston, VA: The Council of Arthur Young Professors.

Dyckman, T.R. 1989. Practice to research—"What have you done for me lately?" *Accounting Horizons* 3(March): 111-118.

Dyckman, T.R., and S.A. Zeff. 1984. Two decades of the *Journal of Accounting Research. Journal of Accounting Research* 22(Spring): 225-297.

Gordon, R.A., and J.E. Howell. 1959. *Higher Education for Business*. New York: Columbia University Press.

Johnson, H.T., and R.S. Kaplan. 1987. *Relevance Lost: The Rise and Fall of Management Accounting*. Boston: Harvard Business School Press.

Kaplan, R.S. 1993. Research opportunities in management accounting. *Journal of Management Accounting Research* 5(Fall): 1-14.

Lev, B., and J. Ronen. 1991. A statement on the state of academic accounting. Unpublished paper presented at the American Accounting Association Annual Meetings, Nashville, TN.

Pierson, F.C. 1959. *The Education of American Businessmen*. New York: McGraw-Hill.

Schlossman, S.L., M. Sedlack, and H. Wechsler. 1987. *The New Look: The Ford Foundation and the Revolution in Business Education*. Los Angeles: Graduate Management Admissions Council).

THE EFFECT OF SEC ENFORCEMENT ON AUDITOR IPO MARKET SHARE

Keith A. Moreland

ABSTRACT

One objective of the enforcement activities of the Securities and Exchange Commission (SEC) is to maintain the credibility of the financial disclosure system in the United States, in which auditors play a key role. One direct effect for auditors found by the SEC to have performed substandard audits is that the audit firm is subject to disciplinary action by the SEC. During recent years auditing firms also have faced rapidly increasing costs associated with litigation for alleged substandard audit work. This study examines whether auditors also experience an indirect effect in the form of decreased market share of initial public offering (IPO) audits following the SEC's reports of enforcement actions issued from 1978 to 1991.

The IPO market is a rich setting to examine the market for audit services because of the significance that client firms attach to auditor selection in order to enhance the attractiveness of the securities offering.

Research in Accounting Regulation, Volume 11, pages 73-98.

ISBN: 0-7623-0168-6

Reports of SEC enforcement actions (or sanctions) and litigation cases against auditors are modeled as information that negatively affects assessed auditor quality. It is hypothesized that some IPO firms will avoid auditors reported in such information.

Post-sanction changes in IPO market shares of criticized auditors and a control group were examined using regression analysis. The regression models also controlled for differences in market shares and levels of litigation across audit firms.

The results suggest that reports of SEC enforcement actions negatively affect auditor IPO market shares during the period from one to three years after the sanction. No market share effects related to litigation were observed. The sanction-related market share decrease suggests that client firm managers use information from the regulatory organization in assessing auditor quality and in auditor selection decisions. These results may have implications for regulators and audit firm executives who are concerned with assessing the impact that disciplinary actions against auditors have in the market for audit services.

INTRODUCTION

This study examines the effects of publicly-reported disciplinary actions by the Securities and Exchange Commission (SEC) and litigation cases from 1978 to 1991 on the initial public offering (IPO) market shares of the criticized audit firms. During recent years auditing firms have faced rapidly increasing costs associated with litigation by investors for alleged substandard audit work. Auditors accused of substandard audit work associated with securities filings in the United States also are subject to disciplinary action (or sanctions) by the SEC. While litigation against Big 6 auditors[1] has increased and overall SEC enforcement activity has not decreased during the last decade, the number of SEC disciplinary actions against these large audit firms has decreased.

Nonetheless, prior research suggests that SEC criticisms of auditors affect the market for audit services in the form of lower client retention rates (Wilson and Grimlund 1990) and lower first-year audit fees on clients that switch auditors (Davis and Simon 1992). This SEC enforcement action study on auditor IPO market share extends prior research by focussing on a setting where auditor selection and audit services have heightened importance. This is because the audited financial statements typically are associated with the sale of a significant (partial) ownership interest in the entity and a high quality auditor potentially can reduce uncertainty associated with the discount in the selling price (Datar et al. 1991). In addition, because client firms are more inclined to change auditors prior to an IPO, concerns about perceived auditor quality are more likely to be manifested in auditor selection decisions. Hence, this is a rich setting in which to examine the effects of information about auditor quality on the market for audit services.

Regression analysis of changes in IPO market shares for auditors recently criticized by the SEC and a control group of "uncriticized" auditors is performed. The results suggests that audit firms disciplined by the SEC experience negative market-share effects from approximately one to three years after the criticism. No IPO market share effects related to litigation against auditors were detected.

These results suggest that managers use information included in SEC reports of disciplinary actions in auditor selection decisions. Consequently, the results are useful to regulators and audit firm executives who are concerned with the impact that disciplinary actions against auditors have on decisions in the market for audit services.

The remainder of this paper includes sections on the background of the role of auditors in IPOs, SEC enforcement activities, litigation, and development of the hypotheses; research methodology; the empirical results; and a conclusion.

BACKGROUND AND HYPOTHESIS DEVELOPMENT

The Role of Auditing in Initial Public Offerings

IPOs have been modelled as a setting where a risk-averse entrepreneur with private information regarding firm value seeks to raise capital from and share risk with external investors. Datar et al. (1991) show that external investor uncertainty regarding the firm's value causes underpricing of the firm and the security offering, absent communications revealing the entrepreneur's private information.

Entrepreneurs may employ various signals to reduce uncertainty regarding the firm's value, attract investors, and reduce underpricing. For example, Grinblatt and Whang (1989) suggest entrepreneurs use two signals, retained ownership percentage and some underpricing, to convey the mean and variance of the firm's projects. Underpricing on IPOs is argued to exist, in part, to attract investors to subsequent offerings. Datar et al. (1991) show that the report of a credible auditor is a signal that can be used to reduce the ownership percentage required to be retained by the entrepreneur and still communicate private information regarding firm value.

Studies of the role of auditing in IPOs suggest credible financial statement assertions are of increased importance at this stage of a firm's life. The significant portion of the firm that generally is offered for sale, the importance of historical financial statements in assessing value, and the potential severe penalties for inadequate financial reporting are argued to cause IPO firms to focus on auditor selection. Carpenter and Strawser (1971) find that firms frequently change to a Big 6 auditor prior to going public in order to make the offering more attractive.

Datar et al. (1991) and Feltham et al. (1991) argue that the enhanced ability to fully signal entrepreneur private information should cause IPO firms with greater firm-specific risk to select high-quality audit firms (referred to as a "demand-side effect"). Empirical evidence relating to IPOs in the United States generally does not support this expectation. Feltham et al. (1991) suggest that a "supply-side effect," in the form of increased litigation and other costs, works to counter the expected association between high-quality auditors and higher-risk IPO firms. Clarkson and Simunic (1994) observe the expected association between high-quality audit firms and higher-risk IPO firms in Canada, where expected auditor costs associated with higher-risk IPOs (e.g., litigation) are argued to be not as great.

Actual and Perceived Auditor Quality

Auditor quality has been described as the ability to detect and willingness to report client errors (DeAngelo 1981). These qualities, in turn, depend on the auditor's knowledge, expertise, thoroughness, and ability not to acquiesce to client pressure regarding the report (Feltham et al. 1991; O'Keefe and Westort 1992).

Actual audit quality is largely not observable because audit services generally include neither "search charactistics," which can be ascertained prior to purchase, nor "experience characteristics," which are evaluated in consumption (Darby and Karni 1973; Blair and Kaserman 1980). Dopuch and Simunic (1982) suggest that the only audit characteristic disclosed to outside users is the audit firm name. Davis and Simon (1992) argue that client firm managers are better able than outside users to observe audit quality characteristics, but cite Wallace (1989) in noting that these managers' quality assessments are incomplete nonetheless. Blair and Kaserman (1980) suggest that the inability of users to evaluate audit quality gives rise to external and self regulation. The inability to observe actual audit quality has caused researchers to focus on perceived or reputed auditor quality.

Dopuch and Simunic (1982) and DeAngelo (1981) argue that large audit firms with well-known brand names have economic incentives and the wherewithal to provide high quality in order to develop and retain a large portfolio of audit clients. Their large size enables them to invest in development of expertise and specialization. At the same time, it is argued that these firms will go to greater lengths to ensure quality because news of a single audit failure would have further reaching effects. As a result, they have reputations for providing higher quality audits.

Numerous studies have employed the dichotomous Big 6/non-Big 6 measure of audit firm size and brand name as a proxy for audit quality. Simunic and Stein (1987), Balvers et al. (1988), and Beatty (1989) observe reduced uncertainty and initial returns (underpricing) in IPOs audited by Big 6 firms.

Dopuch and Simunic (1982) and Wilson (1983) suggest that an audit firm quality assessment is driven by overall reputation because of lack of specific knowledge. These researchers identify potential information sources regarding assessed auditor quality, such as litigation or regulatory actions, and argue that a quality assessment can change as new information becomes available. Some evidence suggests positive associations among the various measures of assessed audit quality. For example, Palmrose (1988) finds that Big 6 firms, which have reputations for high quality, experienced lower rates of litigation than smaller audit firms.

Researchers have further suggested that a change in quality assessment can affect a firm's position in the market for audit services and the information content of the auditor's report. Davis and Simon (1992) find that, from 1978 to 1988, auditors criticized by the SEC experience lower first-year audit fees from switching clients than do other auditors. Wilson and Grimlund (1990) find that criticized auditors experience somewhat lower client retention rates during the same period. Moreland (1995) reports that, from 1974 to 1990, earnings/returns associations are weaker for clients of recently sanctioned auditors. Firth (1990) finds clients of auditors criticized by the United Kingdom Department of Trade from 1969 to 1983 experience small declines in market value at the time of the release of the criticism. These results suggest that criticized auditors experience a decline in the assessed level of credibility they provide to client financial information. This in turn causes a weakened competitive position for the auditor and/or more uncertainty regarding client firm financial information and values. In this study, the SEC sanction effect on auditor market share is examined in the IPO setting where financial, legal, and other ramifications are thought to heighten the importance of auditor selection.

SEC Enforcement Activities

Enforcement activities are a key part of the SEC's programs directed at improving capital markets and preventing fraud. The specific objective of the SEC's accounting and auditing enforcement activities is to maintain the credibility of the financial disclosure system, in which the SEC believes auditors play a key role (Burton 1975). With respect to auditors, the SEC noted in a 1991 *Accounting and Auditing Enforcement Release* that "...(i)t is of utmost importance that investors be able to rely on the independence of public accountants and their audit reports when making investment decisions" (*AAER 301*, June 13, 1991).

The SEC conducts investigations of auditors in cases where it has reason to believe there may be auditor knowledge of a client's deficient financial reporting or scheme to mislead the public, or other serious professional deficiency. Burton (1975) notes that the SEC believes that sanctions impact the reputation of an audit firm.

The number of audits cited, the seriousness of the audit problems, and the severity of penalties against an audit firm vary. Sanction-related penalties and remedial actions include a censure of the firm, a temporary suspension or permanent ban from practicing before the SEC, a temporary prohibition from accepting new SEC clients, a peer review of the firm's practice (before they became mandatory), and implementation of specific continuing professional education programs. Actions can be directed at the firm as a whole, specific practice offices, or individuals.

Generally, an enforcement investigation is confidential until completion, when the details of the investigation and the sanctions against the auditors are publicly reported in AAERs, or prior to 1982, in *Accounting Series Releases* (ASRs). The details reported in AAERs and ASRs provide an indication of the severity of the sanction. Table 1 identifies the enforcement actions included in this study. The Appendix summarizes the most recent enforcement action included in this study.[2]

Reports of enforcement actions are issued in response to actual audit weaknesses (in the view of the SEC) pertaining to a small number of specific audits. To affect the perception of an audit firm in the IPO market, the sanction must degrade managers', underwriters', and/or investors' assessments of quality across the firm's practice. Palmrose (1991b) describes SEC enforcement actions as a type of "non-routine" or "highly visible" litigation which audit report users may be more likely to consider in assessing auditor quality.

Relationship Between SEC Enforcement Actions and Litigation

Civil litigation cases against auditors that do not involve SEC enforcement actions are a more common or "routine" source of information to assess auditor quality. Palmrose (1988) identifies 240 litigation cases against Big 6 auditors from 1973 to 1985. During the same period, there were 11 enforcement actions against these firms reported in ASRs and AAERs. Since 1985, the frequency of reported enforcement actions against Big 6 firms has decreased while the number of litigation cases against this group has increased (Lys and Watts 1994). The relative infrequency and source (the SEC) of the enforcement actions suggest a greater importance may be attached to an individual enforcement action than to an individual litigation case.

Both civil litigation occurrences and outcomes against auditors have been modelled as information that could affect auditor quality assessments. Both measures are regarded as noisy because of factors such as frivolous lawsuits, "deep pockets," alternative lawsuit settlement strategies, and varying levels of litigiousness across client industries. These factors and the relatively routine nature of lawsuits against auditors may work against detection of an association between litigation-related auditor quality assessments and audit market effects, such as changes in market share (Palmrose 1991b).

Nonetheless, high levels of litigation potentially can affect an assessment of auditor quality. Further, the impact on assessed audit quality from public disclosure of an SEC enforcement action may depend, in part, on the audit firm's litigation experience. For example, an enforcement action against an audit firm that has been identified in recent, adverse litigation may, in effect, confirm the audit quality assessment information resulting from the litigation. Conversely, information about a sanction against an audit firm that has been relatively litigation-free may more dramatically affect assessed audit quality.[3]

SEC Enforcement Action and Litigation Hypotheses

Various factors including incumbency, industry specialization, fees, and service level affect auditor selection. Carpenter and Strawser (1971) argue that, prior to an IPO, many firms change from smaller to larger audit firms that have more recognizable brand names in order to enhance the perceived credibility of the financial statements and the offering. Similarly, if an SEC enforcement action is thought to degrade assessed audit quality and the credibility added to client financial information, some IPO firms may elect to avoid a sanctioned auditor. At the same time, the approximately zero-sum nature of the IPO audit market suggests that client firm decisions to avoid sanctioned auditors would benefit audit firms not identified in a sanction, in the form of increased market share.

The cost of not avoiding a sanctioned auditor may be affected by the status of the sanctioned auditor (incumbent or not) and characteristics of the client firm. Client firm management may decide that the costs of retaining an incumbent sanctioned auditor are less than the costs of switching to a new "unsanctioned" auditor. Also, the effect of a sanction on the credibility that auditors provide to financial statements may be of less concern to client firms with characteristics such as large size, familiarity within the investing community, relative financial strength, or a reputation for being well-managed. Thus, only those client firms for whom the alternatives are considered to be less costly are expected to avoid sanctioned auditors. The SEC enforcement action market share hypothesis (in the alternative form) is:

H_1. The market share of IPO client firms declines for an audit firm after it is criticized in an SEC enforcement action.

Likewise, some IPO firms are expected to avoid audit firms that have experienced significant litigation that may degrade assessed auditor quality. The litigation/market share hypothesis (in the alternative form) is:

H_2. The market share of IPO client firms declines for an audit firm that has experienced an increase in litigation against it.

RESEARCH METHODOLOGY

Data

Panels A and B of Table 1 list each sanctioned auditor, a brief description of the enforcement action outcome, the associated control groups of "unsanctioned" Big 6 auditors, and the time periods and number of firm-commitment IPOs from which market shares were calculated for the enforcement actions included in this study. The sample included 889 monthly market share observations; 228 for criticized auditors and 661 for control firms. The time periods from which the observations were taken are discussed below. Prior research suggests that excluding "best-efforts" and non-Big 6-audited IPOs creates a more homogenous sample in examining IPO auditor selection (Balvers et al. 1988; Beatty 1989). The numbers of IPOs related to each enforcement action listed in Table 1 reflect the dramatic increase in public offerings during the last 20 years.

Empirical Test the Enforcement Action and Litigation Hypotheses

The SEC enforcement action and litigation effects on auditor market share are tested as follows. First, the difference between monthly market share during the period expected to be affected by the sanction and litigation and the average monthly market share of the preceding (unaffected or base) period is calculated. Consequently, observations included in this study consist of these individual monthly market share differences, stated in percentage points. Next, these monthly market share differences are regressed against a variable identifying the audit firm, a measure of the change in litigation against the audit firm, and a variable indicating whether the audit firm is assumed to be under sanction or a control firm. The period assumed to be affected by the sanction is divided into two sub-periods to study the length of time of a "sanction effect." The control groups include Big 6 auditors not sanctioned by the SEC for three years before and after the sanction in question. Accordingly, the control groups vary for each sanction. Also, although an audit firm could represent a "control" against two or more sanctioned firms because of the chronological proximity of some enforcement actions, a monthly market share for such a control firm is included as one and only one observation.

Table 1. Summary SEC Enforcement Actions

Panel A. Enforcement Actions and Control Firms

Sanctioned Audit Firm		
Enforcement Action/Date	*Enforcement Action Outcome*	*Related Control Group Audit Firms*
Ernst & Young[a]/ 06/90-06/91	Firm's New York Region SEC practice restricted and one partner suspended (1990)/SEC accused firm of lack of independence (1991).	Arthur Andersen Coopers & Lybrand Deloitte & Touche[b] KPMG Peat Marwick Price Waterhouse
Price Waterhouse/ 06/85	SEC requested permanent injunction against the firm and three of its associates seeking ban on fraudulent securities activities.	Arthur Andersen Arthur Young Deloitte Haskins & Sells Ernst & Whinney KPMG Peat Marwick
Coopers & Lybrand/ 11/84	SEC issued an opinion and order criticizing the audit firm.	Arthur Andersen Arthur Young Deloitte Haskins & Sells Ernst & Whinney KPMG Peat Marwick
Touche Ross/11/83	SEC issued an opinion and order criticizing and censuring the audit firm.	Arthur Young Deloitte Haskins & Sells Ernst & Whinney KPMG Peat Marwick
Arthur Andersen/ 06/81	SEC issued an opinion and order criticizing and censuring the audit firm.	Arthur Young Coopers & Lybrand Deloitte Haskins & Sells Ernst & Whinney KPMG Peat Marwick Price Waterhouse
Touche Ross/06/79	SEC censured firm, required peer review, and suspended two firm partners.	Arthur Young Coopers & Lybrand KPMG Peat Marwick
Ernst & Ernst/05/78	SEC censured firm and suspended two firm partners.	Arthur Andersen Arthur Young Coopers & Lybrand
Haskins & Sells/ 02/78	Firm agrees to undergo SEC practice review and sponsor internal control research. SEC work of one practice office restricted.	Arthur Andersen Arthur Young Coopers & Lybrand
Price Waterhouse/ 01/78	Firm required to return audit fees and undergo practice review. Three associates suspended from SEC practice.	Arthur Andersen Arthur Young Coopers & Lybrand

(continued)

Table 1. (Continued)

Panel B. Sample Information for Criticized and Control Firms

Criticized Firms	*Dates*	*Months*	*IPOs*[c]	*Control Firms*	*Dates*[d]	*Months*	*IPOs*[c]
Ernst & Young	7/91-6/94	36	445	Arthur Andersen	7/91-6/94	36	568
				Coopers & Lybrand	7/91-6/94	36	416
Price Waterhouse	7/86-6/88	24	131	Deloitte & Touche	7/91-6/94	36	691
				KPMG Peat Marwick	7/91-6/94	36	524
Coopers & Lybrand	12/85-11/87	24	182	Price Waterhouse	7/91-6/94	36	339
				Arthur Andersen	12/85-6/88	31	264
Touche Ross	12/84-11/86	24	130	Arthur Young	12/84-6/88	43	228
				Deloitte Haskins & Sells	12/84-6/88	43	227
Arthur Andersen	7/82-6/84	24	113	Ernst & Whinney	12/84-6/88	43	285
				KPMG Peat Marwick	12/84-6/88	43	336
Touche Ross	7/80-6/82	24	57	Arthur Young	7/82-6/84	24	97
				Coopers & Lybrand	7/82-6/84	24	82
Ernst & Ernst	6/79-5/81	24	18	Deloitte Haskins & Sells	7/82-6/84	24	89
				Ernst & Whinney	7/82-6/84	24	98
Haskins & Sells	3/70-2/81	24	7	KPMG Peat Marwick	7/82-6/84	24	153
				Price Waterhouse	7/82-6/84	24	86
Price Waterhouse	2/79-1/81	24	20	KPMG Peat Marwick	7/80-6/82	24	66
				Arthur Andersen	2/79-5/81	28	58
				Arthur Young	2/79-6/82	41	62
				Coopers & Lybrand	2/79-6/82	41	65
Total		228	1,103			661	4,734

Notes: [a] Ernst & Young was formed by a merger of Ernst & Whinney (formerly Ernst & Ernst) and Arthur Young.

[b] Deloitte & Touche was formed by a merger of Deloitte Haskins & Sells (formerly Haskins & Sells) and Touche Ross. For three months during the "preceding period" Deloitte Haskins & Sells and Touche Ross were operating separately. For those months the Deloitte & Touche market share consists of the combined market shares of these two firms.

[c] IPOs AUDITED = The number of IPOs audited by sanctioned and control-group auditors during the sanction-effected period (13 to 36 months after the sanction).

[d] Note that in several cases an audit firm serves as a "control firm" for two or more enforcement actions that occurred in chronological proximity. A monthly market share observation for such a control firm is included once and only once in the study. The monthly periods and number of months reported here refer to the consecutive months for which an audit firm represented a control firm for one or more sanctions.

Identification of sanction-affected time periods is problematic. The process of selecting an auditor, which may involve discussions, interviews, and negotiations with several firms, is lengthy and variable. As a result, there is a time lag between a management decision to avoid a sanctioned auditor and its manifestation in the form of change in market share. Wilson and Grimlund (1990) focus on this length and uncertainty of the auditor selection process when they measure market share at the end of the year following the year of the sanction (i.e., 13 to 24 months after the sanction).

In an IPO setting many activities in addition to the audit, such as discussions and negotiations with underwriters and investors, are necessary. Consequently, the time lag for manifestation of a sanction-related auditor change decision in IPO market share is expected to be at least as long as that of a non-IPO auditor change decision. In this study monthly market shares from 13 to 36 months after the sanction are examined. This time period is based on that used by Wilson and Grimlund and the expectation that manifestation of a sanction-related change in auditor IPO market share is expected to be at least as long as manifestation of auditor changes in non-IPO settings. The preceding (base) period that is assumed to be unaffected by the sanction and that is used in computing the differences in market shares ends 12 months after the sanction (and begins 12 months before the sanction).

The following empirical models of two measures of IPO auditor market share were developed. Model 1 relates to the change in each audit firm's average monthly percent of the total number of Big 6-audited IPOs. Model 2 relates to the change in each audit firm's average monthly percentage of total IPO client firm sales volume, because client firm size has been shown to be associated with auditor revenues in an IPO setting (Beatty 1989).

$$\text{CMSN}_i = f[\sum_{i=1}^{9} \text{AUD}_i, (\text{SANC*TIME1})_i, (\text{SANC*TIME2})_i, (\text{LIT*TIME1})_i, (\text{LIT*TIME2})_i] \quad (1)$$

$$\text{CMSS}_i = f[\sum_{i=1}^{9} \text{AUD}_i, (\text{SANC*TIME1})_i, (\text{SANC*TIME2})_i, (\text{LIT*TIME1})_i, (\text{LIT*TIME2})_i] \quad (2)$$

where:

$CMSN_i$ and $CMSS_i$ = the percentage point change in audit firm monthly IPO market share in terms of number of clients and client sales volume, respectively, measured for each month from 13 to 36 months after the sanction, in comparison to the monthly average of the preceding two years (see Note 4),

$AUD1_i \ldots AUD9_i$ = a series of indicator variables used to distinguish among the ten audit firms included in this study (the original Big 8 and the two firms created by mergers),

$SANC_i$ = 1 if the audit firm was criticized by the SEC, and 0 otherwise,

LIT_i = the difference between the number of litigation cases against the audit firm reported in *The Wall Street Journal* during the 12 months leading up to the SEC sanction (standardized by the firm's relative market share before the sanction) and the same measure for the preceding 12 months,[5]

$TIME1_i$ = 1 if the audit firm monthly market share is for the period from 13 to 24 months after the sanction, and 0 otherwise, and

$TIME2_i$ = 1 if the audit firm monthly market share is for the period from 25 to 36 months after the sanction, and 0 otherwise (see Note 4).

Evaluation of Validity of Variables

CMSN and CMSS. Client firm size, which is often measured in sales volume, is frequently argued to be associated with auditor revenues (for example, Beatty 1989). This suggests that incorporating client sales volume (CMSS) into the calculation may be expected to produce a more refined measure of change in auditor market share. Conversely, part of the appeal of IPO clients to audit firms is relatively rapid expected client growth and audit fee increases. The current level of client sales volume may not be a good indicator of this expected expansion and fee increase. As a result, it could be argued that the number of IPO clients, or change in that number (CMSN), is a better indicator of auditor success in this market. Consequently, both measures are examined in this study.

AUD1…AUD9 are used to control for differences in market shares and market share changes across audit firms.

SANC is used to distinguish criticized audit firms from those in the control group. Hypothesis H_1 predicts a significant negative coefficient on SANC. Audit firms that had avoided SEC enforcement actions for the three years before sanction and three years after the sanction were considered "unsanctioned" and included in the control group. This time period appears to reduce to a very low level the likelihood of incorrectly including an audit firm in the control group, based on previous studies (Wilson and Grimlund 1990; Davis and Simon 1992). The primary risk of measurement error for this variable relates to uncertainty surrounding identification of the "sanction period" for the criticized audit firms.

LIT measures the difference in the number of references to litigation cases against the auditor in *The Wall Street Journal* during the 12 months leading up to the sanction and the preceding 12 months. The counts are standardized by audit firm market share because, ceteris paribus, firms with more clients are expected to face more litigation. This variable is a proxy for the change in litigation-based quality assessment of the audit firm at the time of the enforcement action. Hypothesis H_2 predicts a negative coefficient on LIT.

References in *The Wall Street Journal* serve as a proxy for, and clearly understate, total litigation against an audit firm, but represent the most significant cases (Palmrose 1991b). Uncertainty about the timing (lag) of any litigation-based effects on auditor market share is a source of potential measurement error for this variable. The assumptions underlying the examination of the litigation time periods used in this study are that (1) auditor selectors would examine litigation information over a period of time, and (2) the time lag for litigation-base quality assessments that affect auditor selection is the same as that for sanction-based quality assessments.

TIME1 and TIME2 are used to examine varying market share effects within the "sanction period." They are included in the model because of uncertainty about, and to further study, the time periods affected by the sanction. Nonetheless, there is some ambiguity associated with these variables. Because of the chronological proximity of some enforcement actions, a monthly market share for a "control" firm could fall in TIME2 with respect to one sanction and TIME1 with respect to a later sanction. These observations have been categorized with respect to the first sanction, that is, in TIME2 in this study. Consequently, distinctions between TIME1 sanction effects and TIME2 sanction effects and between TIME2 sanction effects and "multiple sanctions effects"[6] are confounded. This limitation should be considered in evaluating the results of this study.

EMPIRICAL RESULTS

Univariate Analysis

Summary statistics for the variables included in the regression models are reported in Table 2. On a Univariate basis SANC is significantly negatively correlated with CMSS (consistent with Hypothesis H_1), but not with CMSN. LIT is significantly negatively correlated with both CMSN and CMSS (consistent with Hypothesis H_2). The correlations among the independent variables do not indicate the presence of multicollinearity. This issue is discussed more completely below. The similarity between the two market share measures is apparent in the high correlations between CMSN and CMSS.

Regression Results

Table 3 reports the results for the regression models of changes in auditor market share of IPOs (CMSN) and auditor market share of sales volume of IPO firms (CMSS). The models explain approximately 11.1% and 7.2% of the variation in CMSN and CMSS, respectively.

Evidence consistent with a sanction-related decline in auditor market share (Hypothesis H_1) is observed in both models. In the model of market share of IPOs (CMSN), the estimate of the sanction-related decline in market share is 1.6 percentage points in the first sanction period (SANC*TIME1) and 2.6 percentage points in the second sanction period (SANC*TIME2). SANC*TIME2 is statistically significant (p-value less than .01) and SANC*TIME1 is marginally significant (p-value less than .08).

In the model of market share of IPO sales volume (CMSS), the estimate of the sanction-related decline in market share is 4.1 percentage points in the first sanction period (SANC*TIME1) and 5.6 percentage points in the second sanction period (SANC*TIME2). SANC is statistically significant in both the first and second periods (p-values less than .02 and .002, respectively).

In both models the absolute value and significance of the coefficient on (SANC*TIME2) are greater than they are for (SANC*TIME1). One potential explanation for this result relates to uncertainty surrounding the timing of the "sanction-affected period." Wilson and Grimlund (1990) argue that the affected period begins between 13 and 24 months

Table 2. Descriptive Statistics and Pearson Correlation Coefficients[a] (N = 889 observations)

	Mean	*Std.Dev.*	*Correlation Coefficient*[b] *CMSN*	*CMSS*	*SANC*	*LIT*
CMSN	.019	.094				
CMSS	.009	.165	.587 (.001)			
SANC	.256	.437	–.015 (.656)	–.086 (.011)		
LIT	–.204	2.100	–.112 (.001)	–.092 (.006)	.224 (.001)	
TIME1	.394	.489	.003 (.933)	–.018 (.594)	.096 (.004)	.022 (.507)
TIME2	.606	.489	–.003 (.933)	.018 (.594)	–.096 (.004)	–.022 (.507)
AUD1	.121	.327	–.077 (.022)	–.032 (.335)	–.218 (.001)	.003 (.931)
AUD2	.141	.348	.003 (.931)	.048 (.157)	–.060 (.075)	.088 (.009)
AUD3	.102	.303	.036 (.287)	.083 (.013)	.006 (.867)	–.100 (.003)
AUD4	.102	.303	–.029 (.388)	–.057 (.091)	.006 (.867)	.087 (.009)
AUD5	.143	.350	–.026 (.413)	.070 (.038)	–.240 (.001)	–.016 (.626)
AUD6	.121	.327	–.032 (.335)	–.087 (.009)	.160 (.001)	.118 (.001)
AUD7	.054	.226	–.133 (.001)	–.079 (.018)	.407 (.001)	.202 (.001)
AUD8	.040	.197	.275 (.001)	.143 (.001)	.350 (.001)	.020 (.553)
AUD9	.040	.197	.139 (.001)	.113 (.001)	–.121 (.001)	–.712 (.001)

Notes: See text for definitions of variables.

[a]Correlation coefficients among and between audit firm indicator variables and time periods are not presented. Correlations among audit firm indicator variables ranged from –.060 to –.170. Correlations between time periods and audit firm indicators were not significantly different from zero.

[b]Parenthetical amount indicates the probability that the correlation is not significantly different from 0.000.

Table 3. Regression Results of Auditor IPO Market Share Models (1) and (2)

$$\text{CMSN}_i = f[\sum_{i=1}^{9} \text{AUD}_i, (\text{SANC*TIME1})_i, (\text{SANC*TIME2})_i, (\text{LIT*TIME1})_i, (\text{LIT*TIME2})_i] \quad (1)$$

$$\text{CMSS}_i = f[\sum_{i=1}^{9} \text{AUD}_i, (\text{SANC*TIME1})_i, (\text{SANC*TIME2})_i, (\text{LIT*TIME1})_i, (\text{LIT*TIME2})_i] \quad (2)$$

	IPO Market Share Model (1)		*IPO Sales Volume Market Share Model (2)*	
Parameter	*Coefficient Estimate*	*T-Value*[a]	*Coefficient Estimate*	*T-Value*[a]
Intercept	0.018	2.195**	–0.035	–2.362***
AUD1	–0.017	–1.440	0.036	1.685
AUD2	0.006	0.520	0.071	3.502****
AUD3	0.018	1.444	0.103	4.530****
AUD4	–0.001	–0.116	0.028	1.246
AUD5	–0.004	–0.370	0.074	3.595****
AUD6	0.002	0.207	0.024	1.127
AUD7	–0.032	–1.881*	0.029	0.949
AUD8	0.150	8.182****	0.210	6.317****
AUD9	0.079	3.367****	0.175	4.089****
SANC*TIME1	–0.016	–1.492*	–0.041	–2.122**
SANC*TIME2	–0.026	–2.504***	–0.056	–2.286***
LIT*TIME1	0.001	0.129	0.007	1.313
LIT*TIME2	0.003	1.127	0.005	1.043
Adjusted R^2 =	.111		.072	
N = 889				

Notes: CMSN and CMSS = changes in market share of IPO firms and sale volume.
AUD1...AUD9 identify the audit firm to which the market share relates.
SANC indicates whether the audit firm was "under sanction" by the SEC.
LIT measures the change in litigation between the year leading up to the sanction and the preceding year.
TIME1 and TIME2 indicate the first and second years of the sanction period.
[a]Significantly different from zero at p–value < .08(*), .05(**), .01(***), and .001(****), respectively. A one-tailed test is used for SANC and LIT related variables (for which hypotheses were tested) and two-tailed tests for other variables and the intercept.

after the enforcement action. The observed results are consistent with the scenario that the sanction effect is not fully in effect during the first year of the "sanction period." At the same time, the ambiguity in categorizing "control" firm observations (discussed above) may affect the observed timing of a sanction effect.

The coefficient on LIT was positive and statistically insignificant in interaction with both time frames (TIME1 and TIME2) in explaining both measures of market share. Thus, the null hypothesis (H_2) of no decline litigation-related decline in market share cannot be rejected. This is consistent with the notion that "routine" litigation may not be significant enough to produce a detectable market reaction (Palmrose 1991b). Finally, the volatility of IPO market shares, particularly when measured by CMSS, is reflected in statistically significant coefficients on several of the audit firm indicator variables.

Discussion and Validation of Results[7]

Sensitivity to Sanction-Affected Time Period

The regression results are consistent with a decline in market share that is present and increasing during the period from one to three years after the enforcement action. The actual time period affected is an empirical question. The answer likely varies significantly across auditor selection decisions. To consider the sensitivity of the reported results to the identified time frame, several other one-year periods were evaluated. For CMSS, statistically significant market share declines were observed in all one-year time frames that began more than one year after the enforcement action. For CMSN, statistically significant market share declines were not consistently observed in one-year time frames until 18 months after the sanction. In one-year time frames that began within one year of the enforcement action, significant market share declines were not observed for either CMSN or CMSS. Thus, the second year (13 to 24 months) after the sanction represents the earliest observed market share decline and this is sensitive to the measure of market share employed.

Litigation effects on market share during periods involving a shorter time lag also were studied. No litigation effects were observed in these periods.

Validity of Regression Analysis Assumptions

The effects of multi-collinearity, heteroscedasticity, and correlation of residuals on the reported results were considered. The ratio of the largest to smallest eigenvalue in the correlation matrix of the independent variables (the "condition number") in each regression model was less than 6.0. Thus, significant multi-Collinearity does not appear to be present in the models.

Analysis of residuals did not indicate the presence of influential outlying observations.[8] Also, residual analysis did not indicate that residuals (based on their absolute values) are correlated across audit firms.

Analysis did indicate that the regression model residuals are not independent nor homoscedastic across enforcement actions (events). Particularly, residuals related to the first enforcement action are significantly greater, and those related to the last enforcement action significantly less, than the residuals related to other enforcement actions. Consequently, the statistical significance of the reported results (t-values) is potentially overstated because the standard error of the estimate is understated[9] (Bernard 1987).

To evaluate the validity of the reported results two additional tests were performed. First, to consider whether the reported results were due to the influence of market shares around any one sanction, models (1) and (2) were re-developed excluding, one sanction at a time, the market share observations related to each sanction. This was necessary because: (1) the study spanned a long time period, (2) there is great variation in the number of IPOs over this time period, (3) market shares associated with the earlier sanctions were calculated based on a small number of IPOs, (4) the residuals are correlated and heteroscedastic, and (5) confounding factors such as the mergers creating the Big 6 during the late 1980s were present at certain times.

The coefficients on SANC*TIME2 and (generally) on SANC*TIME1 continued to be negative and significant in each of the additional models of CMSS.[10] In each of the additional models of CMSN, the coefficients on SANC*TIME2 continued to be negative and significant. The coefficients on SANC*TIME1 in the CMSN models generally were not significant; this coefficient was marginally significant in the original model.

Second, to address the potential overstatement of statistical significance of the coefficients related to SANC due to heteroscedasticity and correlated residuals, the following test was performed. Reduced regression models of CMSN and CMSS [(3) and (4) below] that exclude the variables in Models (1) and (2) related to SANC were developed.

$$\text{CMSN}_i = f[\sum_{i=1}^{9} \text{AUD}_i, (\text{LIT*TIME1})_i, (\text{LIT*TIME2})_i] \quad (3)$$

$$\text{CMSS}_i = f[\sum_{i=1}^{9} \text{AUD}_i, (\text{LIT*TIME1})_i, (\text{LIT*TIME2})_i] \quad (4)$$

Non-parametric Wilcoxon Rank Sum tests, which do not depend on the distributional assumptions that underlie regression analysis, were performed on the residuals of these reduced models (which were not cross-sectionally correlated across sanctions) (Hollander 1973). Under the alternative Hypothesis H_1, the rank sum of reduced-model residuals for observations where SANC = 1 will be less than expected. Table 4 presents the results of the rank sum tests. Results are reported for residuals from the reduced models of CMSN and CMSS for TIME1, TIME2, and for the two time periods combined.

These tests indicate that for both CMSN and CMSS, SANC is statistically significant in distinguishing among residuals from the reduce model in TIME2 and when the two time periods are combined. SANC is also statistically significant in TIME1 with respect to CMSS. Thus, the non-parametric tests are consistent with the regression results that SANC is significant in TIME2 and the significance of SANC in TIME1 is sensitive to the market share metric.[11]

Omitted Variables

Incumbency and the strength of the audit firm in the audit markets of the client's industry and geographic area are variables that are likely to contribute to explanatory power of models of IPO auditor market share. Ad hoc observations suggest that these factors impact auditor selection decisions. This study is limited by the omission of data pertaining to these variables. Prior research suggests that sanctions vary as to severity (Moreland 1995). Tests of the effect of sanction severity were performed (results not reported). Severity was categorized dichotomously based on descriptions of the reported audit problems and the enforcement action reported in the AAER or ASR. Severity was classified as "low" if the audit firm received only public criticism and a censure from the SEC. The Andersen-1981, Touche-1983, and Coopers-1984 actions fell into this category. Severity was classified as "high" if additional penalties were imposed (see Table 1). The results of this test did not

Table 4. Non-parametric Analysis of Residuals from Reduced Models (3) and (4)

$$CMSN_i = f[\sum_{i=1}^{9} AUD_i, (LIT*TIME1)_i, (LIT*TIME2)_i]^a \quad (3)$$

$$CMSS_i = f[\sum_{i=1}^{9} AUD_i, (LIT*TIME1)_i, (LIT*TIME2)_i]^a \quad (4)$$

	IPO Market Share (Model 3)		*IPO Sales Volume Market Share (Model 4)*	
	SANC = 0	*SANC = 1*	*SANC = 0*	*SANC = 1*
TIME1:				
Observations	242	108	242	108
Rank Sum	43,111	18,315	44,224	17,201
Expected (H_O)	42,471	18,954	42,471	18,954
Z-Value[b]		−0.730		−2.004*
TIME2:				
Observations	419	120	419	120
Rank Sum	115,886	29,644	117,084	28,446
Expected (H_O)	113,130	32,400	113,130	32,400
Z-Value[b]		−1.832*		−2.628**
COMBINED TIME1 and TIME2:				
Observations	661	228	661	228
Rank Sum	300,491	95,114	305,315	90,290
Expected (H_O)	294,145	101,460	294,145	101,460
Z-Value[b]		−1.898*		−3.341***

Notes: [a]See text for descriptions of variables.
[b]Significantly less than zero at *p*-value < .05(*), .01(**), and .001(***), respectively.

indicate that increased sanction severity is associated with greater declines in market share.[12]

CONCLUSIONS AND DISCUSSION

As noted by Blair and Kaserman (1980), the inability of users to fully evaluate quality creates a need for external regulation. In the market for IPO audit services, the results of this study suggest that managers of IPO firms use enforcement action reports by the SEC in formulating auditor quality assessments. This, in turn, affects auditor selection decisions. The observed impact of an approximate 2 to 5% percentage point decline in market share is statistically significant and fairly consistent over the enforcement actions from 1978 to 1991. It was also observed that there is a time lag of at least one year before the effects of the sanction are manifested in market share. This is consistent with the relatively long auditor-selection time frames observed in prior research. Evidence of the presence of a market share effect for up to three years was observed. Although a univariate association (correlation) between litigation and auditor market share was observed, litigation did not impact auditor market share in the regression models.

These results were observed in empirical models of changes in auditor IPO market share regressed against the sanction effect, changes in the level of litigation against the audit firm, and audit firm indicator variables. The regression results were supplemented and supported by non-parametric tests. These non-parametric tests were necessary because analysis indicated that the homoscedasticity and uncorrelated-residual assumptions that underlie inferences drawn from least squares regression were not entirely appropriate.

One limitation of this study was identification of the period where market share was expected to be affected by the SEC criticism. The lag of one to two years between enforcement action and observed market share effect generally supports the time frame suggested by prior research (Wilson and Grimlund 1990 and Davis and Simon 1992). However, it must be noted that auditor selection time periods are variable and as a result subject to measurement error. Further, because some control firm market share observations related to two or more sanctions, there is ambiguity in the observed time lag of sanction effects. Finally, the significance of the market share decline early in the sanction period is sensitive to the measure of market share employed.

Difficulty in distinguishing between observed sanction effects and litigation effects should be considered when drawing conclusions from this study. Generally, the observed sanction effects are consistent with the scenario that enforcement actions are a stronger auditor quality signal than litigation occurrences. Nonetheless, the existence of a misidentified litigation effect cannot be completely ruled out, especially given the correlation between LIT and both CMSN and CMSS.

The explanatory power of the empirical models is limited by the omission of variables measuring incumbency of the auditor, and auditor strength in the client's industry and location. Future research on auditor selection and market share could incorporate these variables.

The observed decline in IPO market share of sanctioned auditors is consistent with the assertion that reports of enforcement actions against auditors impact assessments of auditor quality (Burton 1975). The results suggest that market participants (managers and underwriters) use information generated by the regulatory process to assess the quality of audit service providers. These results may be useful to regulators and auditors who are concerned with the impact that disciplinary actions have in the market for audit services.

APPENDIX:

Summary of 1991 Enforcement Release Against Ernst & Young (*AAER 301*, June 13, 1991)

Summary: The Release announced that the SEC sought a permanent injunction in United States District Court for the District of Columbia against Ernst & Young (EY)and charged that EY and a predecessor firm, Arthur Young & Co., were not independent with respect to two audit clients. The alleged lack of independence relates to membership by over 50 of the firm's partners in a real estate partnership that received loans from an audit client in the banking industry and leased space to another audit client, and because the audit firm maintained non-interest bearing accounts with the banking client. This matter had been referred to the SEC by the Federal Deposit Insurance Corporation.

Note: This AAER differed from most other AAERs in that it announced an alleged violation of SEC rules and regulations, the American Institute of Certified Public Accountants Code of Professional Conduct, and generally accepted auditing standards for which the SEC had not completed its investigations. Typically, an AAER announces SEC findings after completion of its investigation (Moreland 1995). This matter was concluded in 1995 (*AAER* 655 issued on March 15) when EY consented to the entry of a "Final Order" by the Court where EY agreed to undertake to comply with the standards of the SEC and auditing profession regarding the independence of auditors.

ACKNOWLEDGMENTS

The author acknowledges the helpful comments on earlier drafts this paper received from David Willis, the Faculty Workshop at the University of Michigan—Flint School of Management, and the participants at the 1993 American

Accounting Association—Ohio Region Annual Meeting. I thank Randolph Beatty and the Office for the Study of Private Equity Finance at the University of Michigan—Ann Arbor for making the initial public offering data available to me. Discussions with Madhu Angur about several issues in the paper were especially helpful. Finally, I thank Gary Previts, the Editor, and two anonymous referees who made suggestions that greatly improved this paper.

NOTES

1. The term "Big 6" is used in this study. Mergers among the eight largest audit firms (the Big 8) during the late 1980s, near the end of the time period studied, reduced this group to the Big 6.

2. Feroz et al. (1991) and Campbell and Parker (1992) provide thorough summaries of the SEC enforcement process. Moreland (1995) summarizes the reported audit weaknesses for the enforcement actions from 1978 to 1990 listed in Table 1 that are included in this study.

3. Another possibility is that the SEC criticism may be viewed as an aberration and discounted.

4. There are two exceptions to these time frames. First, auditor market share data prior to June 1977 was not available. Consequently, the "preceding period" for the 1978 Price Waterhouse, Haskins & Sells, and Ernst & Ernst sanctions begin, 6, 7, and 11 months prior to the sanction, respectively. This caused the number of IPOs and months from which the average "base" (preceding) market shares were calculated for these sanctions to be reduced. Second, the 1990 and 1991 enforcement actions against Ernst & Young were combined because of their chronological proximity. As a result, the "preceding period" began 12 months before and ended 12 months after the 1990 action. The "sanction effect" was investigated in the period that began 13 months after the 1990 sanction and ended 36 months after the 1991 sanction (48 months after the 1990 sanction). This caused the number of IPOs and months from which market share changed were calculated to be increased.

5. Data regarding litigation (LIT) are available from the author upon request.

6. This "multiple sanction" efffect refers to the scenario where audit report users focus to a greater extent on SEC criticisms of auditors because several enforcement actions, rather than only one, occurred in a relatively short time period. Examination of this issue is beyond the scope of this study.

7. The results referred to in the Dicussion and Validation of Results section are available from the author upon request.

8. A priori, no monthly change observation was considered to be an outlier. The largest "Cook's D" statistic, which represents a composite measure of influence on the vector of coefficients for a given observation, was less than .20. This is not significant by traditional benchmarks (Belsley 1980).

9. The coefficient estimates are unbiased (Maddala 1977, 259-283).

10. The coefficient on (SANC*TIME1) was always negative and significant in all but one case.

11. As expected, the significance levels for the non-parametric tests generally are lower.

12. In assessing sanction severity the objectivity of the report in the AAER or ASR should be considered. The descriptions are relatively detailed and generally were not disputed by the criticized auditor. However, Palmrose (1991b) cites an unpublished working paper by Loebbecke and Willinghan (1988) that describes the reports in AAERs and ASRs as biased against the criticized auditor.

REFERENCES

Balvers, R., B. McDonald, and R. Miller. 1988. Underpricing of new issues and the choice of auditor as a signal of investment banker reputation. *The Accounting Review* (October): 605-622.

Beatty, R. 1989. Auditor reputation and the pricing of initial public offerings. *The Accounting Review* (October): 693-709.

Belsley, D., E. Kuh, and R. Welsch. 1980. *Regression Diagnostics: Identifying Influential Data and Sources of Collinearity.* New York: Wiley & Sons.

Bernard, V. 1987. Cross-sectional dependence and problems in inferences in market-based accounting research. *Journal of Accounting Research* (Spring): 1-48.

Blair, R., and D. Kaserman. 1980. Preservation of quality and sanctions within the professions. *Regulating the Professions*: 185-198.

Burton, J. 1975. SEC enforcement and professional accountants: Philosophy, objectives and approach. *The Vanderbilt Law Review* (January): 19-29.

Carpenter, C., and R. Strawser. 1971. Displacement of auditors when clients go public. *Journal of Accountancy* (June): 55-58.

Clarkson, P., and D. Simunic. 1994. The association between audit quality, retained ownership, and firm-specific risk in U.S. versus Canadian IPO markets. *Journal of Accounting and Economics* 17: 207-228.

Darby, M., and E. Karni. 1973. Free competition and the optimal amount of fraud. *Journal of Law and Economics* 16: 67-80.

Datar, S., G. Feltham, and J. Hughes. 1991. The role of audits and audit quality in valuing new issues. *Journal of Accounting and Economics* 14: 3-49.

Davis, L., and D. Simon. 1992. The impact of SEC disciplinary actions on audit fees. *Auditing: A Journal of Practice and Theory* (Spring): 58-68.

DeAngelo, L. 1981. Auditor size and audit quality. *Journal of Accounting and Economics* (December): 183-199.

Dopuch, N., and D. Simunic. 1982. Competition in auditing research: An assessment. In *Fourth Symposium on Auditing Research.* Urbana: University of Illinois, 403-450.

Ernst & Whinney. 1984. *Deciding to Go Public: Understanding the Process and the Alternatives.* Akron, OH: Ernst & Whinney.

Feltham, G., J. Hughes, and D. Simunic. 1991. Empirical assessment of the impact of auditor quality on the valuation of new issues. *Journal of Accounting and Economics* (December): 375-399.

Feroz, E., K. Park, and V. Pastena. 1991. The financial and market effects of the SEC's accounting and auditing enforcement releases. *Journal of Accounting Research* (Supplement): 107-142.

Firth, M. 1990. Auditor reputation: The impact of critical reports issued by government inspectors. *Rand Journal of Economics* (Autumn): 374-387.

Hofmeister, S. 1987. The seller's intent. *Venture* (October): 53-56.

Hollander, M., and D. Wolfe. 1973. *Nonparametric Statistics*. New York: Wiley & Sons.

Ibbotson, R., J. Sindelar, and J. Ritter. 1988. Initial public offerings. *Journal of Applied Corporate Finance* (Summer): 37-45.

Loebbecke, J., and J. Willingham. 1988. Review of SEC accounting and enforcement releases. Unpublished Working Paper.

Lys, T., and R. Watts. 1994. Lawsuits against auditors. *Journal of Accounting Research* 32 (Supplement): 65-93.

Maddala, G. 1977. *Econometrics*. New York: McGraw-Hill.

Moreland, K. 1995. Sanctions of auditors and the earnings and returns of client firms. *Auditing: A Journal of Practice and Theory* (Spring): 94-104.

O'Keefe, T., and P. Westort. 1992. Conformance to GAAS reporting standards in municipal audits and the economics of auditing: The effects of audit firm size, CPA examination performance, and competition. In *Research in Accounting Regulation*, Vol. 6, 39-78, ed. by G.J. Previts. Greenwich, CT: JAI Press.

Palmrose, Z. 1988. An analysis of auditor litigation and audit service quality. *The Accounting Review* (January): 55-73.

______. 1991a. Trials of legal disputes involving independent auditors: Some empirical evidence. *Journal of Accounting Research* (Supplement): 149-185.

______. 1991b. An analysis of auditor litigation disclosures. *Auditing: A Journal of Practice and Theory* (Supplement): 54-71.

Perry, L. 1984. The SEC's enforcement activities. *CPA Journal* (April): 9-13.

Pincus, K., W. Holder, and T. Mock. 1988. The SEC and fraudulent financial reporting. In *Research in Accounting Regulation*, Vol. 2, 167-185, ed. by G.J. Previts. Greenwich, CT: JAI Press.

Sack, R., A. Barr, J. Burton, and C. Sampson. 1988. A journal round table discussion: Frank talk from former SEC chief accountants. *Journal of Accountancy* (December): 76-84.

Securities and Exchange Commission. 1986. *The Work of the SEC* (October): 26-33.

Simunic, D., and M. Stein. 1987. *Product Differentiation in Auditing: Auditor Choice in the Market for Unseasoned New Issues*. The Canadian Certified General Accountants' Research Foundation.

Sutton, P., and M. Benedetto. 1990. *Initial Public Offerings*. Chicago: Probus Publishing Company.

Wallace, W. 1989. Are audit fees sufficiently risk adjusted? In *Advances in Accounting*, Suppl. 1, 3-37, ed. by J.S. Gangolly. Greenwich, CT: JAI Press.

Wilson, R. 1983. Auditing: Perspectives from multi-person decision theory. *The Accounting Review* (April): 305-318.

Wilson, T., and R. Grimlund. 1990. An examination of the importance of an auditor's reputation. *Auditing: A Journal of Practice and Theory* (Spring): 43-59.

THE EFFECTS OF FINANCIAL REPORTING DISPUTES WITH THE SEC ON THE INFORMATIVENESS OF EARNINGS

Obeua S. Persons

ABSTRACT

This study provides evidence concerning the impact of regulatory enforcement actions on the return/earnings relationship. In particular, it examines the effect of financial reporting disputes with the SEC on the perceived informativeness of earnings. Financial-reporting-dispute firms are defined as those that were investigated by the SEC for possible violations related to accounting practices and these investigations were reported in the *Wall Street Journal*. Because reporting disputes are likely to increase the perceived uncertainty or noise in present and future earnings, this study hypothesizes that market and analyst reactions to earnings following dispute disclosures will be less pronounced than those

Research in Accounting Regulation, Volume 11, pages 99-123.

ISBN: 0-7623-0168-6

before the disclosures. An earnings response coefficient model (a return model) and an analyst earnings revision model are used to test this hypothesis. This study controls for information environment, management change, growth/persistence, systematic risk and risk-free interest rate. Results, which are robust against several diagnostic tests including the use of matched nondispute firms, strongly support the hypothesis. The evidence here suggests that a regulatory enforcement action, such as the SEC's financial reporting investigation, is an important mechanism in maintaining public confidence in the reported earnings numbers.

INTRODUCTION

An important role of the earnings number is to communicate to investors a firm's future prospects. Findings of many studies since Ball and Brown (1968) about the positive association between stock returns and unexpected earnings support the contention that accounting earnings reflect value-relevant information. Recently, return/earnings research has progressed into a new research arena, the earnings response coefficient (ERC). The ERC is defined as the effect of a dollar of unexpected earnings on stock returns, and is typically measured as a slope coefficient in a regression of abnormal returns on unexpected earnings.

Recent ERC studies have focused on the ERC determinants. Kormendi and Lipe (1987) document a positive relation between the ERC and earnings persistence (defined as the magnitude of revision in future earnings resulting from unexpected earnings). Easton and Zmijewski (1989), and Collins and Kothari (1989) found that, in addition to earnings persistence, the ERC varies inversely with systematic risk of a firm. Collins and Kothari (1989) also found that the ERC is increasing in growth opportunities and decreasing in risk-free interest rates. Several researchers (e.g., Lang and McNichols (1990), Imhoff and Lobo (1992), Teoh and Wong (1993)) have also begun to examine factors which affect the informativeness (quality) of the reported earnings number. None of these studies, however, investigate the impact of accounting regulatory actions on earnings informativeness.

This study responds to the public's concerns over increasing numbers of fraudulent financial reporting cases by examining the effect of financial reporting disputes with the Securities and Exchange Commission (SEC) on the informativeness of earnings.[1] The study defines financial-reporting-dispute firms as those that were investigated by the SEC for possible violations related to accounting practices, and the investigations were reported in the *Wall Street Journal*. This study has two major contributions. First, the study adds to our understanding about a return/earnings relationship by identifying another specific factor affecting the relationship. Second, from a regulatory perspective, this study provides additional evidence on the influence of enforcement actions by a regulatory body, the SEC, in the financial reporting environment.[2]

Prior studies (Ohlson 1983; Collins and DeAngelo 1990) provide supporting evidence that the perceived informativeness of earnings may be measured in two ways: an earnings response coefficient (ERC) and an analyst revision coefficient. The ERC is estimated by the return model (regressing unexpected returns on unexpected earnings).[3] The ERC is assumed to be positively related to the extent to which the current period's unexpected earnings lead to market revisions in future periods' dividends and earnings (Garman and Ohlson 1980; Ohlson 1983). The analyst revision coefficient is estimated by regressing analysts' earnings forecast revisions on unexpected earnings. The revision coefficient is assumed to be positively related to the extent to which the current unexpected earnings lead analysts to revise their forecasts of future earnings (Collins and DeAngelo 1990).

Holthausen and Verrecchia (1988) and Choi and Salamon (1989) demonstrate that the ERC is inversely related to the market's expectation about the amount of uncertainty or noise in a firm's present and future earnings numbers. A disclosure of a financial reporting dispute with the SEC has the potential to negatively affect the market's and the analysts' expectations of future earnings because the dispute disclosure serves as a negative signal concerning the integrity and credibility of the firm's management. Consequently, the market and the analysts are likely to perceive the earnings number generated by the firm as having more noise or uncertainty than expected, and is less informative in predicting future earnings than previously assumed.

This study, therefore, hypothesizes a decrease in the informativeness of dispute firms' earnings following the first disclosure of reporting disputes, that is, a smaller earnings response coefficient and a smaller revision coefficient subsequent to the first dispute disclosure. Regression results, which control for information environment, management change, growth/persistence, systematic risk, and risk-free interest rate, strongly support the hypothesis. Several diagnostic tests including the use of matched nondispute firms further support the hypothesis.

The rest of this paper is organized as follows. The next section describes selection of the sample and data collection. Test methods which describe the models for testing the impact of reporting disputes on the ERC and the analyst revision coefficient are presented in the third section. Results of hypothesis testing and diagnostic tests are in the fourth section. Conclusions are stated in the fifth section.

SAMPLE SELECTION

A sample of firms that experienced reporting disputes is obtained from the Index to the *Wall Street Journal* (WSJ) under the topics of "Securities and Exchange Commission" from 1973 through 1993. This study uses the WSJ to identify reporting dispute firms because an examination of the SEC's annual reports reveals that not every reporting dispute is included in the *Accounting and Auditing Enforcement Releases* (AAER).[4] Several reporting disputes are disclosed in the *Litigation Releases* (LR) and not in the AAER.[5] Therefore, using the AAER to locate reporting disputes can understate the size of the population. Another reason for using the WSJ is that investors and analysts are *first* aware of a reporting dispute through the news release which precedes the LR and the AAER.[6] Although not all disputes are disclosed in the WSJ, those that are not covered are less likely to receive investors' attention.[7] In order to test the effects of reporting disputes on the informativeness of earnings, it is crucial to focus on those disputes that receive significant attention from investors.

Pincus, Holder, and Mock (1988) report that the SEC's accounting enforcement actions are triggered from several sources including: (1) reviews of financial reports; (2) financial press, public complaints and referrals from other law enforcement agencies; and (3) the market surveillance programs of the New York and the American Stock Exchanges and the National Association of Securities Dealers. These enforcement actions may involve an informal investigation or a formal investigation. During an informal investigation, the SEC invites individuals with relevant information to cooperate by providing testimony and documents. The SEC does not need to notify its target in such an investigation. If an outcome of the informal investigation warrants further scrutiny, the SEC will issue a formal order for a private investigation which grants subpoena power to compel testimony and the production of documents. The agency is required to formally notify a firm that it has been a target of the SEC investigation. This private investigation can become public knowledge because the formal investigation is considered as material information and the securities laws require the target firm to publicly disclose the investigation.

According to the WSJ Index, there are 205 firms which experienced reporting disputes with the SEC. The WSJ articles for these 205 firms are read to ensure that only firms that experienced financial reporting (accounting) disputes are included in the sample. This procedure excludes nine firms which made misleading nonaccounting statements related to their securities offering.[8] For the remaining 196 firms, the corporate index to the WSJ is searched for the *first* disclosure of the dispute *subject matter.* The subject matter of a dispute may first appear in the SEC investigation announcement, a firm's internal investigation announcement, a stockholder lawsuit, an auditor qualification, etc. This first disclosure is used to determine a pre-reporting dispute period and a post-reporting dispute period. The pre-reporting dispute period spans up to five years before the first disclosure. The post-reporting dispute period covers one year after the first disclosure.

Sample size and selection criteria for testing the earnings response coefficient (ERC) are presented in tabular format below.

Firms experiencing accounting disputes	196
Less: Firms with missing CRSP stock return data	(86)
Firms with insufficient number of "clean" unexpected earnings during the pre- and post-dispute periods	(27)
Final sample for the ERC test	83

"Clean" unexpected earnings are those without potential confounding events during three days before and three days after the announcement. The confounding events include dividends increase/decrease, stock splits, takeover announcements and other events with possible pricing implications. To maximize the sample size, insufficient number is defined as less than six clean unexpected earnings during the pre-dispute period and less than two clean unexpected earnings during the post-dispute period.

Sample size and selection criteria for testing the analyst revision coefficient are presented in tabular format below.

Firms experiencing accounting disputes	196
Less: Firms with insufficient number of Value Line (VL) forecast errors and VL forecast revisions during the pre- and post-dispute periods	(142)
Final sample for the analyst revision test	54

To maximize the sample size, insufficient number is defined as less than six VL forecast errors and forecast revisions during the pre-dispute period and less than two during the post-dispute period. Except for two firms, all analyst-revision-test firms are part of the 83 ERC-test firms. As a result, the final sample is comprised of 85 firms. Thirty-two out of 85 firms do not have related AAERs. Among these 32 no-AAER firms, 16 were charged by the SEC for violations of generally accepted accounting principles.[9] The other 16 firms were investigated by the SEC but were not charged.[10] These later 16 firms are included in the sample to prevent any hindsight bias because, at the time of the first reporting dispute disclosure, investors and analysts do not know which firms will later be charged by the SEC.

Among these 85 firms, 62 are exchange-listed firms and 23 are OTC firms. Firm size (market value of common stock) ranges from $1.72 million to $844.37 million, with the median value of $140.26 million. The sample includes 25 industries based on two digit SIC code, with the largest clusters of 17 firms in financial services industries (SIC 60-67) and 16 firms in electronics industries (SIC 35 and 36). The sample spans 22 years from 1971-1992, 35 out of 85 firms are from 1982-1985. The average number of unexpected earnings and analyst forecast errors/revisions for the sample is 14 for the pre-dispute period and four for the post-dispute period. There are a total of 1,494 unexpected earnings for the ERC test and 979 analyst forecast errors/revisions for the analyst revision test.

Among the first dispute disclosures of these 85 firms, the leading source of the disclosures is an announcement of the SEC investigation (60 firms or 70.6%).[11] The other sources of the first dispute disclosures are firm's internal investigations (8 firms or 9.4%), shareholder lawsuits (7 firms or 8.2%), auditor qualification/resignation (5 firms or 5.9%), other government agencies' investigations (4 firms or 4.7%), and WSJ rumor (1 firm or 1.2%).

Data in Table 1 shows that 49% of sample firms overstated revenues due mostly to premature revenue recognition. Another 51% of the sample understated expenses due mostly to failure to writedown inventory or insufficient reserve for uncollectible receivables. Table 1 also shows that most cases of the alleged reporting violations (46 cases or 45%) involve overstatement of receivables. Another 20 disputes or 20% involve overstatement of inventory. These results parallel those in Feroz et al. (1991). Two accounts with the highest average amount of misstatements are

Table 1. Accounts Misstated Among Final Sample Firms Experiencing Accounting Disputes and the Average Misstated Amount in Millions

Accounts Misstated	*Number*	*% of N (= 85)*	*Amount ($)*
Revenues	44	49%	23.16
Expenses	45	51%	78.57
Total	99[a]	100%	
Receivables	46	45%	57.74
Inventories	20	20%	29.27
Liabilities	10	10%	53.57
Investments	9	9%	37.62
Long-term assets	6	6%	12.62
Marketable securities	2	2%	24.20
Miscellaneous assets	8	8%	39.33
Total	101[a]	100%	

Note: [a]The total number of accounts misstated exceeds the number of firms because some reporting disputes affect more than one income statement and balance sheet account.

expense account (an average of $78.57 million understatement) and receivable account (an average of $57.74 million overstatement).

TEST METHODS

This study measures the perceived informativeness of earnings by two proxies: (a) the earnings response coefficient (ERC test based on the return model), and (b) the analyst revision coefficient (analyst revision test).

Estimation of the ERC requires the use of unexpected earnings (earnings forecast error, FE) and cumulative abnormal returns (CAR). FE is computed as actual earnings per share before extraordinary items (EPS) minus expected earnings per share. FE is scaled by the stock price two days before the quarterly earnings announcement date.[12] This study measures expected earnings based on the seasonal random walk model for quarterly earnings because the evidence in Bernard and Thomas (1990) supports the use of this model.[13] An abnormal return is defined as the difference between the daily return for each stock and the return on a portfolio comprised of similar beta risk stocks. Beta values are computed using the techniques described in Scholes and Williams (1977). The abnormal returns are cumulated over two days, CAR(–1,0), the day before and the day of the quarterly earnings announcements.

Estimation of the analyst revision coefficient requires the use of earnings forecast errors (FE) and quarter-to-quarter revisions (REV) in analysts' earnings forecasts. FE for this estimation is computed as actual

EPS minus the *Value Line* (VL) earnings forecast. FE is scaled by the stock price two days before the quarterly earnings announcement date. REV for quarter q is computed as the VL earnings forecast for quarter $q+1$, made after quarter-q earnings announcement, minus the VL earnings forecast for quarter $q+1$, made before quarter-q earnings announcement. REV is also scaled by stock price two days before the earnings announcement for quarter q.[14]

In order to test the hypothesis that dispute firms' earnings informativeness is decreased following the first disclosure of reporting disputes, six variables suggested by earlier studies as ERC determinants are controlled. These variables are included as independent variables in the return model and the analyst revision model. These six variables are systematic risk, risk-free interest rate, growth, earnings persistence, management change, and information environment (firm size).

Systematic Risk and Risk-Free Interest Rate. In the capital asset pricing model framework, stock price is assumed to be the present value of expected future dividends. The higher the systematic risk and risk-free interest rate, the smaller the present value of a given increase in expected future dividends caused by unexpected earnings. Therefore, a negative association is expected between ERC and the systematic risk and the risk-free interest rate. This negative association is supported by Collins and Kothari (1989). This study uses beta (market model slope coefficient) as a proxy for the systematic risk and uses yields of long-term U.S. Government bonds reported in Coleman et al. (1993) as a proxy for the risk-free interest rate.

Growth and Earnings Persistence. Collins and Kothari (1989) also argue that: (1) the future earnings and dividend streams will be larger in the presence of higher growth opportunities, and (2) higher earnings persistence (i.e., current period's unexpected earnings persist in the future and affect future earnings expectations) will lead to a greater revision in dividend expectations. The ERC is, therefore, expected to be a positive function of growth and earnings persistence. Collins and Kothari's results support their arguments. Similar to Collins and Kothari, this study uses the ratio of market to book value of equity to proxy for growth and earnings persistence.[15]

Management Change. Prior studies (Moore 1973; DeAngelo 1988) find that new management has a tendency to take an earnings "bath," that is, using discretionary accounting decisions to reduce earnings in the first year and blame it all on old management. As a result, much higher earnings is reported in a later year when the new management takes credit. Sample firms of this study have relatively high incidents of management changes, that is, 36 out of 85 sample firms changed management during the study period, 23 of which occurred during one year after the first reporting-dispute disclosure.[16] The earnings bath has a potential dampening effect on the informativeness of earnings because it is a transitory element of earnings. Hence, a negative relation is expected between ERC and management change.

Information Environment (Firm Size). Atiase (1985) argues that the amount of predisclosure information production and dissemination is an increasing function of firm size. This difference in information environment between large versus small firms could contribute to differential market and analyst reactions, that is, larger firms are likely to have less market and analyst reactions than smaller firms. A negative relation is, therefore, expected between ERC and the information environment proxied by firm size (the natural log of market value of common stock).

Model Estimation

Both return model and analyst revision model are estimated as pooled cross-sectional regressions using the ordinary least-squares method. Both models and the definition of their variables are presented in Table 2.

Return Model

$$\begin{aligned}\text{CAR}(-1,0)_{iq} = a_1 &+ b_1(FE_{iq}/P_{it-2}) + b_2(\text{DUM1}*FE_{iq}/P_{it-2}) \\ &+ b_3(\text{LNSIZE}_i*FE_{iq}/P_{it-2}) + b_4(\text{MGT}*FE_{iq}/P_{it-2}) \\ &+ b_5(\text{MB}*FE_{iq}/P_{it-2}) + b_6(\text{BETA}*FE_{iq}/P_{it-2}) \\ &+ b_7(\text{RFINT}*FE_{iq}/P_{it-2}) + u_{iq}\end{aligned}$$

Analyst Revision Model

$$\begin{aligned}\text{REV}(q+1)_{iq}/P_{it-2} = a_1 &+ b_1(FE_{iq}/P_{it-2}) + b_2(\text{DUM1}*FE_{iq}/P_{it-2}) \\ &+ b_3(\text{LNSIZE}_i*FE_{iq}/P_{it-2}) + b_4(\text{MGT}*FE_{iq}/P_{it-2}) \\ &+ b_5(\text{MB}*FE_{iq}/P_{it-2}) + b_6(\text{BETA}*FE_{iq}/P_{it-2}) \\ &+ b_7(\text{RFINT}*FE_{iq}/P_{it-2}) + u_{iq}\end{aligned}$$

In the return model, coefficient b_1 is the "normal" earnings response coefficient (market reaction to earnings in the absence of reporting dispute) whereas in the analyst revision model, b_1 is the "normal" forecast revision coefficient (analyst reaction to earnings in the absence of

Table 2. Return Model and Analyst Revision Model

Return Model

$$\begin{aligned}\text{CAR}(-1,0)_{iq} = {} & a_1 + b_1(FE_{iq}/P_{it-2}) + b_2(\text{DUM1}*FE_{iq}/P_{it-2}) + b_3(\text{LNSIZE}_i*FE_{iq}/P_{it-2}) \\ & + b_4(\text{MGT}*FE_{iq}/P_{it-2}) + b_5(\text{MB}*FE_{iq}/P_{it-2}) + b_6(\text{BETA}*FE_{iq}/P_{it-2}) \\ & + b_7(\text{RFINT}*FE_{iq}/P_{it-2}) + u_{iq}\end{aligned}$$

Analyst Revision Model

$$\begin{aligned}\text{REV}(q+1)_{iq}/P_{it-2} = {} & a_1 + b_1(FE_{iq}/P_{it-2}) + b_2(\text{DUM1}*FE_{iq}/P_{it-2}) + b_3(\text{LNSIZE}_i*FE_{iq}/P_{it-2}) \\ & + b_4(\text{MGT}*FE_{iq}/P_{it-2}) + b_5(\text{MB}*FE_{iq}/P_{it-2}) + b_6(\text{BETA}*FE_{iq}/P_{it-2}) \\ & + b_7(\text{RFINT}*FE_{iq}/P_{it-2}) + u_{iq}\end{aligned}$$

where:

$\text{CAR}(-1,0)_{iq}$	= Cumulative abnormal returns over the two days around earnings announcement of firm *i* for quarter *q*, where day 0 is an earning announcement date.
$\text{REV}(q+1)_{iq}$	= Revision in the *Value Line* earnings forecast of firm *i* for quarter $q+1$ following the earnings announcement of quarter *q*.
FE_{iq}	= Earnings forecast error of firm *i* for quarter *q*.
P_{it-2}	= Stock price two days before an earning announcement of firm *i*.
DUM1	= 1 if an earnings announcement occurs during one year after a reporting-dispute disclosure, and 0 if the announcement occurs before the dispute disclosure.
LNSIZE_i	= Natural log of the market value of common stock of firm *i*.
MGT	= A dummy variable that takes on the value of 1 if an earnings announcement occurs during one year after management change, and 0 otherwise.
MB	= Market to book value of common equity (growth and persistence).
BETA	= Market model systematic risk.
RFINT	= Long-term U.S. Government bond yield (risk-free interest rate).
u_{iq}	= An error term.

reporting dispute). This coefficient is expected to be positive. Coefficient b_2 in the return model represents differential market reaction to earnings announcements during one year after a reporting-dispute disclosure. This same coefficient in the analyst revision model measures differential analyst reaction to earnings announcements during the same period. The hypothesis of decreased earnings informativeness following reporting dispute will be supported if b_2 is significantly negative. The coefficients, b_3 (the information environment/size effect), b_4 (the management change effect), b_6 (the systematic-risk effect), and b_7 (the risk-free interest rate effect), are expected to be negative. The coefficient b_5 (the growth/persistence effect) is expected to be positive. This study uses interaction terms between the control variables and earnings forecast error to avoid the assumption that ERCs are cross-sectionally constant. As discussed earlier, these control variables determine ERC and they vary across firms. Collins and Kothari (1989) also use interaction terms to circumvent this problem.

The return model and the analyst revision model are estimated over the full sample and over a reduced sample excluding extreme outliers (FE and REV) that are attributable to special, *nonrecurring* items such as asset write-offs and losses/gains from discontinued operations or corporate restructuring.[17] An exclusion of these extreme outliers is consistent with the evidence in Elliott and Shaw (1988), and Hoskin, Hughes, and Ricks (1986) that the market will discount these transitory shocks to earnings which are known to investors prior to or at the time of the earnings announcement. Including such observations may bias our estimate of the "normal" earnings response coefficient downward. Large special adjustments can also distort the "normal" relation between revisions in analysts' earnings forecasts and the current quarter's earnings surprise. Distortions in estimated analyst revision coefficients can result if previously announced special adjustments are incorporated in analyst forecast revisions (REV) but not in the previous quarter's actual EPS (hence, the FE). Similarly, bias can be introduced in the estimated revision coefficients if the current FEs reflect transitory special adjustments that are not expected to influence future earnings.

This study identifies extreme FEs based on these two criteria: (a) |FEs| > 1, and (b) the WSJ earnings announcement mentions special adjustments or non-recurring items of unknown magnitude. If the WSJ indicates the magnitude of special items, FEs are adjusted for these items. These adjusted FEs are not considered as extreme. In all, there are 48 extreme FEs, 42 of which are negative. This relatively large proportion of negative extreme FEs implies poor performance of dispute firms which, in turn, suggests that these firms may have used unacceptable accounting practices to disguise their poor performance.[18]

Extreme REVs are identified by these two criteria: (a) |REVs| > 1 and (b) the VL reports mention impending asset write-offs, corporate restructurings and/or discontinued operations as the reason for the forecast revision.[19] In all, there are 17 extreme REVs. Consistent with extreme FEs, the vast majority of extreme REVs are negative (13 out of 17). This suggests that analysts expect lower future earnings (poor performance), therefore they use the special nonrecurring items to revise downward their earnings forecasts for the subsequent quarter.

RESULTS

This section is divided into two parts. Part one, Main Results, presents summary statistics and the estimated return model and analyst revision model. Part two, Additional Tests, describes additional tests for checking the robustness of the results.

Main Results

Table 3 shows summary statistics for the full sample of reporting-dispute firms. The table includes statistics for both the pre-dispute and the post-dispute periods for the following variables: two-day abnormal return (CAR(-1,0)), scaled forecast error (FE/P), absolute value of scaled forecast error (|FE/P|), scaled forecast revision (REV/P), absolute value of scaled forecast revision (|REV/P|), return on equity (ROE), end-of-quarter price (PRICE), firm size (LNSIZE), market to book ratio (MB), systematic risk (BETA), risk-free interest rate (RFINT), CACL, TATL and Z-score.[20]

A comparison (two-sample *t*-test) between the pre-dispute and post-dispute periods suggests the following significant results.[21]

1. Greater variability of forecast errors (|FE/P|) and forecast revisions (|REV/P|) in the post-dispute period. These results suggest that there is more uncertainty in predicting future earnings after reporting-dispute disclosures.
2. Smaller ROE in the post-dispute period. This indicates poorer profitability which may be attributable to an earnings bath by new managers.
3. Smaller end-of-quarter stock price and firm size in the post-dispute period. This may be interpreted as a negative market response to a revelation that a firm's financial condition is poorer than expected. Another plausible explanation is that the market may anticipate class-action lawsuits which typically follow the dispute disclosure and can adversely affect a firm's future cash flows.
4. Smaller market to book ratio in the post-dispute period. This implies that reporting-dispute disclosure reduces a firm's growth opportunities possibly due to its decreasing ability to raise needed capital as evidenced by a significant decline in stock price.
5. Smaller liquidity (CACL), higher debt level (TLTA) and smaller overall financial condition (Z-score) in the post-dispute period. These results suggest that firms' financial conditions are poorer after the reporting dispute disclosure.

Table 3. Summary Statistics for Reporting Dispute Firms

	N	*Mean*	*Std. dev.*	*t-values*
CAR(–1,0)[a]				
Pre-Reporting Dispute	1182	–0.0014	0.0583	
Post-Reporting Dispute	312	0.0042	0.0959	–0.9869
FE/P[b]				
Pre-Reporting Dispute	1182	–0.0163	0.1263	
Post-Reporting Dispute	312	–0.0246	0.8884	0.1646
|FE/P|[c]				
Pre-Reporting Dispute	1182	0.0302	0.1238	
Post-Reporting Dispute	312	0.1756	0.8711	–2.9433**
REV/P[d]				
Pre-Reporting Dispute	766	–0.0089	0.0436	
Post-Reporting Dispute	213	–0.0144	0.0769	0.9827
|REV/P|[e]				
Pre-Reporting Dispute	766	0.0147	0.0420	
Post-Reporting Dispute	213	0.0315	0.0716	–3.2679***
ROE[f]				
Pre-Reporting Dispute	1182	0.1931	0.7435	
Post-Reporting Dispute	312	–0.0975	1.6382	3.0525***
PRICE[g]				
Pre-Reporting Dispute	1182	20.9082	16.2331	
Post-Reporting Dispute	312	15.0994	13.7831	6.3690****
LNSIZE[h]				
Pre-Reporting Dispute	1182	18.8702	1.8325	
Post-Reporting Dispute	312	18.5797	1.8881	2.5535**
MB[i]				
Pre-Reporting Dispute	1182	1.7302	1.3282	
Post-Reporting Dispute	312	1.3154	1.2206	5.2374****

(continued)

Table 3. (Continued)

	N	*Mean*	*Std. dev.*	*t-values*
BETA[j]				
Pre-Reporting Dispute	1182	1.0705	0.5692	
Post-Reporting Dispute	312	1.1097	0.6170	−1.0654
RFINT[k]				
Pre-Reporting Dispute	1182	9.8862	2.3028	
Post-Reporting Dispute	312	9.7453	1.9460	1.1445
CACL[l]				
Pre-Reporting Dispute	1182	2.6253	1.9492	
Post-Reporting Dispute	312	2.0592	0.9657	2.7904**
TLTA[m]				
Pre-Reporting Dispute	1182	0.6244	0.2404	
Post-Reporting Dispute	312	0.7184	0.2643	−2.6688**
Z-score[n]				
Pre-Reporting Dispute	1182	0.0416	0.0394	
Post-Reporting Dispute	312	0.0261	0.0248	3.3817***

Notes: [a] Two-day cumulative abnormal returns around earnings announcement.

[b] Earnings forecast error scaled by stock price two days before an earnings announcement. Median FE/P is 0.0 for pre-dispute period and −0.0029 for post-dispute period.

[c] Absolute value of earnings forecast error scaled by price.

[d] Forecast revision scaled by stock price two days before an earnings announcement.

[e] Absolute value of forecast error scaled by price.

[f] ROE or Return on equity = (Net income/Average stockholders' equity).

[g] The end-of-quarter price.

[h] LNSIZE = Natural log of the market value of common stock.

[i] MB = Market to book value of common equity as a proxy for growth and persistence.

[j] BETA = Market model systematic risk.

[k] RFINT = Long-term government bond yield (risk-free interest rate).

[l] CACL = Current assets/Current liabilities.

[m] TLTA = Total liabilities/Total assets.

[n] Z-score measured overall financial condition (Altman and McGough 1974).

** Significant at 0.01 level for two-tailed unequal-variance *t*-statisitc.

*** Significant at 0.001 level for two-tailed unequal-variance *t*-statisitc.

**** Significant at 0.0001 level for two-tailed unequal-variance *t*-statisitc.

Table 4 presents test results for differential market reaction to earnings surprises (ERC-return model) during the pre-reporting dispute period relative to the post-reporting dispute period, both before and after deletion of extreme forecast errors (FEs). For both sample groups, b_1 ("normal" ERC) is significantly positive at < .005 level and b_2 (differential market reaction to earnings announcements during one year after the dispute disclosure) is significantly negative at < .01 level. Both b_1 and b_2 are larger and more statistically significant after deletion of extreme FEs. Adjusted R^2 and F-value for the model are also more than double after the deletion. These findings support the earlier contention that special nonrecurring items are transitory elements which contribute to lower ERCs. Since the market is likely to place a higher value on the permanent component of earnings (Beaver et al. 1980), the isolation of this component from the transitory one results in a significant improvement in earnings and return relation. The control variables b_3 (the information environment effect) is significantly negative as expected after deletion of extreme FEs. This confirms the finding of Atiase (1985) that larger firms have less market/analyst reactions to their earning announcements than smaller firms. Another significantly negative control variable is b_4 (the management change effect). This confirms the earnings bath among new managers. All other control variables: the growth/persistence effect, the systematic-risk effect and the risk-free interest rate effect, are not statistically significant.

Table 5 presents test results for differential analyst reaction to earnings surprises during the pre-reporting dispute period relative to the post-reporting dispute period, both before and after deletion of extreme REVs and FEs. For both sample groups, b_1 ("normal" revision coefficient) is significantly positive at < 0.0001 level, and b_2 (differential analyst reaction to earnings announcements during one year after the dispute disclosure) is significantly negative at < 0.0001 level. These results suggest that analysts make less extensive revisions in their forecasts of future earnings during one year after the dispute disclosure. Similar to ERC results, b_1, b_2, adjusted R^2 and F-value are larger and more significant after deletion of extreme REVs and FEs. All control variables are statistically significant in the expected directions for both sample groups.

In sum, the ERC and the analyst revision coefficient results strongly support the hypothesis, that is, the market and the analysts perceive earnings after the reporting dispute to be less informative than before

Table 4. Regression Results for Differential Earnings Response Coefficients (Return Model) for Pre-Reporting Dispute versus Post-Reporting Dispute Periods

$$\begin{aligned} CAR(-1,0)_{iq} = {} & a_1 + b_1(FE_{iq}/P_{it-2}) + b_2(DUM1*FE_{iq}/P_{it-2}) \\ & + b_3(LNSIZE_i*FE_{iq}/P_{it-2}) + b_4(MGT*FE_{iq}/P_{it-2}) \\ & + b_5(MB*FE_{iq}/P_{it-2}) + b_6(BETA*FE_{iq}/P_{it-2}) \\ & + b_7(RFINT*FE_{iq}/P_{it-2}) + u_{iq}{}^{a} \end{aligned}$$

Coefficients	*Predicted Sign*	*Before Deletion of Extreme FEs*[b] *(N = 1494)*	*After Deletion of Extreme FEs (N = 1446)*
a_1	?	0.0010	0.0011
(t-value)		(0.577)	(0.665)
b_1	+	0.9121	1.3341
(t-value)		(2.772)***	(5.280)****
b_2	–	–0.0836	–0.0954
(t-value)		(–2.462)**	(–2.709)***
b_3	–	–0.0080	–0.0628
(t-value)		(–1.564)	(–5.784)****
b_4	–	0.0108	–0.1163
(t-value)		(0.5234)	(–3.223)***
b_5	+	0.0313	0.0178
(t-value)		(2.607)	(1.119)
b_6	–	0.0303	0.0358
(t-value)		(1.515)	(1.544)
b_7	–	–0.0060	–0.0170
(t-value)		(–1.377)	(–1.588)
R^2		0.0294	0.0665
Adjusted R^2		0.0248	0.0619
F-value		6.4972****	14.6342****

Notes: [a]CAR = two-day cumulative abnormal return around an earnings announcement.
FE = earnings forecast error.
P = stock price two days before an earnings announcement.
DUM1 = 1 for earnings announcements during one year after a dispute disclosure and 0 otherwise.
LNSIZE = natural log of the market value of a firm's common stock.
MGT = 1 for earnings announcements during one year after a management change and 0 otherwise.
MB = Market to book value of common equity.
BETA = Market model systematic risk.
RFINT = Long-term government bond yield.
[b]Extreme FEs = |FEs| > \$1.00 and the earnings announcement mentions special adjustments or one-time occurrences of unknown magnitude.
**Significant at < 0.01 level, one-tailed test.
***Significant at < 0.005 level, one-tailed test.
****Significant at < 0.0001 level, one-tailed test.

Table 5. Regression Results for Differential Revision Coeffcients for Pre-Reporting Dispute versus Post-Reporting Dispute Periods

$$REV(q+1)_{iq}/P_{it\text{-}2} = a_1 + b_1(FE_{iq}/P_{it\text{-}2}) + b_2(DUM1^*FE_{iq}/P_{it\text{-}2}) + b_3(LNSIZE_i^*FE_{iq}/P_{it\text{-}2}) + b_4(MGT^*FE_{iq}/P_{it\text{-}2}) + b_5(MB^*FE_{iq}/P_{it\text{-}2}) + b_6(BETA^*FE_{iq}/P_{it\text{-}2}) + b_7(RFINT^*FE_{iq}/P_{it\text{-}2}) + u_{iq}{}^{a}$$

Coefficients	*Predicted Sign*	*Before Deletion of Extreme REVs and FEs*[b,c] *(N = 979)*	*After Deletion of Extreme REVs and FEs (N = 929)*
a_1	?	–0.0065	–0.0047
(*t*-value)		(–4.347)****	(–4.994)****
b_1	+	1.3814	1.7294
(*t*-value)		(7.603)****	(7.919)****
b_2	–	–0.1386	–0.3195
(*t*-value)		(–4.293)****	(–6.633)****
b_3	–	–0.0664	–0.0556
(*t*-value)		(–7.269)****	(–3.927)****
b_4	–	–0.2679	–0.2640
(*t*-value)		(–12.044)****	(–4.059)****
b_5	+	0.0595	0.1036
(*t*-value)		(4.316)****	(6.092)****
b_6	–	–0.1166	–0.0953
(*t*-value)		(–4.434)****	(–1.789)*
b_7	–	–0.0292	–0.0700
(*t*-value)		(–5.162)****	(–6.145)****
R^2		0.2488	0.3181
Adjusted R^2		0.2434	0.3129
F-value		45.952****	61.371****

Notes:
[a]REV = the *Value Line* forecast revision.
P = stock price two days before an earnings announcement.
FE = earnings forecast error.
DUM1 = 1 for earnings announcements during one year after dispute disclosure and 0 otherwise.
LNSIZE = natural log of the market value of a firm's common stock.
MGT = 1 for earnings announcements during one year after a management change and 0 otherwise.
MB = Market to book value of common equity.
BETA = Market model systematic risk.
RFINT = Long-term government bond yield.

[b]Extreme FEs = |FEs| > \$1.00 and the earnings announcement mentions special adjustments or one-time occurrences of unknown magnitude.

[c]Extreme REVs = |REVs| > \$1.00 and the Value Line report mentions impending special adjustments or one-time occurrences.

*Significant at < 0.05 level, one-tailed test.

****Significant at < 0.0001 level, one-tailed test.

the dispute. Two diagnostic tests important for a study that uses pooling of time-series and cross-section data are also performed. The first test, based on White (1980), is a test for the possibility of heteroscedastic disturbances. The second test, Durbin-Watson *d* statistic, is a test for a possible autocorrelation in the disturbance term. These two tests do not indicate the problems of heteroscedasticity or autocorrelation.[22]

Additional Tests

Six additional tests for checking the robustness of the results are conducted.

1. The smaller ERC and analyst revision coefficient in the post-dispute period may be explained by alternative hypotheses such as the market and analysts become desensitized to earnings surprises in this period or earnings temporarily become more difficult to predict after the dispute disclosure. To eliminate these alternative hypotheses, each of the 85 dispute firms is matched with a firm not in dispute with the SEC. This matched pair is required to be in the same industry (four digit SIC code) and has similar size (market value of common stock). Similar data collection criteria in the second section are applied to these nondispute firms. The same return model and analyst revision model are reestimated for these 85 matched nondispute firms. Results of this model estimation are similar to those for dispute firms except that b_2 is *not* statistical significant, that is, there is *no* difference in market/analyst reactions to nondispute firms' earnings announcements before versus after the dispute disclosure of their matched dispute firms. This insignificant b_2 for nondispute firms serves to eliminate alternative hypotheses, and renders support for the earlier inference that accounting disputes with the SEC negatively affect the perceived informativeness of dispute firms' earnings.
2. The models are estimated with an intercept dummy that takes on the value of 0 if an earnings announcement occurs before the dispute disclosure and the value of 1 if an earnings announcement occurs after the dispute disclosure. This intercept dummy measures the shift in the intercept for post-dispute period from that for pre-dispute period. Without this intercept dummy, the slope dummy coefficient will pick up intercept difference. The estimated intercept dummy is not statistically significant and the results remain virtually the same.

3. Prior studies (Freeman and Tse 1992; Cheng et al. 1992) suggest nonlinear return/earnings relation. Because of the possibility of nonlinearity, this study uses two alternative measures for all nondummy variables (earnings forecast error, firm size, beta, market to book ratio and risk-free interest rate). The first alternative is a binary measure, that is, a variable takes the value of 1 when it is above the median and 0 otherwise. The binary measure reduces noise from mismeasurement of a variable, and so, reduces the possibility of undue influence by large variable values. Freeman and Tse (1992) use this binary measure. The second measure is the standardized rank, that is , rank of each variable is divided by the number of observations plus 1 ($N + 1$). The standardized rank is relatively insensitive to outliers and provides more efficient significance tests than the binary measure. The standardized rank was first suggested by Beaver et al. (1979), and used by Freeman and Tse (1992), and Cheng et al. (1992). These two alternative measures yield similar inferences as those reported earlier.

4. Because the sample spans over 22 years, it is possible that a group of firms clustering in a certain time period may have undue influence on the results. To examine this possibility, sample firms are partitioned into four equal-size groups based on the year in which their first dispute disclosures were made. Group 1 covers 1971-78 (21 firms), group 2 covers 1979-83 (22 firms), group 3 covers 1983-85 (21 firms), and group 4 covers 1986-92 (21 firms). The three models were estimated for each of these four groups. Consistent results, similar to those reported earlier, are found for all groups.

5. This study also examines whether different sources of first dispute disclosures (SEC investigation announcements, 60 firms, versus the other sources such as shareholders' lawsuits and firms' internal investigation announcements, 25 firms), have differential effects on market and analyst reactions. In particular, another variable, SEC*DUM1*FE/P, is included in the models. SEC is equal to 1 if SEC investigation announcement is the source of the first dispute disclosure and 0 otherwise. DUM1 is equal to 1 for earnings announcements during one year after a dispute disclosure and 0 otherwise. An estimated coefficient of this variable is expected to be negative if SEC investigation announcement is perceived as a more negative signal than the other announcement sources. Results indicate an insignificant coefficient for this variable. This suggests that investors and analysts do not perceive sources of first dispute disclosures as important factors in

assessing the dispute effects. It is the reporting dispute disclosure per se that matters.

6. In order to assess the effect of using the AAERs versus the WSJ index as data sources, the models are reestimated after excluding 32 no-AAER firms. The inferences with respect to the analyst revision model remain the same but the inferences based on the return model have changed. The coefficient b_2 (differential market reaction to earnings announcements during the post-dispute period) in the return model is no longer significant. This finding suggests that using the AAERs vs. the WSJ to identify reporting dispute firms can lead to different inferences especially for the ERC-return model. This finding provides a caution against using the AAERs as the only sources of reporting dispute identification, especially in a return/earnings study.

CONCLUSIONS

This study investigates the effects of regulatory enforcement actions on perceived earnings informativeness. In particular, the study examines market and analyst reactions to earnings announcements of sample firms involved in financial reporting disputes with the SEC. These reactions are measured by an earnings response coefficient (ERC) from the return model and by an analyst-revision coefficient from regressing analyst forecast revisions on analyst forecast errors. The coefficient which measures differential market/analyst reactions to earnings in the post-dispute period is tested in order to assess potential effects of reporting dispute disclosures on the informativeness of earnings.

A disclosure of reporting disputes is hypothesized to have a negative impact on the ERC and the analyst-revision coefficient because the dispute disclosure serves as a signal that the earnings number has more noise or uncertainty than previously assumed. Regression analysis, which controls for information environment, management change, growth and/or persistence of earnings, systematic risk and risk-free interest rate, yields supporting results for the hypothesis. The results show a smaller ERC and a smaller analyst-revision coefficient after reporting-dispute disclosures, suggesting a negative effect of regulatory enforcement actions on the perceived informativeness of earnings. These results are robust against several diagnostic tests including the use of matched nondispute firms. Evidence provided here strongly suggests that regulatory enforcement actions, such as the SEC's financial reporting investigations, are viable sanctions in maintaining public confidence in financial reporting.

In addition, this study documents that there are several reporting-dispute WSJ firms that are not included in the AAERs. This understatement in sample size of reporting dispute firms when using the AAERs as the data sources can lead to different inferences especially for the ERC-return model. Therefore, future studies may want to use not only the AAERs but also the WSJ to identify reporting dispute firms.

ACKNOWLEDGMENTS

The author acknowledges the financial support of Rider University during this project. Comments of the Work-In-Progress Seminar participants at Rider University on an earlier version of this paper are also acknowledged.

NOTES

1. This public concern is supported by the 1994 fraud survey of KPMG Peat Marwick. The survey states that "The increase in the number of organizations reporting large false financial reporting frauds appears to bear out the conclusion of the Treadway Commission indicating that false financial reporting was one of the fastest growing financial crimes."

2. Prior studies concerning the SEC enforcement actions are Pincus, Holder, and Mock (1988) which describe the SEC investigation procedures; Feroz, Park and Pastena (1991) which document negative market reaction to the reporting dispute disclosures; and Dechow, Sloan, and Sweeney (1994) which examine causes and consequence of financial reporting disputes. *None* of these studies investigate the impact of SEC enforcement actions on the informativeness of earnings.

3. Following the suggestion of Kothari and Zimmerman (1992), the ERC is also estimated by the price model (regressing stock prices on the level of earnings). Because results of both return and price models are virtually the same, only the return model is presented.

4. See Feroz et al. (1991) for a detailed description of the AAER which is a publication of the SEC.

5. The Litigation Release is another publication of the SEC. This study examines these reporting disputes to identify any common situations where disputes are not included in the AAERs. The examination does not reveal any common charactistic or any apparent reason.

6. Thompson, Olsen, and Dietrich (1987) indicate that firm-specific news reported in the WSJ was disclosed in the Dow Jones newswire releases one day earlier. This one-day-earlier disclosure of reporting disputes does not affect this study's hypothesis test-

ing since this study tests the market/analyst reactions to unexpected earnings on the earnings announcement dates before versus after the dispute disclosure. *No* earnings announcement dates of sample firms are within one week of the first reporting dispute disclosure in the WSJ.

7. This argument is supported by Nourayi's (1994) findings that investors do not react significantly to announcements of the SEC enforcement actions in the LRs but investors react significantly to the announcements made in the WSJ.

8. In particular, these misleading statements include overstating potential return on investments, using investors' funds for purposes other than those communicated to investors, understating risk associated with investments, failing to inform investors about disciplinary history of promoters and misleading investors with respect to the plan of distribution of securities.

9. These 16 firms were reported in the *Litigation Releases*.

10. These 16 firms did not appear in any SEC publications.

11. Fifty-seven of these 60 firms experience formal investigations and three firms experience informal investigations.

12. Several studies use stock price to scale FE, for example, Collins and DeAngelo (1990), Ahmed (1994). The purpose of this scaling is to minimize heteroscedasticity problems in subsequent regression analyses and to enhance cross-sectional comparability. Results based on the use of FE scaled by expected earnings are virtually the same as those reported here.

13. According to the seasonal random walk model, expected earnings are earnings for the same quarter a year earlier. Bernard and Thomas (1990) find that stock prices on announcement of quarterly earnings behave as if quarterly earnings follow a seasonal random walk model.

14. The purpose of this scaling is stated in note 12. Again, results based on the use of FE and REV scaled by expected earnings are virtually the same as those reported here.

15. Using market to book ratio as a proxy for earnings persistence also avoids a significant reduction in sample size as compared to using time series of earnings. When book value of equity is negative, MB is set equal to zero because negative MB values do not have an economic interpretation in this context. When MB is greater than 5, MB is set equal to 5 to avoid undue influence of very large MB values. These truncating criteria follow Collins and Kothari (1989).

16. Management change is defined as a change in at least one of the positions of president, chief executive officer, or chairman of the board.

17. This study does not screen for extreme CAR because the study has already excluded any earnings announcements with potential confounding events as a part of sample selection.

18. The poor performance of reporting-dispute firms is supported by significantly negative cumulative abnormal returns (–15.92%, *t*-value = –4.117) during approximately one year before the first disclosure of disputed reporting.

19. These criteria for identifying outliers are similar to Collins and DeAngelo's criteria except that REV threshold here is $|REVs| > 1$. Using Collins and DeAngelo's threshold of 0.50 does not change any inferences.

20. CACL = Current assets/Current liabilities. TLTA = Total liabilities/Total assets. *Z*-score is computed according to Altman and McGough (1974).

21. Inferences based on the Wilcoxon signed rank tests are virtually the same.

22. The heteroscedasticity is a condition where regression error terms have unequal variance. The autocorrelation is a condition where the error terms are serially correlated.

REFERENCES

Ahmed, A.S. 1994. Accounting earnings and future economic rents: An empirical analysis. *Journal of Accounting and Economics* (May): 377-400.

Altman, E.R., and T. McGough. 1974. Evaluation of a company as a going concern. *The Journal of Accountancy* (December): 50-57.

Atiase, R.K. 1985. Predisclosure information, firm capitalization, and security price behavior around earnings announcements. *Journal of Accounting Research* (Spring): 21-36.

Ball, R., and P. Brown. 1968. An empirical evaluation of accounting income numbers. *Journal of Accounting Research* 6: 159-177.

Beaver, W., R. Clarke, and W.F. Wright. 1979. The association between unsystematic security returns and the magnitude of earnings forecast errors. *Journal of Accounting Research* (Autumn): 316-340.

Beaver, W., R. Lambert, and D. Morse. 1980. The information content of security prices. *Journal of Accounting and Economics* (March): 3-28.

Bernard, V., and J. Thomas. 1990. Evidence that stock prices do not fully reflect the implications of current earnings for future earnings. *Journal of Accounting and Economics* (December): 305-340.

Cheng, C.S., W.S. Hopwood, and J.C. McKeown. 1992. Non-linearity and specification problems in unexpected earnings response regression model. *The Accounting Review* (July): 579-598.

Choi, S.K., and G. Salamon. 1989. Accounting information and capital asset prices. Working Paper, Vanderbilt University.

Coleman, T.S., L. Fisher, and R.G. Ibbotson. 1993. *Historical U.S. Treasury Yield Curves*. Ibbotson Associates.

Collins, D.W., and S.P. Kothari. 1989. An analysis of intertemporal and cross sectional determinants of earnings response coefficients. *Journal of Accounting and Economics* (July): 143-181.

Collins, D.W., and L. DeAngelo. 1990. Accounting information and corporate governance: Market and analyst reactions to earnings of firms engaged in proxy contests. *Journal of Accounting and Economics* (October): 213-247.

DeAngelo, L. 1988. Managerial competition, information costs, and corporate governance: The use of accounting performance measures in proxy contests. *Journal of Accounting and Economics* (January): 3-36.

Dechow, P.M., R.G. Sloan, and A.P. Sweeney. 1994. Causes and consequence of agressive financial reporting policies. Working Paper, University of Pennsylvania.

Easton, P., and M. Zmijewski. 1989. Cross-sectional variation in the stock market response to accounting earnings announcements. *Journal of Accounting and Economics* (July): 117-141.

Elliott, J.A., and W.H. Shaw. 1988. Write-offs as accounting procedures to manage perceptions. *Journal of Accounting Research* (Suppl.): 91-119.

Feroz, E.H., K. Park, and V.S. Pastena. 1991. The financial and market effects of the SEC's accounting and auditing enforcement releases. *Journal of Accounting Research* (Suppl.): 107-142.

Freeman, R.N., and S.Y. Tse. 1992. A nonlinear model of security price responses to unexpected earnings. *Journal of Accounting Research* (Autumn): 185-209.

Garman, M., and J. Ohlson. 1980. Information and the sequential valuation of assets in arbitrage-free economics. *Journal of Accounting Research* (Autumn): 420-440.

Holthausen, R., and R. Verrecchia. 1988. The effect of sequential information releases on the variance of price changes in an intertemporal multi-asset market. *Journal of Accounting Research* (Spring): 82-106.

Hoskin, R.E., J.S. Hughes, and W.E. Ricks. 1986. Evidence on the incremental information content of additional firm disclosures made concurrently with earnings. *Journal of Accounting Research* (Suppl.): 1-32.

Imhoff, E.A., and G.J. Lobo. 1992. The impact of ex ante earnings uncertainty on earnings response coefficient. *The Accounting Review* (April): 427-439.

Komendi, R., and R. Lipe. 1987. Earnings innovations, earnings persistence and stock returns. *Journal of Business* (July): 323-345.

Kothari, S.P., and J. Zimmerman. 1992. Price versus return models. Working Paper, University of Rochester.

KPMG Forensic and Investigation Services. 1994. *1994 Fraud Survey.* KPMG.

Lang, M. 1991. Time-varying stock price response to earnings induced by uncertainty about the time-series process of earnings. *Journal of Accounting Research* (Autumn): 229-257.

Lang, M., and M. McNichols. 1990. Earnings quality, financial distress and the incremental information content of cash flows. Working Paper, Stanford University.

Moore, M.L. 1973. Management changes and discretionary accounting decisions. *Journal of Accounting Research* (Spring): 100-107.

Nourayi, M.M. 1994. Stock price responses to the SEC's enforcement actions. *Journal of Accounting and Public Policy* (December): 333-347.

Ohlson, J. 1983. Price-earnings ratios and earnings capitalization under uncertainty. *Journal of Accounting Research* (Spring): 141-154.

Palmrose, Z. 1987. *Litigation and independent auditors: The role of business failures and management fraud. Auditing: A Journal of Practice & Theory* (Spring): 90-103.

Pincus, W., W.H. Holder, and T.J. Mock. 1988. *Reducing the Incidence of Fraudulent Financial Reporting: The Role of the Securities and Exchange Commission.* Los Angeles: SEC and Financial Reporting Institute of the University of Southern California.

Scholes, M., and J. Williams. 1977. Estimating betas from nonsynchronous data. *Journal of Financial Economics* (December): 309-328.

St. Pierre, K., and J. Anderson. 1984. An analysis of the factors associated with lawsuits against public accountants. *The Accounting Review* (April): 242-263.

Teoh, S.H., and T.J. Wong. 1993. Perceived auditor quality and the earnings response coefficient. *The Accounting Review* (April): 346-366.

Thompson, R.B., C. Olsen, and J.R. Dietrich. 1987. Attributes of news about firms: An analysis of firm-specific news reported in the Wall Street Journal index. *Journal of Accounting Research* (Fall): 245-274.

White, H. 1980. A heteroskedasticity-consistent covariance matrix estimator and a direct test for heteroskedasticity. *Econometrics* (September): 817-838.

COMMENT LETTERS AS INDICATORS OF OVERALL CORPORATE MANAGER PREFERENCES:
EMPLOYERS' ACCOUNTING FOR PENSIONS

Georgia Saemann

ABSTRACT

The underlying objective of this study was to determine if comment letters filed in the FASB's due process are indicative of overall corporate opinions or just a select interest group, and to offer explanations for the relationship between filing choice and accounting preferences. The study examines models of corporate positions (support or oppose) on seven controversial requirements of *SFAS 87* with four explanatory variables including filing choice, firm size, and pension plan size and status. The analyses are unique in that prior studies of the lobbying process have examined differences between filers and nonfilers (using filing choice as a proxy for accounting preference), or have investigated the positions stated by a relatively homogenous group—comment filers. The results

Research in Accounting Regulation, Volume 11, pages 125-142.

ISBN: 0-7623-0168-6

confirm prior researchers' assumptions that filing choice relates inversely to positions taken on certain issues and, more importantly, the findings suggest that filers and nonfilers have differing accounting concerns. Large companies, who tend to be more active filers than their smaller peers, were more likely to oppose and comment on measurement issues that led to increases in reported income level and volatility.

INTRODUCTION

The Financial Accounting Standards Board (FASB) is committed to developing neutral standards that are useful to those who rely on financial statements. The FASB's mission statement, however, constrains the Board to "promulgate standards only when the expected benefits exceed the perceived costs." To assess the views of its constituents and to identify the benefits and costs of mandated accounting changes, the FASB solicits comment letters through open due process procedures. Accounting researchers also use comment letters to study corporate accounting preferences. For example, Watts and Zimmerman (1978), Dhaliwal (1982), and McKee, Bell, and Boatsman (1984) read comment letters to determine the positions corporate managers took on general price level and oil and gas accounting proposals. Other researchers used corporate willingness to file comment letters with the Board as a surrogate for accounting preferences (e.g., Griffin 1982, 1983; Kelly 1982, 1985; Francis 1987; Deakin 1989) under the assumption that companies are more likely to incur costs of filing as the perceived costs associated with an accounting change increase.

Using comment letters to assess corporate accounting preferences presents several methodological difficulties. First, and most obviously, the views apply solely to those who file the comment letters; the views of nonfilers can only be assumed. Second, comment filers seldom address all issues in an accounting proposal. Therefore, even the views of filers apply only to a limited number of issues within a proposed standard. Although Schalow (1995) shows that companies tend to file on standards they oppose, other unrelated factors may also apply. As an example, the decision to not file a comment letter on a specific issue may merely reflect the perception that the FASB's position on that issue is unshakable. Similarly, some companies may not have the necessary resources, including manpower, to develop informed arguments for their accounting preferences.

One approach to overcoming these difficulties and the one used here is to survey both filers and nonfilers of comment letters about their positions on major accounting issues. This allows a direct investigation of positions taken by a more heterogeneous sample than one that includes only comment filers. It also provides empirical evidence about the relationship between position and filing choices.

This study investigates corporate reaction of filers and nonfilers, to each of seven controversial requirements of the *Exposure Draft: Employers' Accounting for Pensions* (*ED*; FASB 1985). Pension accounting remains an important standard to investigate not only because of its impact on the primary financial statements and related note disclosures but also because of the widespread attention it received in the financial press. This widespread attention increased the likelihood that corporations were aware of the proposed changes and able to take informed positions on the various issues, whether or not they filed comment letters. The diverse impact of the proposed standard also increased the likelihood that existing differences between filers and nonfilers in the types of accounting changes they opposed would emerge.

This study addresses the following questions which are relevant to the standard-setting process.

1. Do comment filers and nonfilers have similar concerns over accounting standards?
2. Do comment letters focus on issues of most widespread concern to the corporate population as a whole?
3. How are firm size, financial statement effects from an accounting change, and filing choice related to corporate positions on accounting issues?

The study's underlying objective is to determine if comment letters filed in the FASB's due process are indicative of overall corporate opinions or just a select interest group, and to offer explanations for the relationship between filing choice and accounting preferences. The evidence is relevant to public policy issues related to the effectiveness of the FASB's due process procedures.

THE MODEL

This study examines models of the relationship between corporate preferences (1 = support, 0 = oppose) on proposed accounting changes and four explanatory variables: filing choice, firm size, and pension plan size and status. Separate analyses are performed on each of seven proposed accounting changes, using survey data to measure corporate preferences. A discussion of the changes and the hypothesized relationships between accounting preference and the explanatory variables follows.

The Proposed Accounting Changes

The seven accounting changes come from the *ED*, which identified key requirements in an introductory synopsis. The changes address liability recognition for underfunded (1) vested and (2) unvested accumulated benefit obligations, (3) standardization of pension cost measurements, (4) discount rates used to determine present values of the pension obligation, and disclosures for (5) the effect of a one-percent change in compensation or discount rate, (6) the components of periodic pension cost, and (7) a reconciliation of the plan as funded with balance sheet amounts.

The first two questions relate to balance sheet recognition of a liability for vested and unvested benefits in an underfunded pension plan. The *ED* required companies to record a liability for the amount by which accumulated pension obligations, including both vested and unvested benefits, exceeded the fair market value of plan assets. Note that, because this requirement did not include booking the liability based on the projected benefit obligation, the financial statement effect was significantly mitigated. Nevertheless, Norton (1989) reports that a sizable number of companies faced recognizing a minimum pension liability for the first time under the *ED* requirements.

The second two questions address measurement issues regarding pension cost standardization and a settlement-based discount rate. The *ED* required all companies to apply the projected unit credit method to calculate pension expense using a discount rate based on rates implicit in current prices of annuity contracts or rates of return on high-quality fixed-income investments. Subsequent adoption studies on *SFAS 87* (e.g., Norton 1989; Sami and Welsh 1992; Senteney and Strawser 1990; Stone and Ingram 1988) confirmed projections that these changes would reduce reported pension expense for most companies. In terms of standardization, the reduction derived from the fact that only a small number of companies used the projected unit credit method in 1985. One survey of 924 pension plans found that only 18% used this method; the remainder of the plans used methods that resulted in greater pension expense (Arthur Young 1985, 2). An increase in the discount rates further reduced pension expense because most companies used rates between 8 and 9% compared to newly required rates based on current long-term yields at a time when the yield on U.S. Treasury Securities was about 11.75%.

The last three questions address footnote disclosures, including the effect of a 1% change in the discount or compensation rates used to calculate pension expense, components of net periodic pension cost, and reconciliation of the plan's funded status with amounts reported in the balance sheet. These disclosures substantially extended the already expanded requirements of *SFAS 36*, and opposers generally viewed them as excessive.

Filing Choice

The FASB maintains listings of comment filers in its due process for the public record. Companies included in the study were matched to these listings to determine their filing activity (1 = filer, 0 = nonfiler) on the *ED*. The FASB also provided copies of these letters for comparative analysis with survey responses.

As discussed earlier, filing choice studies basically assume that a company's decision to file on a proposed accounting standard proxies for an opposing position on that standard. Hussein (1981) further asserts that companies are more likely to file on a proposed standard that materially impacts reported income than on one that affects financial statement form, because contracting and monitoring costs are most closely associated with changes in reported income and recorded assets and liabilities. In support of this assertion, Hussein found that corporations filed comment letters significantly more often on accounting standards that affected financial statement content (*SFAS 2, 5, 8, 12, 13*) than on those that affected form (*SFAS 1, 4, 6, 14*). Although the present study recognizes that filers and nonfilers on the *ED* are most likely to differ in the positions they take on the liability recognition and cost measurement requirements, it hypothesizes that filers are more likely than nonfilers to oppose each of the seven *ED* requirements:

H_1. Filing choice relates inversely to corporate positions on the seven *ED* requirements.

Empirical support for this hypothesis would endorse the use of filing choice as a proxy for corporate accounting preferences wherein opposers equal filers. A significant relationship between filing choice and corporate positions on the disclosure requirements would suggest that opposition to some disclosures is enough to motivate companies to file comment letters.

Firm Size

Accounting changes have a potential effect on corporate cash flows because accounting numbers are used in monitoring corporate performance. For example, management compensation and debt covenant agreements (private monitoring) provide incentives for managers to adopt income- or asset-maximizing accounting principles. Alternatively, "excessive profits" provide politicians and regulators with a justification to penalize corporations (political monitoring), most frequently in the tax code or in fee regulation. Concern over the costs of reporting "excessive profits" increases with firm size, offsetting the benefits of higher reported profits or assets associated with contracts related to management compensation and debt financing (Watts and Zimmerman 1978). This leads to the *firm size hypothesis* which states that a company's tendency to oppose income-increasing accounting standards increases with firm size.

Existing support for the firm size hypothesis remains uneven. Studies of positions taken in comment letters have provided very weak evidence, and studies of lobbying choice are inconclusive because alternative explanations for large versus small firm filing choices reduce the validity of such tests. Studies of adoption timing decisions also provide inconclusive results. Ayres (1986) reports a tendency for smaller companies to have early-adopted *SFAS 52*, increasing reported income, but Sami and Welsh (1992) report that larger companies early-adopted *SFAS 87*, which also increased reported income. In explaining these contradictory findings, Sami and Welsh suggest that the cost of early adopting *SFAS 87* precluded small companies from taking early advantage of the change in accounting. The issue, however, remains that large companies did early-adopt an income-increasing accounting standard.

For this study, net sales provides a proxy to measure potential managerial concern with private versus political monitoring costs. Net sales is preferable to total assets because the measure is in current rather than historical dollars. Thus between-firm comparisons are more reliable for current monitoring costs. Net sales is also less variable over time and less subject to differences in reporting than income before taxes or net income.[1]

This study hypothesizes that the likelihood of corporate opposition to standardization and new discount rates increases with firm size given that most companies faced reductions in reported pension expense from these changes:

H_2. Firm size relates inversely to corporate positions on income-increasing changes—cost standardization and discount rates.

Although no hypotheses are offered for the relationships between firm size and requirements affecting the balance sheet or footnote disclosures, these models include firm size to avoid a problem from omitting potentially explanatory variables.

Pension Plan Size

If contracting and monitoring costs drive corporate filing activity in the standard-setting process, that activity should be directly related to the potential magnitude of a proposed accounting change's financial statement effects. Francis (1987) provided such evidence for filing choice on *SFAS 87* using reported pension expense to proxy for financial statement effect. He showed that, as potential financial statement effect increased, companies were more likely to file comment letters on *Preliminary Views: Employers' Accounting for Pensions*. The potential benefits from influencing the requirements of a proposed standard, in other words, became large enough to offset the cost and effort of filing a comment letter with the FASB.

This study asserts that there is a relationship between corporate positions on a proposed accounting standard and its expected financial statement effect independent of filing choice; the greater the impact on the financial statements, the more likely companies are to oppose, rather than support, a proposed accounting change. This assertion is based on two premises. First, any mandated accounting change that reduces the number of acceptable reporting alternatives or requires increased disclosures is likely to affect corporations adversely. This is because management has already chosen what they perceive as the most favorable method of accounting, including the nature and extent of disclosures. Second, the greater the financial statement effect, the more likely the company will face private and/or public contracting and monitoring costs as described earlier.

To measure the magnitude of financial statement effect, this study uses the accumulated benefit pension plan obligation, as defined in the *ED* and *SFAS 87*, relative to the company's total assets (accumulated benefit obligations/total balance sheet assets). The study hypothesizes an inverse relationship between pension plan size and position choices on all *ED* requirements on the premise that only materially affected companies must comply:

H_3. Relative pension plan size relates inversely to corporate positions on all seven *ED* requirements.

Once a plan meets a materiality threshold, companies are likely to further consider the magnitude of the *ED*'s effect on reported income and liabilities. For footnote disclosures, this relationship is not expected to be as strong since pension plan size is likely to only marginally affect the complexity, length, or cost of disclosures once the compliance threshhold is met.

Pension Plan Status

A second variable used to proxy for the *ED*'s financial statement effect addresses pension plan status, which is measured by the ratio of accumulated benefit obligations to pension assets. Francis (1987) asserted and found that companies with more significantly underfunded pension plans were more likely to lobby against the liability recognition requirements proposed in the FASB's *Preliminary Views* on pension accounting. Similarly, this study hypothesizes that a lower level of funding motivates companies to oppose liability recognition:

H_4. Pension plan status relates inversely to corporate positions on liability recognition.

Although no hypotheses are offered for the relationships between pension plan status and income statement and footnote disclosure requirements, these models include plan status to avoid a problem from omitting potentially explanatory variables.

RESEARCH METHODOLOGY

The Sample

This research is based on a survey of a random sample of all companies whose stock was listed on the New York Stock Exchange (NYSE) in 1985. The single sample approach attempts to draw a representative sample of the NYSE population that provides overall generalizability of results that is not possible with the more commonly used two sample approach (from separate populations of filers and nonfilers).

The final sample includes 107 companies from a survey of 269 randomly selected NYSE companies, reflecting an overall 40% survey response rate and representing almost 8% of the NYSE population in 1985 when the *ED* was issued.[2] Table 1 reports evidence of response bias in that 100% of the filers responded to the survey as compared to 32% of the nonfilers.

From a research perspective, the nonresponse bias reduces generalizability of the results and may reduce power. Excluded companies may follow decision models that differ from those in the sample, introducing bias, or analyses may not reveal existing relationships because the sample is more homogenous than the population from which it was drawn. Most likely, the population excluded from this study was less interested and less informed about the proposed changes in pension accounting making their preferences less defined, reliable, and important.[3]

From a standard-setting perspective, the 32% response rate among *ED* nonfilers suggests that the Board could obtain a wider range of constituent views on proposed standards. Unclear, however, is how valuable this information would be. The standard-setting process is not intended to culminate in a simple voting tally; the Board is clearly looking for sound arguments for and against proposed accounting changes (FASB 1995). The primary advantage of survey results from this study is that political motivations should have little impact on corporate responses, especially given that the survey was distributed near the end of the *ED* comment period, suggesting a very low likelihood that any results could be used to influence the FASB's decision on the pension accounting standard.

The Survey Instrument

Data for this study on pension accounting preferences come from a two-part survey which addressed corporate views of the standard-set-

Table 1. Comparisons Between Survey Respondents and Nonrespondents

	Respondents	*Nonrespondents*	*Test of Differences*[a]
Number of companies	107	162	
Filing Activity on *ED*			
Number of filers	32 (100%)	0 (0%)	
Number of nonfilers	75 (32%)	162 (68%)	11.63***
Median Sales (000's)	$743	$479	1.44
Median Pension Size (Obligation/Total Assets)	.05	.04	.34
Median Plan Status (Obligation/Pension Assets)	.73	.68	.80

Notes: ***Significant at .01
[a]Mann Whitney U for sales and pension size; chi square for pension plan status

ting process and specific positions on the pension *ED*.[4] The financial managers of two companies, one filer and one nonfiler provided input on the form and content of the survey instrument, which was mailed in September 1985, near the end of the *ED*'s comment period. This mailing date enhanced the likelihood that respondents would be aware of the nature of the proposed changes, which were described by many CPA firms in widely distributed informational brochures. The survey also addressed relatively straightforward, nontechnical aspects of the *ED* that had received considerable attention.

The cover letter for the survey was addressed to a senior financial officer, either the CFO or the controller, of each company in the sample, by name, to ensure that the most reliable respondent would be contacted. The letter assured managers that survey results would be presented only in the aggregate and that their individual responses would be kept confidential. Each survey returned was identified by number, and second requests were mailed to nonrespondents. No significant differences were found between first and second request respondents in filing choice, firm size, pension plan size, or status. Almost half of the respondents requested a summary of the survey results, identifying themselves in most cases as the financial officers to whom the surveys had been addressed. Although filer survey respondents tended not to be the same individuals who signed comment letters, they stated congruent positions in 44 of 55 possible comparisons between the two instruments.[5] Eight of the differences in position were on footnotes disclosures where companies stated support in the survey but opposition in their comment letters to the FASB. Of three differences on pension cost standardization, two companies stated opposition in the survey and support in their comment letters.

RESULTS

To test the relationships between positions taken on the seven *ED* requirements and the proposed explanatory variables, this study uses multivariate logistic regression analyses.[6] Logistic regression provides a more appropriate analytical tool than multiple linear regression when the dependent variable is binary and the underlying data are not normally distributed, as in these models.

Filing Choice

As hypothesized (**H_1**), results from the analyses of positions taken on cost standardization and discount rates reveal significant inverse relationships with filing choice (Table 2) which suggest that filers were more likely than nonfilers to oppose these issues. No relationship, however, is evident between filing choice and positions taken on the liability recognition or footnote disclosure issues which suggest that filers and nonfilers took similar positions on these issues. Importantly, Table 2 shows that cost standardization received the highest number of comments from filing survey respondents, inferring that this was the most strongly opposed *ED* requirement. While this is probably true for the 14 filers who addressed the issue, the survey data indicate that a majority of companies actually supported standardization. In fact, this is the only issue which received majority support.

Notably, the proportion of respondents stating support for *ED* requirements indicates that corporate managers do not blanketly oppose all accounting changes; they are just more likely to comment when they oppose certain issues. Further, while heavy filing activity in itself indicates a high level of opposition to some issues, the evidence shows that comment letters may not indicate the specific requirements that are most widely opposed.

Table 2. Logistic Regression Analyses on Position Choices (as stated in Survey)

Issue	*Survey* Yes	No[a]		*Model* χ^2	*β Coefficients (Wald Test in Parentheses)* Filing Choice	Log Sales	Pension Plan Size[b]	Plan Status[c]
Liability for								
Vested benefits	47	60	(5)	7.96*	–.59	–.10	–3.03*	0.06
					(1.30)	(0.51)	(2.65)	(0.01)
Unvested benefits	14	93	(7)	5.94	–.85	0.11	–9.43	0.04
					(1.16)	(0.30)	(2.16)	0.01
Cost Standardization	60	47	(14)	25.66***	–1.47***	–.28*	–4.51**	0.73
					(7.06)	(2.68)	(4.50)	(0.98)
Discount Rate	42	65	(5)	13.89***	–.95*	–.27*	–1.55	0.64
					(2.72)	(3.09)	(0.93)	(0.92)
Disclosures for								
1% change in rates	26	81	(6)	3.62	–.39	–.10	1.14	–.98
					(0.41)	(0.40)	(0.62)	(1.90)
Pension cost components	43	64	(11)	11.40**	–.25	–.11	–6.71**	0.31
					(0.22)	(0.58)	(4.77)	(0.20)
Reconciliation of fund status	37	70	(9)	12.50**	–.37	–.41**	–.18	0.21
					(0.39)	(6.01)	(0.01)	(0.10)

Notes: * Significant at 0.10
** Significant at 0.05
*** Significant at 0.01
Dependent variable is position (Yes or No) taken in survey on listed issue.
[a] Number of opposing positions stated in comment letters is shown in parentheses.
[b] Pension plan size = pension obligations/total assets
[c] Pension plan status = pension obligations/pension assets

Firm Size

The regression analyses reported in Table 2 support the hypothesized ($\mathbf{H_2}$) inverse relationships between firm size and position choice on cost standardization and discount rates. The analyses also provide evidence of a similar, unhypothesized relationship between firm size and the reconciliation disclosure. One explanation for the latter finding is that companies' positions on cost standardization and the reconciliation disclosure were related; there would, after all, have been no need to reconcile fund status with balance sheet amounts without cost standardization. Results from chi-square comparisons between positions taken on the seven individual issues reveal some congruence between cost standardization and the reconciliation disclosure ($p < .10$) that is not evident with other disclosure requirements.

Overall, the findings on firm size are consistent with Watts and Zimmerman's (1978) hypothesis that larger firms resist accounting changes that increase reported income and volatility. This evidence is unique in that it comes from a study of position choice, not filing or adoption timing choices. The evidence also differentiates income statement effects from liability recognition and footnote disclosure issues and shows that larger companies are not simply more likely to oppose any issue. Given that smaller companies participate less readily in the accounting standard-setting process, this introduces a real danger that their views are not heard and potentially reduces the effectiveness of the due process.

Relative Pension Plan Size

Relative pension plan size is a significant factor in three of the seven models of position choice (Table 2), providing some support for the hypothesis ($\mathbf{H_3}$) that more affected companies are more likely to oppose accounting changes. Companies with larger pension plans relative to total assets showed a greater tendency to oppose recognition of a liability for vested benefits, cost standardization, and the disclosure of pension cost components. The insignificance of plan size in four models may reflect a weak proxy for the projected costs from these specific requirements. For example, if companies are primarily concerned with the length of disclosures, and not the disclosed information, pension plan size would have little impact on position. Of course, an alternative explanation is that financial statement effect and associated costs did not significantly impact corporate positions on these issues.

Previous studies report a relationship between financial statement effects and corporate decisions to lobby in the standard-setting process, arguing that companies weigh the cost of lobbying against the potential adverse consequences of complying with a newly adopted standard. The present study provides direct evidence of a relationship between financial statement effect and position choice which helps explain why the FASB can gain corporate support for an accounting change by mitigating its effect with extended adoption windows and other implementation compromises.

Pension Plan Status

Results from the logistic regression analyses, as reported in Table 2, do not support the hypothesis ($\mathbf{H_4}$) that funding status is related to positions on liability recognition. This, however, may reflect the homogeneity of funding status for companies in the study. Most companies were overfunded or only marginally underfunded.

OBSERVATIONS AND CONCLUSIONS

This study used data from a survey of comment filers and nonfilers to investigate corporate reactions to seven controversial requirements of the *Exposure Draft: Employers' Accounting for Pensions*, with a primary objective of assessing the extent to which comment letters represent overall corporate views. The results confirm prior researchers' assumptions that filing choice relates inversely to positions taken, but not on all issues. Filers and nonfilers have differing accounting concerns and comment letters do not necessarily focus on the most widely opposed issues. This is, at least in part, because larger companies, who tend to be more active filers, have different accounting preferences than small companies.

The findings from this study on firm size and potential financial statement effects indicate that both factors relate to corporate accounting preferences, not just filing choice as shown in prior studies. Large companies were more likely than their smaller peers to oppose measurement issues that led to increases in reported income level and volatility, a finding which is consistent with Watts and Zimmerman's theory of political visibility. The magnitude of a proposal's effect, even when potentially positive also motivated corporate opposition. Moreover, companies appeared less inclined to comment on opposed standards that had little financial statement effect as is evident in the small number of companies that commented on cost standardization versus liability recognition of unvested benefits.

Some researchers and standard-setters may argue that they are most concerned with the views of companies that deem an accounting change sufficiently important to lobby in the due process. From a purely political perspective, comment letters indicate the strength of individual companies' preferences and the likelihood that the FASB will face subsequent lobbying in another, more threatening form. However, from an ethical perspective, the FASB's mission, and a goal of the due process procedure it follows, is to adopt standards that give consideration to views of all affected parties, not just those with the resources to lobby. Further, the availability of a broader-based set of corporate positions may help the FASB more efficiently identify changes that will and will not cause implementation problems or lead to misinterpretation.

Survey research on accounting standards not yet promulgated, offer academics an opportunity to better understand financial statement preparers' views and, based on an objective analysis, provide the FASB a broader information-base. While the results from this and prior studies indicate that financial statement effect and related consequences influence corporate preferences and lobbying behavior, the evidence is not so strong that it precludes the importance of other factors. Identification of arguments unique to requirements that incite the greatest opposition may help the FASB anticipate and respond to opposition more effectively and, in the process, gain acceptance for sound accounting standards.

APPENDIX A

The Survey

The following questions relate to the position of *your company* on several aspects of the pension accounting issue.

	Yes	No
Should a *liability* for unfunded accumulated benefits be recognized on the balance sheet?		
1. For vested benefits	____	____
2. For nonvested benefits	____	____

	Yes	No
Should pension cost measurement be standardized as to the allocation of costs?	____	____
Should the discount rate used to calculate the present value of *pension liabilities* be based on current prices for settling the employer's obligation?	____	____
Should the following disclosure be required?		
1. The effect of the projected benefit obligation and net periodic pension cost of a one percentage point change in the discount rate or rate of compensation	____	____
2. The components of net periodic pension cost	____	____
3. Reconciliation of the funded status of the plan with amounts reported in financial statements	____	____

ACKNOWLEDGMENT

I wish to thank Anne-Lee Bain and two anonymous reviewers for their helpful comments.

NOTES

1. The log of net sales is used in the multivariate analyses to provide a better fit for the model.
2. Thirty companies were dropped from a sample of 300 companies because of missing financial statement data and one survey respondent was omitted because of its outlier position.
3. The 100% response rate from comment filers provides reasonable assurance that this group is representative of the filing population.
4. A copy of the total survey is available from the author upon request.
5. Before survey responses were received, three coders determined positions taken on the seven issues ($32 \times 7 = 224$) in comment letters filed with the FASB. Agreement among the three coders:

	2 of 3	*3 of 3*	*Total*
indeterminable	5	164	169
oppose	3	44	47
support	0	8	8

6. Univariate comparisons provided substantially the same results as the multivariate analyses and are, therefore, not reported separately.

REFERENCES

Arthur Young. 1985. FASB issues exposure draft on employers' accounting for pensions. *Accounting and Auditing Newsletter* (May): 1-9.

Ayres, F.L. 1986. Characteristics of firms electing early adoption of SFAS 52. *Journal of Accounting and Economics* (June): 143-158.

Deakin, E.B. 1989. Rational economic behavior and lobbying on accounting issues: Evidence from the oil and gas industry. *Accounting Review* (January): 137-151.

Dhaliwal, D.S. 1982. Some economic determinants of management lobbying for alternative methods of accounting: Evidence from the accounting for interest costs issue. *Journal of Business, Finance and Accounting* (Spring): 255-265.

Financial Accounting Standards Board. 1985. *Exposure Draft: Employers' Accounting for Pensions.* Stamford, CT: FASB.

______. 1995. *Facts about FASB*. Stamford, CT: FASB.

Francis, J.R. 1987. Lobbying against proposed accounting standards: The case of employers' pension accounting. *Journal of Accounting and Public Policy* (June): 35-37.

Griffin, P.A. 1982. Foreign exchange gains and losses: Impact on reported earnings. *Abacus* (June): 50-69.

______. 1983. Management's preferences for FASB Statement No. 52: Predictive ability results. *Abacus* (Spring): 130-138.

Hussein, M.E. 1981. The innovative process in financial accounting standards setting. *Accounting, Organizations and Society* (Winter): 27-37.

Kelly, L. 1982. Corporate lobbying and changes in financing or operating activities in reaction to FAS No. 8. *Journal of Accounting and Public Policy* (Winter): 153-173.

______. 1985. Corporate management lobbying on FAS No. 8: Some further evidence. *Journal of Accounting Research* (Autumn): 619-632.

McKee, A.J., T.B. Bell, and J.R. Boatsman. 1984. Management preferences over accounting standards: A replication and additional tests. *Accounting Review* (October): 647-659.

Norton, C. 1989. Transition to new accounting rules: The case of FAS 87. *Accounting Horizons* (December): 40-48.

Sami, H., and M.J. Welsh. 1992. Characteristics of early and late adopters of pension accounting standard SFAS No. 87. *Contemporary Accounting Research* (Fall): 212-236.

Schalow, C.M. 1995. Participation choice: The exposure draft for postretirement benefits other than pensions. *Accounting Horizons* (March): 27-41.

Senteney, D.L., and J.R. Strawser. 1990. The impact of financial statement effects on the adoption of accounting pronouncements: The case of SFAS 87. In *Advances in Accounting,* Vol 8, 37-60, ed. by B.N. Schwartz. Greenwich, CT: JAI Press.

Stone, M., and R.W. Ingram. 1988. The effect of Statement No. 87 on the financial reports of early adopters. *Accounting Horizons* (September): 48-61.

Watts, R.L., and J.L. Zimmerman. 1978. Towards a positive theory of the determination of accounting standards. *The Accounting Review.* (January): 112-134.

PART II

RESEARCH REPORTS

THE SEC's AUDIT REQUIREMENTS FOR COMPANIES ACQUIRED AND EQUITY INVESTEES

Jerry L. Arnold and William W. Holder

ABSTRACT

In some circumstances the Securities and Exchange Commission (SEC) requires acquiring businesses to file audited financial statements of businesses or portions of businesses acquired. This article addresses the nature and content of the applicable SEC rules, difficulties in compliance and recommendations for entities, auditors and policy-setters. The article initially discusses the underlying framework and content of the SEC's Regulation S-X, the accounting regulation. It then examines the nature of significant acquisitions under Regulation S-X and focuses on the specific requirements for audited financial statements. Those requirements apply at both the time of acquisition and on a continuing basis for entities accounted for under the equity method. Difficulties in compliance with such rules are discussed as are recommendations to overcome such problems as well as implications for standard-setters and regulators.

Research in Accounting Regulation, Volume 11, pages 145-157.

ISBN: 0-7623-0168-6

INTRODUCTION

Practitioners providing services to companies that may "go public" in the near future are generally well aware of the requirements of the Securities and Exchange Commission (SEC) for audited financial statements of such enterprises. Generally, three years of audited financial statements are necessary for a company to initiate a public offering subject to the filing requirements of the Commission. Much less appreciated, however, is the need for companies going public or already public to obtain audited financial statements of companies or portions of companies that are acquired in corporate mergers and acquisitions. This article describes the issues that can arise in such circumstances, emphasizes the need for vigilance in advising clients of the possible need for audited financial statements, and provides additional guidance to help avoid such potential "deal killing" problems. In addition we identify issues to consider for auditing standard setters and regulators.

The following examples illustrate common scenarios that practitioners encounter and should anticipate in assisting clients in proper planning. Assume, for example, that a growing private company is interested in being acquired by a public company. Perhaps, a division of a major corporation is being considered for acquisition by another public company. As a third example, consider a company planning to go public that is contemplating the acquisition of another private company. In each case, the parties agree on terms of the purchase and face no apparent obstacles. Many times, however, a hidden factor can be a deal breaker: the SEC requires audited financial statements for all "significant acquisitions." Many private companies do not have audited financial statements and divisions of public companies seldom do. This "sleeper" can prove to be a nightmare. Consider the dilemma a potential acquirer may face: The company can do the deal or raise public capital, but not both. The Commission's regulatory requirements need to be factored into the acquisition decision just as do the price, form of payment, compensation of management and other economic variables.

THE SEC AND REGULATION S-X

The Securities Exchange Act of 1934 (Exchange Act) established and empowered the SEC to set accounting and auditing requirements for public companies. The Commission has chosen to look to the private sector, e.g., FASB, to establish accounting standards regarding recognition and measurement of assets, income, liabilities and expenses. The Commission has not, however, limited its rulemaking to questions of recognition and measurement. It has determined conditions and situations in which audited financial statements must be filed in order for the entity to comply with the Federal securities laws. One difficult rule with which to comply is that requiring audited financial statements for businesses acquired or to be acquired. The specific requirements applicable to such situations are included in the accounting regulation adopted by the Commission, Regulation S-X.

Regulation S-X applies to filings with the Commission and governs the form and content of financial statements. The regulation is divided into twelve articles identified in Exhibit I.

Each article relates to specific aspects of accounting requirements for filings with the Commission. Article 1 indicates that the regulation applies to filings of financial statements under the various applicable securities laws, most notably the Securities Act of 1933 (Securities Act) and the Exchange Act. Rule 1-02 provides definitions of terms relevant to Regulation S-X. An important definition in the context of this paper is that of a "significant subsidiary," included in Rule 1-02(w). Article 2 enumerates the qualifications necessary for an outside accountant to practice before the Commission. The rules under this article also specify the nature and types of auditor reports which are acceptable in filings with the Commission. Article 3 is quite substantive, enumerating the audited financial statements that must be filed with the Commission, including two balance sheets and three income statements and statements of cash flow. Article 3 houses the specific rules which require submission to the Commission of audited financial statements of other entities, the focus of this paper. Article 4 is most relevant for its inclusion of footnotes that must be contained in Commission filings. Article 5 focuses on financial statements of Commercial and Industrial companies. The Article 5 rules provide in effect a suggested "chart of accounts" for inclusion in the audited balance sheets and income statements of such entities. The article also specifies the supplementary schedules, which must be audited, to be included in Form 10-K filings and in registration statements under the Securities Act. Articles 6 through 9 perform the same functions for the specific industries indicated in the title of the Article. Article 10 addresses the requirements for interim financial statements included in Commission filings. The rules under Article 10 are most applicable to quarterly filings on Form 10-Q and to interim financial statements included in registration statements

Article 1	Application of Regulation S-X
Article 2	Qualifications and Reports of Accountants
Article 3	General Instructions as to Financial statements
Article 3A	Consolidated and Combined Financial Statements
Article 4	Rules of General Application
Article 5	Commercial and Industrial Companies
Article 6	Registered Investment Companies
Article 6A	Employee Stock Purchase, Savings and Similar Plans
Article 7	Insurance Companies
Article 8	Rescinded
Article 9	Bank Holding Companies
Article 10	Interim Financial Statements
Article 11	Pro Forma Financial Information
Article 12	Form and Content of Schedules

Exhibit I. Articles of Regulation S-X

under the Securities Act. Article 11 states the requirements for pro forma financial statements. Such requirements often apply to business acquisitions. The resulting pro forma financial statements are most often found in filings related to current events, on Form 8-K and in registration statements filed under the Securities Act. Because they do not involve audited data, the pro formas are not likely to threaten the consummation of the acquisition. Article 12 contains the requirements for schedules, filed in compliance with rules under Articles 5 through 9.

SIGNIFICANT ACQUISITIONS

The major thrust of this article relates to the audited financial statements of acquired entities that may be required to be filed by an SEC registrant. The most typical such situation under the Exchange Act involves filing of the financial statements under cover of Form 8-K. The same discussion applies to inclusion of the financial statements in registration statements under the Securities Act. The requirements for Item 2 of Form 8-K requires filing of the form within 15 calendar days of the acquisition (or disposition) of assets meeting specified materiality criteria. That item states that an acquisition shall:

> be deemed to involve a significant amount of assets (i) if the registrant's and its other subsidiaries equity in the net book value of such assets or the amount paid...therefor upon the acquisition exceeded 10% of the total assets of the registrant and its consolidated subsidiaries, or (ii) if it involved a business which is significant (see Rule 11-01(b)).[1]

Item 2 of Form 8-K references Rule 11-01(b) of Regulation S-X. Rule 11-01(b) states:

> A business combination...shall be considered significant if:
>
> A comparison of the most recent annual financial statements of the business acquired or to be acquired and the registrant's most recent annual consolidated financial statements filed at or prior to the date of acquisition indicates that the business would be a significant subsidiary pursuant to the conditions specified in (Regulation S-X) Rule 1-02(w), substituting 20% for 10% each place it appears therein.[2]

According to Rule 1-02(w) of Regulation S-X, a subsidiary is considered significant if it meets any of the following tests:

1. The registrant's and its other subsidiaries' investments in and advances to the subsidiary exceed 10% of the total assets of the registrants and subsidiaries consolidated as of the end of the most recently completed fiscal year (for a proposed business combination to be accounted for as a pooling of interests, this condition is also met when the number of common shares exchanged by the registrant exceeds 10% of its total common shares outstanding at the date the combination is initiated); or
2. The registrant's and its other subsidiaries' share of the total assets (after intercompany elimination's) of the subsidiary exceeds 10% of the total assets of the registrant and its subsidiaries consolidated as of the end of the most recently completed fiscal year; or
3. The registrant's and its other subsidiaries' equity in the income from continuing operations before income taxes, extraordinary items and cumulative effect of a change in accounting principle of the subsidiary exceeds 10% of such income of the registrant and its subsidiaries consolidated for the most recently completed fiscal year.[3]

The rule then provides computational guidance in relation to the income test (test(3)). Among the approaches endorsed by the Commission are averaging over a period of five years and use of absolute values.[4] Exhibit II provides a summary of the key variables in determining whether a particular business acquisition should be considered significant under Regulation S-X.

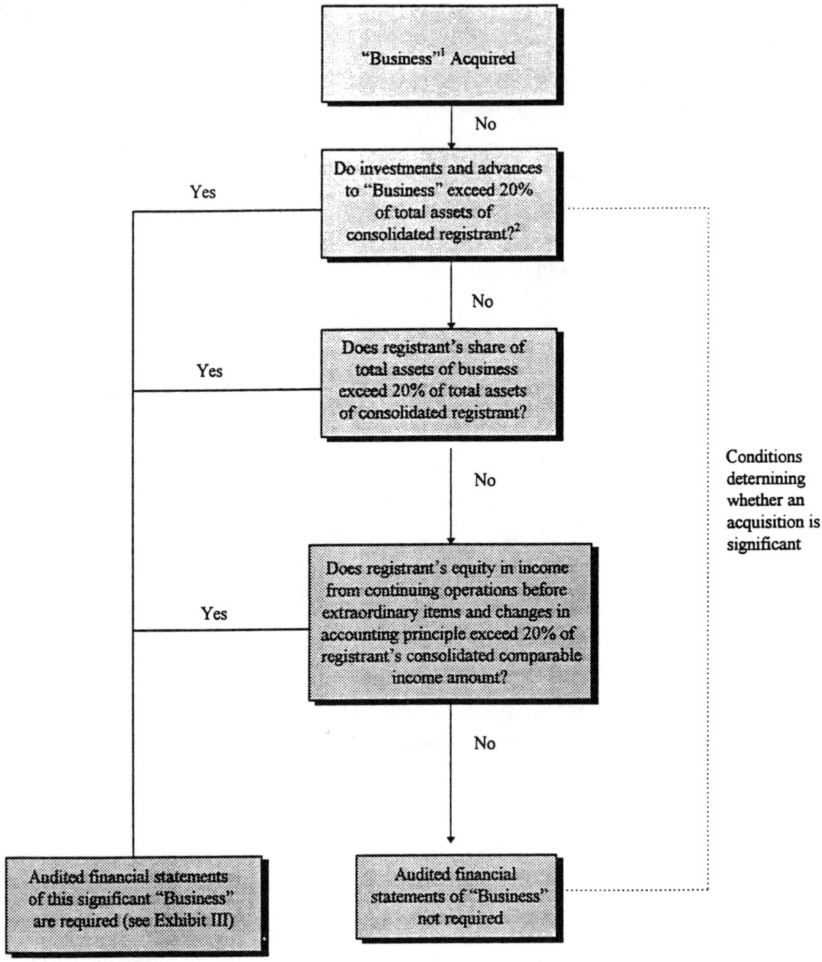

Notes: [1] The "Business" may be the stock of another company or its assets, or a division or other portion of another company.
[2] See text for pooling of interest test.

Exhibit II. SEC Auditing Requirements For Acquisitions

FINANCIAL STATEMENTS OF BUSINESSES ACQUIRED[5]

Item 2 of Form 8-K directs the preparer's attention to Item 7 of the form. That item indicates that audited financial statements must be filed for any acquisitions meeting a significant subsidiary test in Regulation S-X Rule 1-02(w). The periods required are specified in Rule 3-05 of Regulation S-X. This rule is perhaps the most difficult to comply with under the Regulation. Under Rule 3-05, the number of periods required range from zero, for acquisitions significant at less than 20% under Rule 1-02(w), to three years, for acquisitions significant at greater than 50%. Rule 3-05(b) states:

(i) If none of the conditions exceed 20%, financial statements are not required. However, if the aggregate impact of the individually insignificant businesses acquired since the date of the most recent audited balance sheet filed for the registrant exceeds 50%, financial statements covering at least the substantial majority of the businesses acquired shall be furnished. Such financial statements must be for at least the most recent fiscal year and any interim periods specified in (Regulation S-X) 3-01 and 3-02.
(ii) If any of the conditions exceeds 20%, but none exceed 40%, financial statements shall be furnished for at least the most recent fiscal year;
(iii) If any of the conditions exceeds 40%, but none exceed 50%, financial statements shall be furnished for at least the two most recent fiscal years;
(iv) If any of the conditions exceeds 50%, the full financial statements shall be furnished (2 years balance sheets, 3 years income statements and cash flow statements).[6]

An extra 60-day period is provided under Item 7 for filing the required financial statements. Thus, the maximum period from acquisition of the entity to the filing of audited financial statements is 75 days. Further, the required financial statements must be included in any registration statement under the Securities Act prior to it being declared effective. Exhibit III provides a summary of these provisions which can be used determining the number of years' financial statements to be provided for the acquired business.

THE AUDIT PROBLEM

In a typical scenario the auditor of the acquiring entity is asked by the parties to audit the financial statements of the acquired entity. The auditor is incented both from a revenue generation and client service perspective to attempt to accommodate the request. Difficulties arise in that

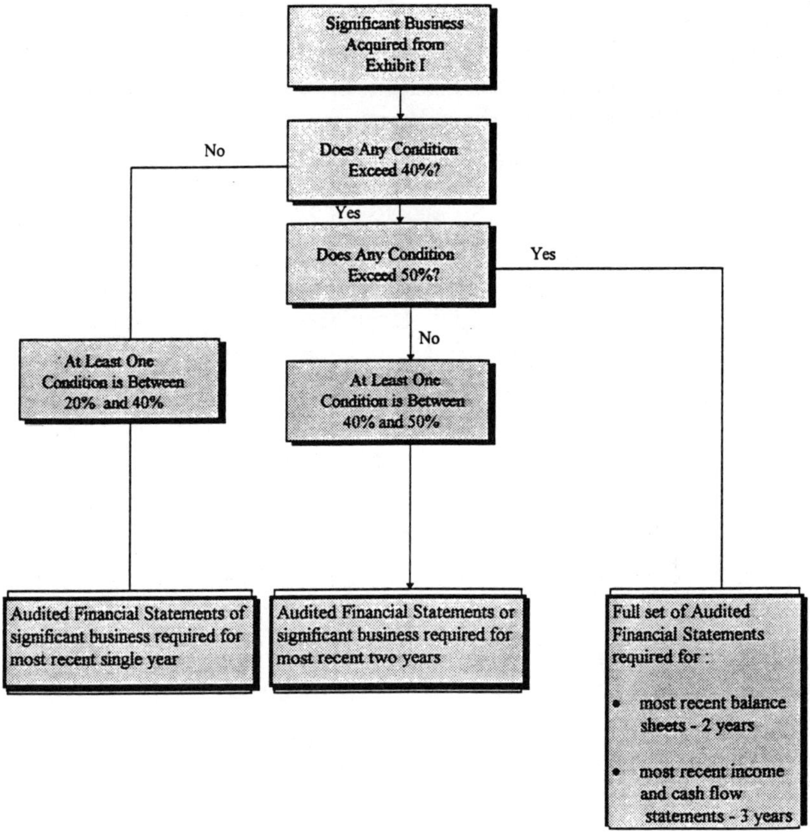

Exhibit III. Number of Required Financial Statements to be Audited

often, even typically, the financial statements of the acquired entity are not auditable for the full three-year period. Even in the situation in which the unaudited company generates substantial evidentiary materials, the auditor is unlikely to be able to obtain satisfaction with respect to the beginning inventory of the earliest year. In this situation or any other in which the full complement of financial statements required by Rule 3-05 cannot be audited, the parties will seek relief or a waiver from the Commission for the unaudited portion. The Commission has a standard response to the question of "will you grant relief?" The answer is typically "yes" and "no," with each applying to different circumstances. The "yes" relates to filings under the Exchange Act. The "no" applies to filings under the Securities Act.

To understand Commission responses to requests for relief, it is necessary to consider the roles and responsibilities of the agency. Documents filed under the Exchange Act are designed to keep the market informed. The Commission selectively reviews such filings for compliance with the various rules and regulations. No affirmative action on the part of the Commission is necessary. Commission reviews under the Securities Act are different. Prior to sales of the securities being registered, the Commission must take the affirmative action of declaring the registration statement effective. Thus, the Commission has determined that it cannot provide the same level of flexibility in regard to deviations from the letter of certain rules, such as Rule 3-05.

The parties to the proposed transaction must factor the audit requirements into the equation and determine how best to proceed. The most difficult decision is apt to lie with the acquirer. Assume that the transaction would be significant at the 55% level, based on one of the tests in Rule 1-02(w). Further assume that the two most recent years of the acquired company's financial statements can be audited with an unqualified opinion. The potential buyer must decide whether the consummation of the transaction warrants preclusion from the capital markets until the earliest year financials become stale—a period exceeding one year. In many cases the proposed "deal" is not deemed to be worth the "lockout."

In some cases the problem that arises relates not to the absence of audited statements, but to the fact that the auditor of the acquired entity does not maintain an SEC practice. While that auditor generally cannot prevent the inclusion of its audit report in any filings under the Exchange Act, it can exercise that prerogative with regard to Securities Act filings. Under the Securities Act, an expert (such as the independent accountant) must furnish written approval in the form of a consent to the inclusion in any registration statement of its audit report. This requirement exists because the threshold for liability is substantially lower under Securities Act filings than for those filed under the Exchange Act. Briefly, gross negligence must be demonstrated for the auditor to be culpable under the Exchange Act, while ordinary negligence can trigger liability under the Securities Act. Because of this exposure, the auditor must explicitly permit its name to be associated with financial statements in registered offerings. A dilemma arises for the parties involved in that the auditor of the acquirer may well be unwilling to assume responsibility for the audit performed by the former accountant and unable to replicate the audit. The former auditor may well conclude that it is economically impractical to consent to the inclusion of its report in a registration statement, with the attachment of the corresponding liability. A solution often involves the joint efforts of the two auditing firms. The auditor of the acquirer assists the former auditor in bringing the audit into conformity with SEC practice, while the latter remains the signatory to the report.

The responsibilities of the auditors with respect to subsequent events also differs in certain public filings. Under Section 11 of the Securities Act the auditor is required to perform a "reasonable investigation" up to the effective date of the registration statement. This requirement is more extensive than the subsequent events procedures required by generally accepted auditing standards (GAAS). Specifically AU Section 560, "Subsequent Events" describes the procedures the auditor should apply between the date of the financial statements and the date that field work ends. The additional requirements to apply subsequent events procedures in a Securities Act filing are described in AU Section 711, "Filings Under the Federal Securities Statutes." In such filings, the auditor should extend the application of subsequent events procedures not only through the date of the audit report but also "...up to the effective date or as close thereto as is reasonable and practicable in the circumstances" (AU Section 711.10). Because field work may have ended significantly before the effective date of the registration statement, the auditing literature recognizes that the likelihood of the auditor discovering new information diminishes. Notwithstanding this circumstance, however, the auditor should make arrangements with management to be kept advised of the progress of the registration process in order to extend certain procedures up to the effective date of the registration statement. In addition to performing the subsequent events procedures described in AU Section 560, the auditor should also perform two other types of procedures described in AU Section 711 and reproduced below:

- Read the entire prospectus and other pertinent portions of the registration statement.
- Inquire of and obtain written representations from officers and other executives responsible for financial and accounting matters (limited where appropriate to major locations) about whether any events have occurred, other than those reflected or disclosed in the registration statement, that, in the officers' or other executives'

opinion, have a material effect on the financial statements included therein or that should be disclosed in order to keep those statements from being misleading.

If an auditor audited the financial statements of a prior period but not the most recent period, the inquiries of management described above need not be performed. The predecessor auditor, however, should obtain and read the prospectus and obtain a representation letter from the successor auditor. The letter from the successor auditor should discuss whether the successor has identified "...any matters that...might have a material effect on the financial statements reported on by the predecessor auditor or would require disclosures in the notes thereto." Complying with these provisions can also pose difficulties of the types discussed in this article and auditors should identify and plan for conducting extended subsequent procedures as necessary.

A CONTINUING PROBLEM

The above discussion has addressed transaction-related issues created by the Commission's audit requirements. The relevance and impact of Regulation S-X does not end when the Rule 3-05 issue is settled. Under Rule 3-09, the acquirer may well need to obtain and furnish audited financial statements every year. That rule requires registrants to include in part IV of Form 10-K, and in any applicable registration statements under the Securities Act, the financial statements of any non-consolidated equity investees which meet certain materiality tests. Rule 1-02(w) again establishes the benchmark against which the significance of the investment is measured. The key portions of Rule 3-09 state:

a. If either the first or third condition set forth in Regulation S-X Rule 1-02(w), substituting 20% for 10%, is met by a 50% or less owned person accounted for by the equity method by the registrant or a subsidiary of the registrant, separate financial statements of such 50% or less owned person shall be filed.
b. In so far as practicable, the separate financial statements required by this section shall be as of the same dates and for the same periods as the audited consolidated financial statements required by Regulation S-X Rule 3-01(two years' balance sheets) and Rule 3-02 (three years' income statements and statements of cash flows). However, these separate financial statements are required

> to be audited only for those fiscal years in which either the first or third condition set forth in Regulation S-X Rule 1-02(w), substituting 20% for 10%, is met.[7]

Note that the investment and income tests (criteria one and three, respectively) apply. The implications of Rule 3-09 can be at least as onerous as those of Rule 3-05. Under this rule, the investor in a less than 50% owned entity faces the possibility of having to secure audited financial statements for that entity every year for inclusion in the investor's Commission filings. The difficulties enumerated above in regard to Rule 3-05 are relevant to this situation, but are compounded by the ongoing need for audited financial statements.

The income test can be especially troublesome in regard to application of Rule 3-09. As discussed above, one criterion for measuring significance is a comparison based on income from continuing operations. If the investor has an off year, with low earnings or a loss, seemingly inconsequential investments can suddenly become significant in terms of the financial statement requirements under Regulation S-X.

RECOMMENDATIONS—AUDITORS, AUDITING STANDARD SETTERS, AND REGULATORS

Auditors generally do not have professional obligations to provide advice to clients beyond the boundaries of the engagements they have agreed to perform. Nevertheless, auditors may choose to provide insights on a variety of matters, including those related to the subject matter of this article. It is in that spirit that the following recommendations are made.

Auditors can add much value to the services they render by taking steps to assist clients avoid the pitfalls in complying with the Commission's rules regarding submission of audited financial statements of other entities. If the client is contemplating an acquisition, the auditor should advise the client of the need for audited financial statements under Regulation S-X Rule 3-05. If the proposed acquiree's financial statements have been audited, the firm performing that audit should be contacted regarding its willingness to be associated with the financial statements in Commission filings, especially those under the Securities Act. If the proposed acquiree's financial statements are unaudited, or if the firm that performed the audit is unwilling to consent to the use of its opinion in Securities Act filings, the client should be advised to engage its auditor to assess the auditability of the financial statements. If possible, the requisite set of financial statements should then be audited. If the auditor determines the financial statements for the relevant number of periods cannot be audited, with an unqualified opinion, the client should be advised prior to the consummation of the acquisition.

The auditor should assure that the client is aware of the continuing requirements to furnish audited financial statements under Regulation S-X Rule 3-09. The client should be advised to secure the agreement of the equity investee to the performance of annual audits. The issues and above discussion relating to attaining the consent of the auditor of such statements also apply in this context.

Finally, the auditor should advise privately-held clients that either plan to go public or to be acquired by a public company of the audit requirements discussed in this paper. Such clients should recognize that proper planning is essential to attaining the required audited financial statements and that inability to comply with the requirements can delay their offering or be a "deal breaker" in a possible acquisition by a public company.

Auditing standard setters and regulators could also consider the need for additional guidance in providing auditing services to prior periods. The need to conduct financial statement audits of previously unaudited past reporting periods is not confined to the circumstances described in this article. Little guidance exists, however, for practitioners confronting such needs or requests. While GAAS does address the ability of the auditor to audit financial statements for relatively distant financial reporting periods a fresh look at the issues and opportunities may be desirable. This recommendation seems particularly appropriate given the increase in mergers and acquisitions coupled with the availability of electronic information.

NOTES

1. SEC's Form 8-K, Item 2.
2. Regulation S-X, Article 11, Rule 11-01(b).
3. Regulation S-X, Article 1, Rule 1-02(w).
4. The averaging rules are contained in Rule 1-02(w). The use of absolute values applies if either the registrant and its other subsidiaries or the subsidiary experienced a loss in the most recent year.
5. The requirement also extends to "probable" acquisitions. Application of the probability criterion is beyond the scope of this paper.
6. Regulation S-X, Article 3, Rule 3-05(b).
7. Regulation S-X, Article 3, Rule 3-09.

THE AUDITOR EXPECTATION AND PERFORMANCE GAPS:

VIEWS FROM AUDITORS AND THEIR CLIENTS

Steven L. Harris and Dale E. Marxen

ABSTRACT

In 1988 the AICPA's Auditing Standards Board issued nine new auditing standards meant to reduce the audit "expectation gap"—the gap between what the public expects to receive from an audit and what auditors feel obligated to deliver. Since then, two published studies have indicated that important public sectors—judges and investors—still appear to hold unrealistic expectations for auditors. This study of 56 auditors and 65 of their clients, however, found that the auditors' clients did *not* hold unreasonable expectations for their auditors, nor did they tend to judge the auditors' actual performances excessively negatively. The clients' most evident concern was the potential conflict of interest caused by accounting firms providing both audit and management advisory services.

Research in Accounting Regulation, Volume 11, pages 159-176.

ISBN: 0-7623-0168-6

INTRODUCTION

Like any profession that deals with the public—and is susceptible to government regulation—the accounting profession has long been concerned about its public image. In the last 15-20 years, however, the legal woes of accounting's largest and most respected firms have only heightened this concern. Although auditors cannot be allowed to perform substandard audit procedures without penalty, are they are being held to unrealistically high standards?

The so-called audit "expectation gap"—the gap between what the public expects to receive from an audit and what auditors feel obligated to deliver—was heavily documented in the 1970's and 1980's in reports such as those by the Opinion Research Corporation (1974), the Cohen Commission (1978), and Louis Harris & Associates (1986). Following many of the 1987 recommendations of the National Commission on Fraudulent Financial Reporting,[1] a private-sector initiative funded by the AICPA, the AAA, and other organizations, in 1988 the AICPA's Auditing Standards Board issued nine new auditing standards known as the "expectation gap" standards (Guy and Sullivan 1988).

One standard, No. 58, was intended to reduce the public's expectations of the audit function by more clearly distinguishing between auditors' and clients' responsibilities, and by further defining the limitations of the audit. The other standards, Nos. 53, 54, 55, 56, 57, 59, 60, and 61—as well as those issued subsequently—have served to close the gap by raising auditor expectations (and performance) via improved and clarified procedures.

Since the issuance of the expectation gap standards, however, little research has been performed to ascertain whether any reduction in the expectation gap has been achieved. Two notable exceptions have been studies by Anderson et al. (1993) and Epstein and Geiger (1994), which reported that judges and investors, respectively, still appear to exhibit unrealistic expectations for auditors.

This research reports the test of whether an expectation gap exists between auditors and another important sector of the public—*their own clients*. Although prior comprehensive surveys have identified business executives as a "key" public, the executives' expectations for auditors have not been directly compared to those held by the auditors themselves. Also, because the auditor and executive subjects in this research were selected from populations that actually interacted on the same audits, their relative opinions may be more directly comparable.

In addition, because the public's judgment of the auditors' *actual* performance is an important factor in any evaluation—as it ultimately becomes in the negligence cases—an evaluation of the auditors' performance by their own clients is also reported herein, and is compared to the auditors' self-judgment of that performance.

PREVIOUS LITERATURE

Studies Conducted Prior to the Expectation Gap Standards

Over the last 45 years, many surveys have been conducted to assess public opinion of the accounting profession. These studies have generally indicated an increasing awareness and acceptance of the profession over time, as well as of the auditors' performance. However, criticisms of the audit function remained in the surveys leading up to the issuance of the "expectation gap" standards. (For a detailed review of these studies, please see Thompson and Jones 1990.)

The three most comprehensive surveys were conducted by the Opinion Research Corporation (ORC) for Arthur Andersen and Company in 1975, by the ORC for Peat Marwick in 1983, and by Louis Harris and Associates for the AICPA in 1986. All surveyed several hundred members of "key publics," including corporate executives, securities analysts, accounting professors, and governmental officials to assess their impressions of the professionalism, personal qualities, and independence of CPA's. In addition, each study collected similar responses from a comparable number of individuals considered to be from the "general public," including shareowners and the news media. None of the studies, however, interviewed actual auditors to provide a self-assessment of the auditors' individual perceived responsibilities, personal qualities, or performances.

Problems highlighted by all studies led to recommendations that the accounting profession address several areas of concern, including: maintaining auditor independence, accepting more responsibility for legitimate oversight in the detection of fraud during audits, and promoting the understanding of auditor responsibilities. The studies generally concluded that the public felt that CPA's are ethical and competent, but may lack creativity and give in too easily to client pressure (Louis Harris 1986).

In the Louis Harris (1986) study, the public's rating of the CPA's' honesty, competence, reliability, and objectivity was substantially lower than similar ratings for other professional groups, although the "key" publics did rate the auditors higher than the general public on most of the pivotal auditor attributes. Particularly germane to the current study, the expectations held by corporate executives for CPA's were generally higher than those held by the academic accountants, whereas the evaluations of the CPA's' performance by the executives were generally lower.

In the academic literature, Wilcox and Smith (1977) surveyed 186 audit clients to determine whether they perceived the CPA's role as significantly different from that prescribed by professional standards. No significant discrepancies were found, either for traditional attest or management advisory services. As no auditors were actually surveyed, however, there was no direct way of determining whether or not a perception gap existed between the two groups, nor were the clients asked to rate their auditors' *actual* performances.

Studies Conducted After the Expectation Gap Standards

Two recent studies indicate the existence of a continuing gap between what the U.S. public expects from auditors and what the auditors perceive themselves as delivering or intending to deliver. Anderson et al. (1993), using an experimental task with 65 judges and 58 auditors as subjects, found that judges provided significantly lower evaluations of the hypothetical performance of an auditor in an audit scenario than those provided by the auditor subjects.

In a recent survey of 246 stockholders, Epstein and Geiger (1994) found that almost half expected complete or absolute assurance that material misstatements in financial statements due to unintentional error would be detected by auditors. Over 70% expected absolute assurance that material misstatement due to fraud would be detected. Current auditing standards, of course, require that auditors provide only reasonable assurance that these misstatements will be found.

Therefore, available research tends to indicate that significant expectation gaps still exist after the issuance of the eight new auditing standards in 1988 for some "key" publics. However, prior to this study, the state of the perception gap relating to the auditors' *clients*, has not been assessed subsequent to the issuance of the above-mentioned standards.

METHODOLOGY

Questionnaire Design

An examination of the "expectation" and "performance" gaps requires an assessment of the perceptions of both auditors and client management. Accordingly, it was decided that identical questionnaires would be prepared for each subject group.[2] Because questions used in past surveys had been carefully formulated to be readily understandable by the many "key" publics, we decided to retain essentially the same wording.

The 18 non-demographic items on our questionnaire were designed to collect the following information: (1) Questions 1 and 2 were used to gather *expectations* for the audit and management advisory (MA) services functions; (2) Questions 4, 5, 7, 8, 9, 10, 11, 16, and 17 were used to *evaluate* the audit and MA services being provided, and (3) Questions 3, 6, 12, 13, 14, and 18 were used to gather feedback on miscellaneous policy matters relating to these services. Question 15 was used to gather perceptions of the auditors' personal qualities.[3]

All questions required the respondent to choose between anchors, which in most cases were strongly agree/strongly disagree, on a 7-point Likert scale. To improve the validity and relevancy of the questions selected, partners from two of the Big 6 accounting firms agreed to evaluate the questionnaires. Following these reviews, only minor modifications were made to the questionnaires to clarify wording and question structure.

Selection of Respondents

The questionnaires were administered to auditors from four of the Big 6 accounting firms—Arthur Andersen & Co., Deloitte & Touche, KPMG Peat Marwick, and Price Waterhouse—and "key" management personnel of their respective clients from a single Rocky Mountain metropolitan area. Auditor questionnaires were hand delivered to the accounting firms, which then distributed them internally among all professional staff levels. The firms assumed responsibility for collecting the completed questionnaires, after which they were picked up. All auditors remained anonymous.

The four Big 6 firms also agreed to create a list of ten to 12 audit clients of varying sizes and industries, and to supply a contact at each client.[4] After receiving the client lists, the researchers explained to the client contacts via telephone that the study was an independent research project intended to ascertain the expectations clients held for their auditors and to gather the clients' evaluations of their auditors' actual performance. Because the survey was intended for "key" management

Table 1. Client Responses by Respondent's Title

President/CEO	4	Assistant Treasurer	1
Senior Vice President	2	Controller	17
Vice President Finance/CFO	13	Assistant Controller	2
Vice President/Other	6	General Accounting Manager	3
Assistant Vice President	1	Cost Accounting Manager	2
Director of Finance	2	Manager of Financial Reporting	1
Director of Accounting	1	Office Manager	1
Treasurer	3	Other	6
		TOTAL	65

personnel associated with the audit—particularly Chief Executive Officers, Vice-Presidents, Treasurers, and Controllers—the client contact was left to determine the appropriate number of questionnaires to be sent to his or her office.

Client questionnaires were then both hand delivered and mailed to the auditors' clients.[5] A cover letter was sent to each client on University letterhead assuring the respondent of anonymity and conveying our gratitude for participating. The surveys completed by client management were returned to the researchers via mail in the postage paid envelope provided. Neither management personnel nor the auditors were asked to sign the questionnaires. However, the questionnaires were identified by audit firm and client prior to respondent solicitation.

Overall, 56 usable questionnaires were returned from the 93 given to the auditors, and 65 of the 124 sent to their clients were received, for response rates of 60% and 52%, respectively. Those returned from the

Table 2. Auditor Responses by Firm and Level

	Firm	*Number Issued*	*Number Returned*	*Response Rate (%)*
By audit firm:	A	25	17	68
	B	30	18	60
	C	18	11	67
	D	20	10	50
	Totals	93	56	60
By level within the firms:	Partner		3	
	Senior Manager		5	
	Manager		9	
	Supervising Senior		7	
	Senior		19	
	Staff Accountant		13	
	Totals		56	

clients represented 26 different firms from various industries including manufacturing, banking, retail, and broadcasting. Table 1 analyzes responses for audit clients by position of the respondents, while Table 2 presents an analysis of the responses by audit firm and by level in the firm. Size distinctions could not be readily identified from public databases for all client firms, and are therefore not included.

RESULTS

Primary Results

The primary results of this study are summarized in Table 3, and are discussed below.

The Expectation Gaps

Our first objective was to determine whether "expectation gaps" existed for the client management and auditors surveyed for this study, in each of the areas of traditional audit and management advisory services.

An audit Watchdog Expectation Index was formed by combining the results of questions 1(a), (e), and (d), which looked at the auditors' responsibility to detect fraud, material errors, and act as the public's "watchdog," respectively. The mean response per item for the auditor group was 4.01, while the mean for the client management group was only slightly greater at 4.22.[6] Not only was this difference insignificant at conventional levels ($F = 1.20$; $p = .28$), but because both responses were close to the midpoint of the scale, the results indicated that both parties carried fairly weak expectations for the auditor as public watchdog.[7] Therefore, for this sample of auditors and their clients, there did not appear to be a serious "expectation gap" concerning the auditors' general role as public watchdog.

To measure any difference in expectations for the *advisory* function of an audit, questionnaire items 1(c) and 2 were combined to form an audit Advisory Expectations Index. This index measured whether the auditors' primary function was to add value to the clients' operations through representations to management and whether a good auditor acts as a "business advisor" to his or her clients. Surprisingly, the mean auditor response of 5.2 per item was significantly ($p = .003$) *higher* than that

Table 3. Summary of Performance Indices

Group	*Per Item Mean*	*F-Value*	*2-Tail Probability*	*df*
	The Expectation Gaps			
Watchdog Expectation Index (expectations for auditor as watchdog)				
Auditors	4.01			
Client Management	4.22	1.20	.28	120
Advisory Expectations Index (expected value of audit advisory services)				
Auditors	5.22			
Client Management	4.39	9.43	.003	120
	The Performance Gaps			
Auditor General Performance Index				
Auditors	4.78			
Client Management	4.58	2.11	.15	120
Audit Function Index (value of audit function)				
Auditors	5.98			
Client Management	5.67	4.94	.03	120
Auditor Attribute Index				
Auditors	5.88			
Client Management	5.04	41.46	.0000	120
MAS Performance Index (actual value of advisory services)				
Auditors	4.71			
Client Management	4.58	0.69	.41	115

of their clients (4.4), indicating that the auditors expected more from their advisory function than their clients did.

Therefore, in the area of advisory services associated with an audit, as in that of the attest function itself, clients did not appear to hold unreasonable expectations for auditors.

The Performance Gaps

Examining the extent of the "performance gaps" for audit as well as management advisory services will proceed in a similar manner to the discussion of expectations for these services. As above, responses to appropriate questions were combined to form overall indices of performance in each of the areas. However, because questions in a particular index were not necessarily designed to measure facets of a specific construct, analyses of the individual items making up each index will be provided when necessary to make interpretation of the results more meaningful.

To measure the auditors' *general performance*, questionnaire items 4, 5, 7, 9, 10, and 17 were combined to form the Auditor General Performance Index. Questions incorporated into this index assessed (1) the use of independent and objective judgment by the auditor, (2) the performance of the profession in comparison to the past, (3) the effect competition has had on overall service, (4) the detection of fraud and illegal acts by the auditor, (5) the effect management services has had on audits, and (6) whether or not the auditors are spending enough time on audits to provide quality service. Although the overall mean rating of the auditors by their clients (4.58) was lower than the auditors' mean rating for themselves (4.78), the difference was not significant at conventional levels ($F = 2.1$; $p = .15$).[8] As both groups' responses were moderately higher than the mean, we can conclude that both groups held a modestly positive evaluation of the auditors' performance.

Second, an Audit Function Index was calculated to assess the audit function based exclusively on the semantic differential scales found in question 3. This question solicited perceptions of the value, benefit, usefulness, desirability, justification, and necessity of an audit. The mean response per item on this index for auditors of 5.98 was significantly greater ($p = .03$) than the mean response given by their clients of 5.67.

Although management was seen to hold the audit function in lower esteem than did the auditors, both were fairly positive. Also, as management's feedback on the audit may be as much a reaction to the SEC policy of requiring an audit as it is to the auditors' performance on that audit, this result does not appear to highlight a significant area of concern.

Third, an Auditor Attribute Index was created by combining the responses from question 15 which measured perceptions of the auditors' pivotal attributes of honesty, reliability, communication skills, objectivity, problem solving, competence, creativity, and concern for public interest. The per item mean result for auditors of 5.88 was significantly higher ($p = .0000$) than the mean result for their clients (5.04)—a result which was not unexpected because previous research has shown that subjects tend to overrate their own good qualities (Meyers and Lamm 1976).

From these results we do not know whether the auditors had inflated perceptions of themselves, or whether their clients were being overly critical. However, because the clients' responses were above the scale's mean—for the index overall and for each of the individual attributes—

they do not appear alarmingly negative. They do, however, leave room for improvement.

An additional index to evaluate the performance of accountants on management advisory services, the MAS Performance Index, was created by combining the responses to items 8, 11, and 16 from the questionnaire. These items solicited perceptions of whether or not the number of advisory services offered by CPA firms was appropriate, the effect increased competition in the marketplace has had on these services, and how the services provided in this area by CPA firms compares to that offered by other consulting agencies. The mean auditor response of 4.71 did not differ significantly ($p = .41$) from the mean response of 4.58 provided by their clients.[9] Neither response, although positive, appeared to be a ringing endorsement of the MAS provided by the CPA firms.

To summarize the above *performance* ratings, on two of the above indices there were no significant differences between the performance ratings of the auditors and their clients. On one of the indices, the Audit Function Index, auditors provided marginally higher evaluations than their clients. However, as mentioned above, this index may measure the clients' feelings toward an audit, rather than to the performance of the auditors. It is only on the Auditor Attribute Index that a substantial difference existed, and this may be artifactual due to the auditors overrating their own good qualities, as mentioned above.

Combining all of the evidence, we conclude that auditors do not appear to be suffering from their clients' unrealistic expectations, nor are their clients tending to be overly critical of the auditors' performance in either the audit or the advisory services functions.

Other Results

We will now turn to the responses to other items contained on the questionnaire which may be classified as recommendations to the accounting profession or as policy items.[10]

Questions 12, 14, and 18 were used to gather perceptions of the effects of management advisory services on the audit function. In all cases, the management personnel were more critical of this relationship than were the auditors. They felt that: (1) expansion beyond traditional services is bad for the accounting profession ($p = .01$), (2) it is not appropriate for an auditing firm to be engaged in management advisory services ($p =$

.001), and (3) management advisory services compromise audits (p = .001).

Question 6 asked whether year-to-year changes in audit personnel lowered audit quality. Although client management tended to believe this more than the auditors did, the difference in mean response was not significant at conventional levels ($p = .11$).

Question 13 was used to determine the perceptions of whether or not increased competition for audits has resulted in decreased audit fees. Auditors tended to much more strongly believe this was true ($p = .0001$).

CONCLUSIONS, LIMITATIONS, AND IMPLICATIONS

Conclusions

Faced with the consequences of litigation, government investigation and intervention, and other problems, the accounting profession moved to narrow the gap between what the public expects and what they believe they are getting from the audit function by issuing a passel of new auditing standards beginning in 1988. This gap can perhaps be better understood by investigating not only the disparity between what the public and auditors expect (the expectation gap), but also the disparity between what the public and the auditors feel is actually being delivered (the performance gap). This study examined one important aspect of the expectation gap by surveying auditors from four large international firms and a selection of their client management.

Results indicated that, relative to the auditors' expectations for themselves, client management did not hold unrealistic expectations for auditors in either the traditional audit function or for its ancillary services. In the area of advisory services, auditors actually expected more from themselves than their clients expected of them. Client management also appeared satisfied with the auditors' *actual* performances.

Auditors and their clients did differ markedly, however, to the extent they perceived a conflict of interest when accounting firms provide both audit and management advisory services. Clients felt that *auditors should be less involved in these activities*—an apparently incongruous position given the overall increase in their utilization (see Armstrong and Vincent 1988, 95).[11] A better understanding of how audit clients can simultaneously promote and criticize use of these services will require further examination.

Limitations and Implications for Further Research

This study was not meant to supplant—or even update—prior comprehensive surveys designed to assess the general state of the auditor expectation gap. Rather, by focusing on a relatively small group of auditors and a selection of their clients in one geographical location, it presented a unique, micro comparison of the perceptions of auditors and one of their "key" publics. As such, its results cannot be applied to general populations, nor can it be used to extrapolate positions taken by a "disinterested" public.

Recently, an advisory panel of the Public Oversight Board (POB) of the SEC practice section of the AICPA division for CPA firms published a report recommending ways to enhance the integrity and objectivity of independent auditors (POB 1994). Among the most important recommendations of this panel (also known as the Kirk panel after chairman Donald J. Kirk), was that auditors should see the client's board of director's—rather than its management—as its true client. Auditors are also asked to increase their interaction with the board and its audit committee, and provide oral feedback to the audit committee regarding the *quality*—not just the acceptability—of management's decisions relating to financial reporting. In short, auditors should work toward combining with the board and the audit committee to form a triumvirate watchdog group monitoring the activities of corporate management on behalf of stockholders. However, how corporate management—themselves often significant stockholders and members of corporate boards—will react to the possible weakening of their relative position is an intriguing question. In addition, investigating the perceptions held by corporate board and audit committee members for the audit expectation gap would also be an interesting extension to this work. At the present time, however, the opinions of corporate management remain, and will likely continue to remain, an important ingredient in the continuing evolution of the auditing function.

APPENDIX: CLIENT QUESTIONNAIRE

For the following questions, please circle the number which corresponds to your best overall answer. Please note that the scale anchors (e.g., Strongly agree/Strongly disagree) are altered from question to question.

1. Based upon my observations, the independent auditor's primary function is to:

   a. detect significant financial fraud and illegal acts by management.

   Strongly agree 1 : 2 : 3 : 4 : 5 : 6 : 7 Strongly disagree

   b. express an opinion about the financial position of the client.

   Strongly disagree 1 : 2 : 3 : 4 : 5 : 6 : 7 Strongly agree

   c. "add value" to the client's operations through recommendations to management.

   Strongly agree 1 : 2 : 3 : 4 : 5 : 6 : 7 Strongly disagree

   d. act as the public's "watchdog".

   Strongly disagree 1 : 2 : 3 : 4 : 5 : 6 : 7 Strongly agree

   e. Detect material errors affecting the financial statements.

   Strongly agree 1 : 2 : 3 : 4 : 5 : 6 : 7 Strongly disagree

2. One of the services a good auditor renders is to be a "business advisor" to clients.

   Strongly agree 1 : 2 : 3 : 4 : 5 : 6 : 7 Strongly disagree

3. In my perception, the audit function is:

Valuable	1 : 2 : 3 : 4 : 5 : 6 : 7	Worthless
Harmful	1 : 2 : 3 : 4 : 5 : 6 : 7	Beneficial
Useful	1 : 2 : 3 : 4 : 5 : 6 : 7	Useless
Desirable	1 : 2 : 3 : 4 : 5 : 6 : 7	Undesirable
Justified	1 : 2 : 3 : 4 : 5 : 6 : 7	Unjustified
Unnecessary	1 : 2 : 3 : 4 : 5 : 6 : 7	Necessary

4. CPA firms exercise independent and objective judgment in performing audits of company financial statements.

   Strongly agree 1 : 2 : 3 : 4 : 5 : 6 : 7 Strongly disagree

5. The accounting profession is performing better today than it has in the past.

   Strongly disagree 1 : 2 : 3 : 4 : 5 : 6 : 7 Strongly agree

6. Year-to-year changes of audit-team personnel lower audit quality.

   Strongly agree 1 : 2 : 3 : 4 : 5 : 6 : 7 Strongly disagree

7. As a client, competition for business by CPA firms has resulted in better overall service.

   Strongly disagree 1 : 2 : 3 : 4 : 5 : 6 : 7 Strongly agree

8. The number of "business advisory services" being offered to my firm is...

   Inappropriate 1 : 2 : 3 : 4 : 5 : 6 : 7 Appropriate

9. The independent auditor generally detects significant financial fraud and illegal acts by management.

   Strongly agree 1 : 2 : 3 : 4 : 5 : 6 : 7 Strongly disagree

10. The "business advisory and consulting services" provided by the audit firm have resulted in...

    Less effective audits 1 : 2 : 3 : 4 : 5 : 6 : 7 More effective audits

11. How has competition among CPA firms affected the availability of "advisory and consulting services"?

    Increased availability 1 : 2 : 3 : 4 : 5 : 6 : 7 Decreased availability

12. Expansion beyond traditional audit and tax practice is bad for the accounting profession in the long run.

    Strongly disagree 1 : 2 : 3 : 4 : 5 : 6 : 7 Strongly agree

13. Competition between CPA firms has resulted in decreased audit fees.

    Strongly agree 1 : 2 : 3 : 4 : 5 : 6 : 7 Strongly disagree

14. It is not appropriate for an auditing firm to be engaged in general management consulting.

    Strongly disagree 1 : 2 : 3 : 4 : 5 : 6 : 7 Strongly agree

15. How would you rate the auditors on...

    a. *Honesty*?

       Dishonest 1 : 2 : 3 : 4 : 5 : 6 : 7 Honest

    b. *Reliability*?

       Reliable 1 : 2 : 3 : 4 : 5 : 6 : 7 Unreliable

    c. *Communication skills*?

       Excellent 1 : 2 : 3 : 4 : 5 : 6 : 7 Poor

    d. *Objectivity*?

       Objective 1 : 2 : 3 : 4 : 5 : 6 : 7 Subjective

e. *Problem solving*?

Poor	1 : 2 : 3 : 4 : 5 : 6 : 7	Excellent

f. *Competence*?

Incompetent	1 : 2 : 3 : 4 : 5 : 6 : 7	Competent

g. *Creativity*?

Uncreative	1 : 2 : 3 : 4 : 5 : 6 : 7	Creative

h. *Concern for the public interest in their work*?

Concerned	1 : 2 : 3 : 4 : 5 : 6 : 7	Unconcerned

16. As management consultants for corporations, how do independent auditors compare to consultants within management consulting firms?

Less able	1 : 2 : 3 : 4 : 5 : 6 : 7	More able

17. On our audit, the auditors spend enough time to achieve…

Highest quality	1 : 2 : 3 : 4 : 5 : 6 : 7	Minimal quality

18. When audit firms serve as advisors to an audit client on tax matters, management systems, or financial matters, their ability to be objective when auditing a client's financial statements is compromised.

Strongly agree	1 : 2 : 3 : 4 : 5 : 6 : 7	Strongly disagree

In the following section, you will be asked to rank various responses to a number of questions. In ranking the responses, you should give a *1* to the best response, a *2* to the next best response and so on. If you feel that one or more of the responses do not apply, give them a *0*. If you feel that two or more of the responses are equal, give them the same ranking.

19. The independent auditor is responsible to: (rank using the scale given above)

a. ____ the public at large	d. ____ the creditors
b. ____ top management	e. ____ the company
c. ____ the stockholders	f. ____ me

20. The audit is useful to: (rank)

a. ____ the public at large	d. ____ the creditors
b. ____ top management	e. ____ the company
c. ____ the stockholders	f. ____ me

21. Independent auditors are most like: (rank)

a. ____ teachers d. ____ lawyers

b. ____ advisors e. ____ policemen

c. ____ consultants f. ____ judges

For the following questions, please check or fill in the blanks where appropriate.

Job title: ________________ Big 8(6) experience __ Yes __ No

Degrees you currently possess:

TYPE	MAJOR	YEAR	SCHOOL
________	________________	________	______________
________	________________	________	______________
________	________________	________	______________
________	________________	________	______________

Male ____ Female ____ Age ______

THANK YOU FOR YOUR TIME AND COOPERATION

ACKNOWLEDGMENTS

The authors wish to thank all those who participated in this study and gratefully acknowledge the kind assistance of the editor and ombudsman referee, as well as the two original anonymous reviewers.

Data Availability: Summary SPSS data used in this study are available from Professor Dale E. Marxen, Department of Accounting, MSU Box 14, Mankato State University, Mankato, MN 56002-8400.

NOTES

1. Commonly referred to as the Treadway Commission after its chairman, James Treadway.

2. The client questionnaire is reproduced in the Appendix. The auditor questionnaire was identical except for minor modifications for the auditor subjects.

3. Questions 1(b) and 19-21, although found on previous expectation gap questionnaires, were not analyzed or included in this report for the following reasons: (1) Question 1(b) was considered to be an essentially neutral question of fact which was not related to a subjective expectation held for audit or advisory service quality; and (2) Questions 19-21were considered to be peripheral to the main intent of this research. In

addition, questions 19-21 were not in Likert-type format, making their responses less comparable to others in the study.

4. The firms were left free to choose the clients, and the contact for each.

5. Except for one accounting firm which took full responsibility for contacting and mailing the questionnaires to its clients.

6. The midpoint of each scale was 4.0; therefore, such a response would be completely neutral. Items that were negatively worded were reverse scored so that those compiling a scale would be additive.

7. Of the three items that made up the index, only the difference in perceptions relating to fraud detection was statistically significant (4.1 vs. 3.4, $\Delta = 0.7$; $p = .02$). Management was more apt to believe that auditors should detect fraud. Interestingly, however, both the auditors' and their clients' ratings of the auditors' *performance* in detecting fraud exceeded the *expectations* held by both parties for the auditors in this area. Therefore, these audit clients appeared to exhibit no perception gap related to the actual detection of fraud.

8. The only items that did differ significantly were items 1 ($p = .005$) and 5 ($p = .05$). Both dealt with auditor independence issues, and in both instances the clients' lower ratings indicated an area of concern.

9. None of the individual items making up the index showed any significant differences either.

10. These results are not tabled herein.

11. As a response to the demands of a competitive marketplace, at least one Big 6 firm has even begun to incorporate such services into its standard audit process.

REFERENCES

Anderson, J.C., D.J. Lowe, and P.M.J. Reckers. 1993. Evaluation of auditor decisions: Hindsight bias effects and the expectation gap. *Journal of Economic Psychology* 14: 711-737.

Armstrong, M.B., and J.I. Vincent. 1988. Public accounting: A profession at a crossroads. *Accounting Horizons* (March): 94-98.

Commission on Auditors' Responsibilities. 1978. *Report, Conclusions, and Recommendations.* New York: AICPA. (Cohen Commission).

Epstein, M.G., and M.A. Geiger. 1994. Investor views of audit assurance: Recent evidence of the expectation gap. *Journal of Accountancy* (January): 60-66.

Guy, D.M., and J.D. Sullivan. 1988. The expectation gap standards. *Journal of Accountancy* (April): 36-46.

Louis Harris & Associates. 1986. *A Survey of Perceptions, Knowledge, and Attitudes toward CPAs and the Public Accounting Profession* (prepared for the AICPA).

Meyers, D.G., and H. Lamm. 1976. The group polarization phenomenon. *Psychological Bulletin* 83: 602-627.

National Commission on Fraudulent Financial Reporting. 1987. *Report of the National Commission on Fraudulent Financial Reporting.* Washington, DC.

Opinion Research Corporation. 1974. *Public Accounting in Transition: American Shareowners and Key Publics View the Role of Independent Accountants and the Corporate Reporting Controversy.* Arthur Andersen & Company.

Public Oversight Board. 1994. *Strengthening the Professionalism of the Independent Auditor.* (Advisory Panel, Donald J. Kirk, Chairman). One Station Place, Stamford, CT.

Thompson, J.H., and K.T. Jones. 1990. The development of public opinion of the accounting profession: The past forty years. *Business and Society* (Spring): 1-9.

Wilcox, K.A., and C.H. Smith. 1977. Role Discrepancies and the auditor-client relationship. *Accounting, Organizations, and Society* 2 (1): 81-87.

THE IMPACT OF *CENTRAL BANK OF DENVER*: SOME EMPIRICAL EVIDENCE

Ross D. Fuerman

ABSTRACT

Until the April 19, 1994 *Central Bank of Denver, N.A.* v. *First Interstate Bank of Denver, N.A.* decision by the United States Supreme Court, auditors could be charged with aiding and abetting a violation of Section 10(b) of the Securities Exchange Act of 1934. Almost immediately after the announcement of the decision, Congress began holding hearings on the question of amending the Securities Exchange Act of 1934 to legislatively overturn the Supreme Court's controversial holding. This is a study of securities disclosure lawsuits commenced from April 20, 1992 through April 19, 1995. The results of the study indicate that *Central Bank* is associated with a significant short-term reduction of auditor litigation risk. However, *Central Bank* is not associated with a reduction of intermediate-term auditor litigation risk. Indeed, *Central Bank* is associated, albeit insignificantly, with an increase in intermediate-term auditor litigation risk.

Research in Accounting Regulation, Volume 11, pages 177-190.

ISBN: 0-7623-0168-6

INTRODUCTION

The United States Supreme Court held in the *Central Bank* decision[1] that there is no private remedy for aiding and abetting a violation of Section 10(b) of the Securities Exchange Act of 1934[2] (hereafter "Section 10(b)"). Aiding and abetting had often been used by plaintiffs against auditors in private securities disclosure litigation. Thus, auditor litigation risk may have been reduced by the Court's April 19, 1994 decision.

On the other hand, the abrogation of the aiding and abetting liability theory may have had little *practical* impact upon auditor litigation risk. Cases can be cited where the complaint against the auditor was completely dismissed due to the dismissal of a claim based on an aiding and abetting liability theory. However, others can be cited where the dismissal of an aiding and abetting claim did not constitute a dismissal of the entire case against the auditor.[3] Alternative legal liability theories may be invoked to impose liability on auditors in securities disclosure lawsuits. These alternative theories include primary liability,[4] claims based on other federal or state statutes, or claims based on common law.

After *Central Bank*, critics of the decision advocated legislative reinstatement of aiding and abetting. Aiding and abetting *was* reinstated as part of the Private Securities Litigation Reform Act of 1995[5] (hereafter "the Act"). However, it was only reinstated for certain Securities and Exchange Commission enforcement actions, and not for private securities lawsuits. Both advocates and opponents of legislative reinstatement of aiding and abetting for private securities lawsuits defend their respective positions on normative economic grounds. Advocates of legislative reinstatement insist that legislative reinstatement would restore investor protection, which would increase investor confidence and facilitate capital formation. Opponents of legislative reinstatement assert that *Central Bank* helped decrease frivolous, costly litigation, and that the decision therefore facilitated capital formation.[6]

This study takes a positive economic approach. Before addressing the normative question of whether legislative reinstatement of private aiding and abetting is in the public interest, policy makers may find it useful to examine the actual impact of the case. This study provides the first empirical evidence of the effect of *Central Bank* on auditor litigation risk.

Segal (1995) surmised that since the decision narrowed the options under which lawsuits against auditors could be filed, certain actions that (before *Central Bank*) would have been asserted against auditors as aiding and abetting claims will likely not be filed at all. Conversely, no analogous narrowing of legal options affected the filing of actions against companies and their management. Section 10(b) private actions against the latter genre of defendants had always been based on primary liability, even before *Central Bank.* Thus, if *Central Bank* lowered auditor litigation risk, after *Central Bank* the proportion of lawsuits that had auditor defendants should have declined.

DEVELOPMENT OF THE HYPOTHESES

An adaptation of the Cooter and Rubinfeld (1989) economic model of litigation provides the theoretical framework for this study. First, financial statements are issued. Then, investors incur losses. Believing that there is a reasonable likelihood of a material misrepresentation, the plaintiff then evaluates the likelihood of auditor culpability. If the plaintiff believes that there is no reasonable likelihood of auditor culpability, no lawsuit is brought against the auditor. If the plaintiff believes that there *is* a reasonable likelihood of auditor culpability, the plaintiff evaluates whether the likely benefits of a lawsuit against the auditor exceed the likely costs of a lawsuit against the auditor.

The plaintiff's evaluation of whether the likely benefits of a lawsuit against the auditor exceed the likely costs of a lawsuit against the auditor can be decomposed into five factors. The first factor is the likelihood of a victory against the auditor (i.e., ability to prove auditor culpability). The second factor is the likelihood of a victory against some defendant(s), not necessarily the auditor (i.e., the strength of the case). The third factor, assuming a plaintiff victory, is the likely amount of the judgment or settlement. The fourth factor is the ability of each potential defendant to pay a judgment or settlement. The fifth factor is the likely increased cost of the litigation if the auditor is named a defendant.

A plaintiff has greater incentive to include the auditor as a defendant if there exists a viable legal liability theory. The *Central Bank* decision eliminated the aider and abettor Section 10(b) legal liability theory. Since 1967,[7] aiding and abetting had been heavily used against auditors in securities disclosure lawsuits. It had seldom been used against defendant companies or their officers and directors. The latter defendants were sued instead under a primary liability theory.

The *Central Bank* decision was announced on April 19, 1994. There were fewer legal theories available to use against auditors after that date. Thus, the proportion of lawsuits commenced in the four months immediately after *Central Bank* with auditor defendants should be smaller than in the lawsuits commenced at other times during the study. This four month window empirically measures the short-term impact of *Central Bank*.

Resourceful plaintiffs' counsel needed only a few months to draft new complaints based on alternative legal theories. Thus, the proportion of lawsuits commenced in the year immediately after *Central Bank* with auditor defendants should *not* be smaller than in the lawsuits commenced at other times during the study. This one year window empirically measures the intermediate-term impact of *Central Bank*. These hypotheses are stated below (in the alternative form).

Hypothesis 1. The proportion of lawsuits that include auditors as defendants, commenced during the *four months* after April 19, 1994, will be significantly smaller than in the lawsuits commenced at other times.

Hypothesis 2. The proportion of lawsuits that include auditors as defendants, commenced during the *year* after April 19, 1994, will *not* be significantly smaller than in the lawsuits commenced at other times.

RESEARCH APPROACH

Sample Selection

The initial sample consisted of 429 securities disclosure lawsuits reported in *Securities Class Action Alert* from the May 1992 issue through the February 1996 issue.[8] All of these lawsuits primarily concerned securities disclosure. They were commenced April 20, 1992, through April 19, 1995. In addition, they were filed in the United States District Courts.[9] Lawsuits against mutual funds or governmental entities were excluded from the study. Six lawsuits were deleted from the study because no audit of a financial statement was performed, there was no private plaintiff, or data was incomplete.[10]

Classification of Lawsuits

Sometimes the auditor was named a defendant in the initial complaint of a lawsuit. Alternatively, there sometimes was a delay of weeks or months until the auditor was named a defendant. Since this study's

Table 1. Time Period of Commencement of Litigation (Period used to operationalize short-term impact of *Central Bank* is bold-faced)

Panel A

	Number (Percentage) of Observations		
	Total Sample (n = 423)	*No Auditor Defendant (n = 388)*	*Auditor Defendant (n = 35)*
4/20/92-8/19/92	62 (15%)	56 (15%)	6 (17%)
8/20/92-12/19/92	55 (13%)	51 (13%)	4 (11%)
12/20/92-4/19/93	37 (9%)	36 (9%)	1 (3%)
4/20/93-8/19/93	44 (10%)	42 (11%)	2 (6%)
8/20/93-12/19/93	40 (9%)	35 (9%)	5 (14.3%)
12/20/93-4/19/94	45 (11%)	39 (10%)	6 (17%)
4/20/94-8/19/94	**58 (14%)**	**57 (15%)**	**1 (3%)**
8/20/94-12/19/94	48 (11%)	43 (11%)	5 (14.3%)
12/20/94-4/19/95	34 (8%)	29 (7%)	5 (14.3%)
	423 (100%)	388 (100%)	35 (100%)

Panel B

	Number (Percentage) of Observations Where Auditor is a Defendant
4/20/92-8/19/92	6 out of 62 (9.7%)
8/20/92-12/19/92	4 out of 55 (7.3%)
12/20/92-4/19/93	1 out of 37 (2.7%)
4/20/93-8/19/93	2 out of 44 (4.5%)
8/20/93-12/19/93	5 out of 40 (12.5%)
12/20/93-4/19/94	6 out of 45 (13.3%)
4/20/94-8/19/94	**1 out of 58 (1.7%)**
8/20/94-12/19/94	5 out of 48 (10.4%)
12/20/94-4/19/95	5 out of 34 (14.7%)
Total	35 out of 423 (8.3%)

experimental explanatory variable is longitudinal, this delay factor had to be addressed. Otherwise, for example, the interpretation of a lawsuit commenced before *Central Bank* with the auditor named a defendant after *Central Bank* would be problematic.

Thus, the time period of the study was divided into nine equal four-month periods (see Table 1) to investigate the short-term impact of *Central Bank* and three equal one-year periods (see Table 2) to investigate the intermediate-term impact of *Central Bank*. First, the period in which each lawsuit commenced was determined. Then, a lawsuit was classified as having an auditor defendant if the auditor was named a defendant, in that same period.[11]

Table 2. Time Period of Commencement of Litigation (Period used to operationalize intermediate-term impact of *Central Bank* is bold-faced)

Panel A

	Number (Percentage) of Observations		
	Total Sample (n = 423)	*No Auditor Defendant (n = 371)*	*Auditor Defendant (n = 52)*
4/20/92-4/19/93	154 (36%)	139 (38%)	15 (29%)
4/20/93-4/19/94	129 (31%)	112 (30%)	17 (33%)
4/20/94-4/19/95	**140 (33%)**	**120 (32%)**	**20 (38%)**
	423 (100%)	371 (100%)	52 (100%)

Panel B

	Number (Percentage) of Observations Where Auditor is a Defendant
4/20/92-4/19/93	15 out of 154 (9.7%)
4/20/93-4/19/94	17 out of 129 (13.2%)
4/20/94-4/19/95	**20 out of 140 (14.3%)**
Total	52 out of 423 (12.3%)

Table 3 presents, based on the four-month window, summary descriptive information about the incidence of lawsuits with auditor defendants. The bottom and top rows denote whether the lawsuit commenced during the four months immediately after the *Central Bank* decision versus at another time during the study, respectively. The right and left columns denote whether the lawsuit had an auditor defendant or did not have one, respectively. The observed proportion of lawsuits having auditor defendants during the four months immediately after the *Central Bank* decision was 1.72%. This compared to 9.32% at other times during the study. Fisher's exact test (Fisher 1934) was used to determine whether the proportion of lawsuits with auditor defendants was significantly smaller in the immediate post-*Central Bank* period. The observed decrease is statistically significant (p = .032, left-tailed) and in the hypothesized direction.

In contrast to the results in Tables 1 and 3 (based on a four month window), the proportion of lawsuits having auditor defendants in the year after *Central Bank* (see Table 2) was *not* significantly smaller. Indeed, the proportion of lawsuits having auditor defendants in the year after *Central Bank* was larger, obviating the need for Fisher's exact test. The proportion of lawsuits having auditor defendants increased from 13.2% in the year before *Central Bank* to 14.3% in the year after *Central Bank*.

Table 3. Summary of Short-term Association Between Auditor Defendant and Period: Lawsuits

	Status of Auditor		
Period	*No Auditor Defendant*	*Auditor Defendant* (SUED)	*Total*
Not after *Central Bank*	331 (90.7%)	34 (9.3%)	365
After *Central Bank* (AFTERCB)	57 (98.3%)	1 (1.7%)	58
Total	368	35	423
Fisher's Exact Test *p*-value = .032			

Also, the proportion of lawsuits having auditor defendants increased from 11.3% in the two years before *Central Bank* to 14.3% in the year after *Central Bank.*

In studying the effect of the explanatory variable (*Central Bank*) on the response variable (auditor named a defendant versus not named a defendant) one should attempt to control covariates that can influence that relationship. In this study, the first step taken to control covariates was to only use recent litigation data from a short time period: lawsuits commenced April 20, 1992 through April 19, 1995. This prevents structural changes that have occurred in recent decades in the auditing and litigation environment from influencing the results. Second, three control variables shown in prior research to influence the plaintiff's decision to include an auditor defendant were taken into account, using logistic regression: culpable restatement of audited annual financial statements (Fuerman 1997), bankruptcy of the defendant company (Gilbertson 1996), and class period length (Fuerman 1997).[12]

Analysis of the logistic regression results provides further support for both hypotheses. The results (based on a four-month window) suggest that after controlling for the culpable restatement of audited annual financial statements, bankruptcy of the defendant company, and class period length, lawsuits were significantly less likely to have an auditor defendant if they were commenced in the four months immediately after *Central Bank.* Conversely, the results (based on a one-year window) suggest lawsuits were *not* significantly less likely to have an auditor defendant if they were commenced in the year immediately after *Central Bank.*

DISCUSSION AND CONCLUSION

A significant decrease in the proportion of lawsuits having auditor defendants (based on a four-month window) during the four months immediately after *Central Bank* period has been documented in this study. Conversely, there was *not* a significant decrease in the proportion of lawsuits having auditor defendants (based on a one-year window) during the year immediately after *Central Bank*. Thus, as hypothesized, empirical evidence suggests that *Central Bank* is associated with a significant, short-term reduction in auditor litigation risk. Also, as hypothesized, *Central Bank* is *not* associated with an intermediate-term significant reduction in auditor litigation risk. Indeed, *Central Bank* is associated with an intermediate, though insignificant, increase in auditor litigation risk. A limitation of this study is that the long-term association of *Central Bank* with auditor litigation risk could not be studied due to the recency of the case.

IMPLICATIONS FOR PUBLIC POLICY

This study is the first to provide empirical evidence on whether auditor litigation risk was reduced by the *Central Bank* decision. *Central Bank*, in the short-term, but *not* the intermediate-term, is associated with a significant reduction of the proportion of securities disclosure lawsuits that included auditor defendants. Opposition to legislative reinstatement of aiding and abetting on the basis that *Central Bank* had no practical impact on auditor litigation risk, is a tenable position.

The 104th Congress did not legislatively reinstate aiding and abetting liability under Section 10(b) of the Exchange Act. It may be irrelevant whether the 105th Congress takes up the reinstatement issue. The evidence from this study suggests that it may not matter. *Central Bank* did not have an intermediate-term impact on auditor litigation risk. Logic suggests that it may not have a long-term impact on auditor litigation risk, either.

APPENDIX A

Appendix A presents details of the logistic regression analysis used to test the hypotheses of the study. As was discussed above, the ability to draw inferences regarding the impact of the *Central Bank* decision is strengthened by using recent litigation data over a short time period, and by controlling for culpable restatement of audited annual financial statements, bankruptcy of the defendant company, and class period length.

There have been two recent empirical studies, both employing multiple logistic regression, differentiating between lawsuits with auditor defendants and lawsuits without auditor defendants (Gilbertson 1996; Fuerman 1997). Gilbertson (1996) was a settlements-only study. Fuerman (1997) was a comprehensive study of both settled and pending securities litigation.

Fuerman (1997) found the culpable[13] restatement of previously issued audited annual financial statements positively associated with naming the auditor a defendant. A culpable restatement of previously released audited annual financial statements is a tacit admission of material financial statement misrepresentation. Similarly, in this study it is expected that a culpable restatement will be positively associated with naming the auditor a defendant. In this study, a culpable restatement is observed as occurring if the restated period(s) overlap the class period of the lawsuit.

Fuerman (1997) also found the length of the class period positively associated with naming the auditor a defendant. The length of the class period is the time during which the defendants allegedly violated the legal rights of the plaintiff.[14] Similarly, in this study it is expected that class period length will be positively associated with naming the auditor a defendant.

Both Gilbertson (1996) and Fuerman (1997) found defendant company bankruptcy positively associated with naming the auditor a defendant. Similarly, in this study it is expected that bankruptcy is observed as occurring if the defendant company filed for bankruptcy within one year before, or one year after, the commencement of litigation.

Culpable restatement, class period length, and bankruptcy were used as control variables in the following logistic regression model:

$$\begin{aligned}\text{SUED} = {} & \beta_0 + \beta_1 * \text{AFTERCB} + \beta_2 * \text{RESTATE} + \beta_3 * \text{BANKRUPT} \\ & + \beta_4 * \text{CLASS} + e\end{aligned}$$

where all variables are defined in Table A1.

Logistic regression is an appropriate statistical technique where, as in this study, there is a single response variable and it is binary. Two-way tables (not shown) show a strong lack of independence between explan-

Table A1.

Variable	Description of Variable
SUED	Coded 1 if auditor named a defendant in same four month period (one year period) in which lawsuit commenced, 0 otherwise
AFTERCB	Coded 1 if lawsuit commenced during four month period (one year period) immediately after *Central Bank*, 0 otherwise
RESTATE	Coded 1 if culpable restatement of previously issued audited annual financial statements, 0 otherwise
BANKRUPT	Coded 1 if defendant company filed for bankruptcy within one year before, or one year after, commencement of lawsuit, 0 otherwise
CLASS	Coded 1 if class period (period of alleged wrongdoing) equals or exceeds its median (ten months), 0 otherwise

atory variables RESTATE and BANKRUPT, between RESTATE and CLASS, and between CLASS and BANKRUPT. However, most important for the purposes of this study, AFTERCB is independent ($p = .33$ or greater in each of the two-way tables) of each of the other three explanatory variables.

Exact logistic regression using LogXact-Turbo, Version 1.3 (CYTEL Software Corporation 1993) was used for the four-month window analysis. Asymptotic logistic regression, due to the extreme cell sparseness, yields unreliable statistical inference results (see Agresti 1996; Mehta and Patel 1995; or Stokes, Davis, and Koch 1995 for discussions of this issue). The results, including exact conditional scores mid-*p* values (Lancaster 1961) are shown in Table A2.

As hypothesized, and consistent with the evidence presented in Tables 1 and 3, the coefficient on the AFTERCB variable (using a four-month window) is −1.9413 and is significant at $p < .05$. The coefficient indicates that after controlling for culpable restatement of audited annual financial statements, class period length, and defendant company bank-

Table A2. Exact Logistic Regression Results (Four-month window) ($N = 423$)

Variables	Parameter Estimate	Exact Conditional Scores Test Statistic	Exact Conditional Scores Mid-p-value	Odds Ratio
Intercept	−3.6969			
AFTERCB	−1.9413	4.3408	.0381	.1435
RESTATE	1.7453	20.0787	.0000	5.7279
BANKRUPT	1.2807	6.2551	.0160	3.5993
CLASS	1.2698	6.6876	.0126	3.5602

Table A3. Asymptotic Logistic Regression Results (One-year window) ($N = 423$)

Explanatory Variable	*Parameter Estimate*	*Standard Error*	*Wald Chi-Square*	*Probability Value*	*Odds Ratio*
Intercept	−3.6383	.4164	76.3600	.0001	
AFTERCB	0.2299	.3552	0.4188	.5175	1.258
RESTATE	2.2802	.3710	37.7791	.0001	9.779
BANKRUPT	1.1145	.5169	4.6493	.0311	3.048
CLASS	1.3865	.4432	9.7864	.0018	4.001

Classification accuracy at .123 (relative frequency of the auditor defendant subscample) = 87.2%; Pseudo R^2 = .1665; Pseudo Adjusted R^2 = .3169.

ruptcy, auditors were less likely to be named defendants in lawsuits commencing in the four months immediately after *Central Bank* than at other times. Expressed in terms of an odds ratio, the estimated odds for auditors to be named defendants in lawsuits not commenced during the four month period after *Central Bank* were $e^{1.9413}$ or 6.97 times the estimated odds for auditors to be named defendants in lawsuits commenced during the four month period after *Central Bank.* Thus, the test of β_1 supports the first hypothesis of the study, that a short-term reduction in auditor litigation risk is associated with *Central Bank.*

Asymptotic logistic regression using SAS' PROC LOGISTIC was used for the one-year window analysis. The results are shown in Table A3. As hypothesized, and consistent with the evidence presented in Table 2, the coefficient on the AFTERCB variable (using a one-year window) is .2299 and is insignificant. Thus, the test of β_1 supports the second hypothesis of the study, that an intermediate-term reduction in auditor litigation risk is *not* associated with *Central Bank.* Indeed, an intermediate-term *increase* in auditor litigation risk is associated (albeit insignificantly) with *Central Bank.*

ACKNOWLEDGMENT

I gratefully acknowledge the assistance of Jeri Ricketts, Norm Bruvold, and Bruce Gaumnitz.

NOTES

1. *Central Bank of Denver* v. *First Interstate Bank of Denver,* 114 S. Ct. 1439 (1994).

2. Section 10(b) provides: "It shall be unlawful for any person, directly or indirectly, by the use of any means or instrumentality of interstate commerce or of the mails, or of any facility of any national securities exchange...(b) To use or employ, in connection with the purchase or sale of any security registered on a national securities exchange or any security not so registered, any manipulative or deceptive device or contrivance in contravention of such rules and regulations as the Commission may prescribe as necessary or appropriate in the public interest or for the protection of investors" 15 U.S.C. 78j(b) (1988).

3. See Goldwasser and Arnold (1996) for examples of both scenarios.

4. Primary liability, in this context, means actual violation of the statute, as contrasted with helping ("aiding and abetting") another defendant to violate Section 10(b).

5. Public Law 104-67.

6. Baum (1995), criticizing the *Central Bank* decision, and Blackman (1995), praising the *Central Bank* decision, provide extensive historical, legal, and public policy analyses of the decision and its aftermath.

7. *Fischer* v. *Kletz,* 266 F. Supp. 180 (S.D.N.Y. 1967).

8. Most lawsuits are disclosed by the newsletter within a few weeks of commencement. However, some are not disclosed for months or even years.

9. The United States District Courts have exclusive jurisdiction over lawsuits that include Section 10(b) claims. 15 U.S.C. 78aa (1949). Thus, they cannot be maintained in a state court. If they are filed nonetheless in a state court, they are generally speedily transferred ("removed") to a United States District Court.

10. All 423 observations had complete data for all variables.

11. A lawsuit is a distinct body of litigation, regardless how many complaints are filed by various plaintiffs. Normally, if multiple complaints are filed, they are consolidated into one proceeding. The commencement date of a lawsuit is the date that the first complaint was filed. This information, as well as the determination of when and if the auditor was named a defendant, was determined via *PACER* (Public Access to Court Electronic Records). *PACER,* maintained by the federal courts, allows users to access via modem any United States District Court host computer database and retrieve official electronic case information and court dockets (see Miro 1995 for a description of *PACER* and how it is used). The last major United States District Court to officially come on-line was the California Northern District in September, 1995.

12. For a detailed discussion of the logistic regression analysis, please see Appendix A.

13. In Fuerman (1997), the following restatements were regarded as *not* culpable: (1) A timely restatement to give retroactive effect to its adoption of a new accounting standard, e.g., *SFAS 96* or *109* (accounting for income taxes; (2) A timely restatement to give retroactive effect to a segment becoming a "discontinued operation;" or to the split-up of one company into two companies; (3) A timely restatement to give retroactive effect to a stock split or a reverse stock split; (4) A timely restatement to give retroactive effect to a pooling of interests merger; (5) A timely restatement to give retroactive effect to owning a greater than (equity method) or less than (cost method) 20% minority stake in another corporation; (6) A timely restatement to give retroactive effect to increasing an ownership stake from a minority interest (equity method) to a 100% ownership stake (consolidated basis); (7) A timely restatement to retroactively create a reserve for a litigation settlement fund; (8) A timely restatement to make prior periods consistent, after

a change to an unclassified balance sheet format from a classified balance sheet format; (9) A timely restatement by an oil and gas producer to give retroactive effect to be consistent after switching from the full cost method to the successful efforts method; (10) A timely restatement to give retroactive effect to the switch to a new fiscal year end; (11) A timely restatement by a foreign company to give retroactive effect to the switch to an accounting policy more in conformance with international and US GAAP; (12) A restatement to retroactively reflect the change in par value of the common stock; (13) A timely restatement by a utility to give retroactive effect to be consistent after changing its accounting policy with respect to spent nuclear fuel.

14. A typical securities class action complaint states as follows: "This complaint is filed on behalf of all purchasers of stock of ABC Company from April 4, 1993 through November 5, 1994."

REFERENCES

Agresti, A. 1996. *An Introduction to Categorical Data Analysis.* New York: John Wiley & Sons, Inc.

Baum, D.J. 1995. The aftermath of Central Bank of Denver: Private aiding and abetting liability under Section 10(b) and Rule 10b-5. *The American University Law Review* (Summer): 1817-1852.

Blackman, S.G. 1995. An analysis of aider and abettor liability under Section 10(b) of the Securities Exchange Act of 1934: Central Bank of Denver v. First Interstate Bank of Denver. *Connecticut Law Review* (Summer): 1323-1376.

Central Bank of Denver, N.A. v. *First Interstate Bank of Denver, N.A.* 114 S. Ct. 1439 (1994).

Cooter, R.D., and D.L. Rubinfeld. 1989. Economic analysis of legal disputes and their resolution. *Journal of Economic Literature* 27: 1067-1097.

CYTEL Software Corporation. 1993. *LogXact-Turbo: Logistic Regression Software Featuring Exact Methods.* Cambridge, MA.

Fischer v. *Kletz,* 266 F. Supp. 180 (S.D.N.Y. 1967).

Fisher, R.A. 1934. *Statistical Methods for Research Workers.* Edinburgh: Oliver and Boyd.

Fuerman, R.D. 1997. Contemporary auditor litigation risk: An empirical investigation based on recent data. Working paper, University of Cincinnati, Cincinnati, OH.

Gilbertson, D.L. 1996. The plaintiffs' decision to sue auditors in securities litigation: An empirical analysis. Working paper, Loyola Marymount University, Los Angeles, CA.

Goldwasser, D.L., and T. Arnold. 1996. *Accountants' Liability.* New York: Practising Law Institute.

Lancaster, H.O. 1961. Significance tests in discrete distributions. *Journal of American Statistics Association* 56: 223-234.

Mehta, C.R., and N.R. Patel. 1995. Exact logistic regression: Theory and examples. *Statistics in Medicine* 14: 2143-2160.

Miro, A.B. 1995. Improve your pace with PACER. *Legal Assistant Today* 12 (May/June): 38-43.

Segal, M.A. 1995. Aiding and abetting after Central Bank of Denver. In *Research in Accounting Regulation,* Vol. 9, 153-162, edited by G.J. Previts. Greenwich, CT: JAI Press.

Stokes, M.E., C.S. Davis, and G.G. Koch. 1995. *Categorical Data Analysis Using the SAS System.* Cary, NC: SAS Institute, Inc.

DECEPTIVE TRADE PRACTICES LEGISLATION:

MORE LITIGATION AHEAD FOR ACCOUNTING FIRMS?

Philip Little and Debra Burke

ABSTRACT

This article addresses the potential for Deceptive Trade Practices Acts (DTPAs) to add to the already substantial litigation burden caused primarily by relaxed privity standards, class action lawsuits, and joint and several liability. Although accounting firms in many states may be able to argue that the provisions of DTPAs do not apply to accounting services, the risk of additional liability exposure looms.

Accounting firms and their lawyers should become familiar with the DTPA in the state in which they practice in order to develop sound defenses against any lawsuits which might develop under the provisions of the legislation. The provisions for treble damages, attorneys' fees, and court costs make DTPA lawsuits appealing for potential claimants and quite costly for those unfortunate accounting firms that unsuccessfully defend such lawsuits.

Research in Accounting Regulation, Volume 11, pages 191-201.

ISBN: 0-7623-0168-6

INTRODUCTION

Over the past two decades, accounting firms have been faced with an alarming number of lawsuits filed and settlements paid out. Fortunately for the accounting profession at least, the U.S. Congress voted in December of 1995 to override a presidential veto and passed the Private Security Litigation Reform Act of 1995. This act affects dramatically the ability of accounting firms to successfully defend themselves against class action suits brought under the federal securities laws. In particular, the act provides reform in areas of joint and several liability, damage limits, and class action proceedings, all of which have contributed greatly to firms' exposure to loss.

Although continuing efforts are needed to solidify the federal reforms, perhaps some of the reform efforts need to be directed to the state level. To complete the reform victory at the federal level, similar successes will be necessary in state legislatures and courts. One such potential for liability at the state level falls under the category of consumer protection laws and is commonly called a Deceptive Trade Practices Act.

These Acts were essentially passed in response to the consumer protection movement of the 1960s. While these statutes are now somewhat dormant with respect to professional liability, they do represent a potential source of liability for the accounting profession especially given the present litigation trend. This article discusses how the accounting profession may be affected by DTP legislation and suggests how accounting firms might defend against lawsuits brought under these acts.

A DESCRIPTION OF DTPA LEGISLATION

Most DTPAs contain a provision similar to the Federal Trade Commission Act of 1938 which prohibits "unfair methods of competition in commerce, and unfair or deceptive acts or practices in commerce" (Arizona, Connecticut, Delaware, Florida, Kentucky, Louisiana, Massachusetts, Minnesota, Missouri, Montana, New Jersey, New York, North Carolina, North Dakota, South Carolina, Vermont, and Washington). Some states couple such a general prohibition with a list of specific violations, many of which represent practices which, under the common law, were considered to be unfair methods of competition, such as trademark infringement, disparagement and false advertising. The Uniform Deceptive Trade Practices Act is one such list which is codified in some states in addition to the general prohibition against all unfair or deceptive acts or practices (Georgia, Hawaii, Illinois, Maine, Nebraska, and Ohio). Other states have enacted lists of specific unfair and deceptive practices, which are more expansive than that of the Uniform Act, in addition to their general prohibition (Alaska, Idaho, Kansas, New Hampshire, New Mexico, Pennsylvania, Rhode Island, South Dakota, Tennessee, Texas, Utah, West Virginia, and Wisconsin). Still others have enacted only a list of specific violations without a corresponding general prohibition (Alabama, Arkansas, California, Colorado, Indiana, Maryland, Michigan, Mississippi, Nevada, Oklahoma, Oregon, Virginia, and Wyoming).

Unlike the Federal Trade Commission Act, however, which is purely regulatory, these state laws allow a private cause of action in addition to the regulatory function, performed by the attorney general in most states. Several states allow class action suits to be brought as well (Connecticut, Massachusetts, New Hampshire, New Mexico, and Hawaii). Only Iowa did not establish a private, civil cause of action. The creation of this private cause of action for aggrieved consumers by DTP legislation is particularly threatening for three reasons. First, it is usually easier to establish a violation of DTPAs than it is to prove a common law cause of action based upon negligence or fraud, because common law defenses are not available against DTP claims, and because *deceptive* practices need not rise to the level of being *fraudulent* to be actionable. Second, the DTP legislation of many states allows for the recovery of treble damages, either automatically, or in the court's discretion, or when the violation is willful (Alabama, Alaska, California, Colorado, Delaware, Louisiana, Massachusetts, Montana, Nevada, New Hampshire, New Jersey, New York, North Carolina, Pennsylvania, South Carolina, Tennessee, Texas, Vermont, Washington, and West Virginia). Third, the overwhelming majority of these acts allow for the recovery of reasonable attorneys' fees and often times court costs. Only a few states do not at least make a provision for fees in appropriate circumstances (Arizona, Arkansas, North Dakota, Rhode Island, and South Dakota). Naturally, if a statute provides for attorneys fees more cases may be litigated than if a suit was simply to be taken upon a contingency fee basis.

Depending upon the state, DTP legislation can embrace a wide variety of commercial activities. In many states the act is applied to the insurance, banking, real estate, and sometimes, securities industries. In some states DTP legislation has been applied to the activities of professionals as well (Texas, Illinois, Massachusetts, Washington, and Minnesota).

However, some states either exempt or fail to include the professional services performed by certain practitioners (New Jersey, Arkansas, North Carolina, Maryland, and Ohio). In the absence of a clear legislative directive, courts typically must decide this issue guided only by the often vague definitions of key words in the statute, such as commerce, consumer, merchandise, or goods and services.

ARE ACCOUNTANTS EXEMPT?

Only two states, Maryland and Ohio, expressly exclude the professional services rendered by accountants from their DTP legislation. The Maryland Act of 1990 exempts the professional services of a certified public accountant, architect, clergyman, professional engineer, lawyer, veterinarian, insurance company authorized to do business in the State, insurance agent or broker licensed by the State, Christian Science practitioner, land surveyor, property line surveyor, chiropractor, optometrist, physical therapist, podiatrist, real estate broker, associate real estate broker, or real estate salesperson, or medical or dental practitioner. The Ohio Act of 1991 prohibits unfair or deceptive practices in consumer transactions. As originally enacted the law exempted from that definition transactions between attorneys or physicians and their clients or patients. The act was amended to exclude the accountant-client relationship from the definition as well.

In an effort to avoid conflicting regulatory schemes, the DTP legislation of most other states only expressly exempts activities which are regulated under other laws. Therefore, since the accounting profession is regulated by state boards, might accountants be exempt under such a provision? The answer is, "It depends." Such provisions are subject to interpretation by courts. For example, the New Hampshire Supreme Court in *Rousseau* v. *Eshleman* (1986), interpreted this provision of its DTP legislation as intending to exempt attorneys because they were regulated by the state bar association. On the other hand, the Connecticut Supreme Court, in *Heslin* v. *Trantolo* (1983), interpreted its act as not precluding dual regulation of attorneys. Even if a court interpreted the exemption as excluding attorneys as already sufficiently regulated professionals, such a precedent may not be applicable to accountants since attorneys, unlike accountants, are subject to regulation by both a licensing board and the state judiciary.

In a different context, some states either expressly or impliedly exempt securities transactions from the application of their DTPAs because of the pervasive regulation of the securities industry under both state and federal law (Louisiana, Michigan, Arkansas, North Carolina, South Carolina, and Washington). Thus, unfair or deceptive practices committed by accountants, which are intricately associated with a securities transaction, might be exempt. However, not all state acts expressly exempt securities transactions. In those states which do not, it is a question for the courts to determine whether or not the legislature impliedly exempted such transactions, given the existence of other regulatory bodies for that industry.

There is one more argument which could be made in favor of recognizing an exemption for accountants. For the most part, state DTP legislation is patterned after the Federal Trade Commission Act, an antitrust law. Historically, antitrust laws were interpreted by courts as impliedly exempting the *professional* activities of members of the *learned professions* from their scope, since antitrust laws [see *FTC* v. *Raladam* (1931)] were designed to regulate competition in the marketplace, not the relationship of professionals with their clients. The classic learned professions are law, medicine, and theology, although recent decisions have expanded the list to include professionals such as architects, engineers, and members of other professions which are characterized by specialized education, confidential relationships, and the adherence to ethical standards. Only North Carolina in 1988, however, has codified such an exception by expressly exempting "professional services rendered by a member of a learned profession." Professional services are those noncommercial activities which distinguish the practitioner as being a professional. Thus, even if a state expressly or impliedly carves such an exception for learned professionals, *and* includes accountants within that definition, the commercial or entrepreneurial aspects of a practice, such as the procedures employed for billing clients, would still be covered by the act.

ARE ACCOUNTANTS INCLUDED?

Like the issue of whether or not accountants are exempt, whether or not accountants are covered by DTP legislation typically is one of statutory construction. If courts broadly construe these remedial acts, the purpose of which is to protect the consuming public, then at a minimum the commercial activities of accountants would fall within the act. Some jurisdictions might refrain from including the professional aspects of a practice for the same reason other courts might consider them exempt. For example, in an Arkansas case, *Robertson* v. *White* (1986), plaintiffs alleged that the defendant accountants had inflated the value of the assets owned, and as a result, included misleading information in an audit. A federal court held that the Arkansas act was not applicable to such a situation because it was not designed to regulate either the attorney-client relationship or the accountant-client relationship.

However, other jurisdictions are not so shy about applying their DTP legislation to the accounting profession. In an Illinois case, *Lyne* v. *Arthur Andersen & Company* (1991), another federal court held that the Illinois act did in fact apply to services rendered by an accounting firm with respect to a securities offering. Even though the court recognized that Illinois state courts had refused to apply the act to attorneys, it justified extending it to accountants because "unlike other commercial services, medical and legal services are regulated by governmental bodies." Even though the accounting profession is regulated, the court determined that it was still not subject to the same type of policing as that of the legal profession. In a subsequent case, *Endo* v. *Albertine* (1993), the district court again held that the state DTPA did apply to accountants who allegedly misstated in a prospectus the potential tax obligation of the corporation and failed to disclose the corporation's contingent environmental liabilities.

Texas is another state where DPTA legislation has been applied to professionals (see Forshey 1978). For example, in *Dominquez* v. *Brackey Enterprises, Inc.* (1988), a Texas Appeals Court held that accountants, who sold accounting services to their clients, consumers of financial advice, could be held liable under the act for breach of a fiduciary duty. A recent amendment to the DTPA, the result of concerted lobbying efforts, now prohibits claims involving professional advice except for those involving misrepresentation or unconscionable conduct. The extent of this new caveat is yet to be tested in Texas courts, however.

Certainly, if accountants perform services not strictly related to their profession, then the potential for liability increases. In a Minnesota case, *Professional Financial Management, Ltd.* (1989), a federal court in Minnesota held that an accounting firm could be held liable under the state's DTP legislation for negligent misrepresentations or omissions in promoting an investment program to its clients.

While there are few cases which specifically address the issue of whether or not accountants are subject to, or exempt from, the act, it is clear that DTP legislation represents yet another source of potential liability for the profession. Rather than leaving the issue to be determined through the process of judicial interpretation, professional associations should lobby state legislatures for an express exemption for professional services, like the legislation of Maryland and Ohio. Unfortunately, if such efforts are unsuccessful, courts might perceive that result as an affirmative choice to include professionals and their services.

Another tactic might be to remove any case brought in state court under DTP legislation to federal court, circumstances permitting. Generally speaking, federal courts would be more apt to narrowly interpret such legislation as not being applicable to professional services because federal courts usually are reluctant to interpret state law broadly in the absence of a guiding precedent from state courts. However, the legislatures of many states have directed courts to liberally construe these remedial measures in order to effectuate their purpose: protecting consumers from unfair or deceptive trade practices. Thus, for example, the federal court in Illinois in *Lyne* v. *Arthur Andersen & Company* (1991) was willing to extend the act to accountants even when state court decisions had interpreted the act as not being applicable to the legal profession.

ACCOUNTING FIRM EXPOSURE TO DTPA LIABILITY

To date, the few cases which have been brought against accountants under DTP legislation have primarily involved summary judgment questions concerning only whether or not accountants were subject to liability. The next logical question then, is if they are subject to liability, what acts or practices committed by accountants might be considered either unfair or deceptive?

While accounting firms do not guarantee that the financial statements with which they are associated are error free, or that the audited entity is in good health, or that fraud was not committed by management in collusion with the audited corporation's board of directors, auditors *do* provide reasonable assurance that the financial statements are free of *material* misstatements, that they are fairly presented in accordance with generally accepted accounting principles (GAAP), and that the audit was conducted in accordance with general accepted auditing standards (GAAS). If such is not the case, then a misrepresentation under DTP legislation may exist. For example, if the audit was not conducted with due diligence, then representing that it was could constitute a violation of the DTPA. Further, if a jurisdiction recognizes an implied contractual warranty in the performance of professional services, then the failure of an auditor to perform in accordance with GAAP could be a breach of that warranty, and as such could be actionable under the DTPA.

Consider too, some of the prohibitions of the Uniform Deceptive Trade Practices Act, which provides that "a person engages in a deceptive trade practice when, in the course of his business, vocation, or occupation, he: ...causes confusion or misunderstanding as to the source, sponsorship, approval or certification of goods or services...causes likelihood of confusion or misunderstanding as to affiliation, connections, or association with, or certification by, another...represents that goods or services have sponsorship, approval, characteristics, ingredients, uses, benefits, or quantities that they do not have, or that a person has approval, status, affiliation or connection that he does not have...represents that goods or services are of a particular standard, quality, or grade, or that goods are of a particular style or model if they are of another...engages in any other conduct which similarly creates a likelihood of confusion or misunderstanding." Some of these provisions could be directly applicable to situations in which auditors have not performed in accordance with GAAP.

Even in states where the Uniform Act has not been specifically enacted, most statutes contain a similar list, or interpret their general prohibition statute as including *at a minimum*, the Uniform Act's prohibitions, which represent the common law's collection of legal wrongs known as unfair trade practices. Most of the general provision statutes allow even greater leeway in interpretation. Such statutes, which follow the federal act, typically require that there be a material misrepresentation, omission or practice that is likely to mislead consumers acting reasonably under the circumstances. This definition of deception does not require a finding of fraud or an intent to deceive.

If a practice is not deceptive, it, nevertheless, may be unfair. In determining unfairness [see *FTC* v. *Sperry Hutchinson* (1972)] courts usually will consider (1) whether the practice, without necessarily having been previously considered unlawful, offends public policy as it has been established by statutes, common law, or otherwise; (2) whether the practice is immoral, unethical, oppressive, or unscrupulous; and (3) whether the practice causes substantial injury to consumers or competitors.

Therefore, under DTPAs deception may not embrace highly culpable conduct, and unfairness could amount to a deviation from professional standards. Again, the only question would be whether or not professional services are to be included as a trade, or in the alternative, excluded from within the purview of the act. While such actionable misrepresentations might also constitute negligent conduct, the threat to auditors could be greater under DTP legislation because of the potential for the recovery of treble damages, attorneys' fees, and costs.

SUMMARY AND CONCLUSIONS

Recently, much press has been given to the spiraling litigation exposure for accounting firms. Certainly the recent Litigation Reform Act of 1995 provides much relief at the federal level. However, this article addresses the potential for Deceptive Trade Practices Acts at the state level to expose accounting firms to litigation. Although accounting firms in many states may be able to argue that the provisions of DTPAs do not apply to accounting services, the risk of additional liability exposure looms.

For more than thirty years, states have enacted DTPAs to prohibit unfair or deceptive acts or practices by business. Several provisions of the acts could be applied to accounting firms especially in the performance of the audit function. DTPAs in several states have been applied to situations in which financial reports are found to be misstated or that the audit was not performed with due diligence. Disturbingly, like similar cases brought under common law, many cases may be decided against accounting firms in situations where the accounting profession's definition of misstatements or due diligence may differ from the court's interpretation. Accordingly, just as the judge in *Ultramares Corp.* v. *Touche-Ross* predicted back in 1931, the accounting profession faces yet another potential source of legal liability that "exposes accountants to a liability in an indeterminate amount for an indeterminate time to an indeterminate class."

This article has sounded the warning alarm. Accounting firms and their lawyers should become familiar with the DTPAs in the state in which they practice in order to develop sound defenses against any lawsuits which might develop under the provisions of the legislation and focus part of its litigation reform efforts on these acts. The provisions for treble damages, attorneys' fees, and court costs make DTPA lawsuits appealing for potential claimants and quite costly for those unfortunate accounting firms that unsuccessfully defend such lawsuits.

REFERENCES

ALA. CODE §§ 8-19-4 to -12 (1975).

ALASKA STAT. § 45.50.531(a) (1986 & Supp. 1992).

ARK. CODE ANN. §§ 4-88-111 to -113 (Michie 1991).

ARIZ. REV. STAT. ANN. §§ 44-1524 to -1531 (1987).

Arthur Andersen & Co., Coopers & Lybrand, Deloitte & Touche, Ernst & Young, KPMG Peat Marwick, and Price Waterhouse, "The Liability Crisis in the United States: Impact on the Accounting Profession," a Statement of Position, August 6, 1992.

CAL. CIV. CODE § 1780 (West 1985).

COLO. REV. STAT. § 6-1-113 (West 1992).

CONN. GEN. STAT. ANN. §§ 42-110(d) to -110 (West 1992).

DEL. CODE ANN. tit. 6, §§ 2514 to -22 (1974).

Dominquez v. *Brackey Enterprises, Inc.*, 756 S.W. 2d 788 (Tex. CI. App. 1988).

Endo v. *Albertine*, 812 F. Supp. 1479 (N.D. Ill. 1993).

FLA. STAT. ANN. §§ 501.205 to .210 (West 1988 & Supp. 1993).

Forshey, J.R. 1978. Applicability of the Texas Deceptive Trade Practices Act to attorneys. *30 Baylor Law Review 65.*

FTC v. *Raladam Co.*, 283 U.S. 643 (1931).

FTC v. *Sperry Hutchinson Co.*, 405 U.S. 233 (1972).

GA. CODE ANN. § 10-1-399(a) (Harrison 1992).

HAW. REV. STAT. § 480-13 (1985 & Supp. 1987).

Heslin v. *Connecticut Law Clinic of Trantolo & Trantolo*, 461 A. 2d 938 (Conn. 1983).

IDAHO CODE § 48-608 (1977 & Supp. 1992).

ILL. ANN. STAT. ch. 815, paras. 505/3-7 (Smith-Hurd Supp. 1992).

IND. CODE ANN. § 24-5-0.5-4(a) (Burns 1991).

KAN. STAT. ANN. § 50-634 (1983 & Supp. 1992).

KY. REV. STAT. ANN. §§ 367.190 TO .240 (Michie 1987).

LA. REV. STAT. ANN. §§ 51.1407 to .1417 (West 1987).

Lyne v. *Arthur Andersen & Company*, 772 F. Supp. 1064 (N.D. Ill. 1991).

MD. COM. LAW CODE ANN. § 13-104 (1990).

MD. COM. LAW CODE ANN. § 13-408(a) (1990).

ME. REV. STAT. ANN. tit. 5, § 213 (West 1989 & Supp. 1992).

MASS. GEN. LAWS ANN. ch. 93A, §§ 2(c) to 8 (West 1984).

MICH. COMP. LAWS ANN. § 445.911 (West 1989).

MINN. STAT. ANN. § 8.31 (West 1981 & Supp. 1991).

MISS. CODE ANN. § 75-24-15(1) (1991).

MONT. CODE ANN. §§ 30-13-121 to -132 (1991).

MO. ANN. STAT. §§ 407.030 to .130 (Vernon 1990).

NEB. REV. STAT. §§ 87-303, 59-1602 (1988).

NEV. REV. STAT. ANN. § 598A.210 (Michie 1991).

N.H. REV. STAT. ANN. § 358-A:10 (1984).
N.J. STAT. ANN. §§ 56:8-3 to -18 (West 1989).
N.Y. GEN. BUS. LAW § 349(h) (McKinney 1988).
N.M. STAT. ANN. § 57-12-10 (Michie 1990).
N.C. GEN. STAT. § 75-1.1(b) (1988).
N.C. GEN. STAT. §§ 75-9 to -15 (1988).
N.D. CENT. CODE §§ 51-15-04 to -08 (1989 and Supp. 1991).
OHIO REV. CODE ANN. §13-45.01(a) (Anderson 1991).
OHIO REV. CODE ANN. § 1345.09 (Anderson 1979).
OKLA. STAT. ANN. tit. 15, § 761.1 (West Supp. 1993).
OR. REV. STAT. § 646.638 (1988).
PA. CONS. STAT. ANN. tit. 73, § 201-9.2 (Supp. 1992).
Professional Financial Management, Ltd., 703 F. Supp. 1388 (D. Minn. 1989).
R.I. GEN. LAWS § 6-13.1-5.2 (1992).
Robertson v. *White*, 633 F. Supp. 954 (W.D. Ark. 1986).
Rousseau v. *Eshleman*, 519 A. 2d 243 (N.H. 1986).
S.C. CODE ANN. §§ 39-5-50 to -130 (Law. Co-op. 1985).
S.D. CODIFIED LAWS ANN. § 37-24-31 (1986).
TENN. CODE ANN. § 47-18-109 (1988 & Supp. 1992).
TEX. BUS. & COM. CODE ANN. § 17.50 (West 1987 & Supp. 1993).
UTAH CODE ANN. § 13-11-19 (1992).
VA. CODE ANN. §§ 59.1-201 to -203 (Michie 1992).
VT. STAT. ANN. tit. 9, §§ 2458 to 2460 (1984).
WASH. REV. CODE ANN. §§ 19.86.080 to .110 (West 1989).
W. VA. CODE § 46A-6-106 (1992).
WIS. STAT. ANN. §§ 100.18 (11) to .20 (West 1988).
WYO. STAT. §§ 40-12-106 to -107 (1990).

PART III

PERSPECTIVE PAPERS

ADDRESS TO THE DECEMBER 1996 AICPA CONFERENCE ON SEC REGULATIONS

Dennis R. Beresford

As I've said many times, this conference is *always* a highlight of my year. It's an opportunity to address a large and well-informed audience. And it's also a great learning experience for me to hear the many other distinguished speakers.

This is my final appearance and by that I mean as FASB Chairman because my term ends next June. I hope, however, to attend many future meetings as an enthusiastic learner like all of you.

While I certainly don't think of myself as having a short-timer's attitude, it is interesting to start seeing the light at the end of the tunnel and not view it as still another train about to run us over. In fact, I'm beginning to get a few of the obligatory requests for interviews inquiring about what the FASB has accomplished during my tenure. The first such inquiry came in a few months ago before I'd thought much about it. When the reporter asked, "What have *you* accomplished," I said that she should have asked instead, "what have *we* accomplished," because the

Research in Accounting Regulation, Volume 11, pages 205-213.

ISBN: 0-7623-0168-6

FASB is very much a group effort. But I then went on to say that the greatest accomplishment is that we have survived and, in particular, that I have survived! That may not sound like much, but given the importance of our activity and, in particular, the great controversy that surrounds it, I'm very proud that we continue to be an extremely viable and relevant organization. In fact, with recent progress on most major technical projects, some excellent trustees added to our governing Board, and a strategic plan for the next 5 years now in place, I am very optimistic about the FASB's future.

Having said all that, I decided to start with the following quote:

> The FASB appears to feel that the business community has too strong a role in the rule-making process and has a disproportionate influence on standard-setting. There seems to be a basic distrust of the business community's motives for taking certain positions on accounting issues...

Now that quote probably sounds like it came from a recent letter on one of our technical projects from a corporation or a similar source. But it actually was part of an October 1987 letter to me from John Reed of Citicorp, then chairman of the Accounting Principles Task Force of the Business Roundtable. The reason for mentioning it again today is not to reopen any old wounds, but simply to point out that I quoted that letter in my first speech to this conference 10 years ago. "*The more things change, the more they stay the same.*"

My point in that first talk was not to criticize the business community. In fact, I emphasized the critical importance of substantial involvement by the business community in our process. But I also cited the need for greater involvement by other interested parties, particularly users of financial statements. Ten years later we've made a little progress in getting users more involved, but it's still a real challenge for us.

That first talk also described significant political involvement in one of our technical projects. No, it wasn't the stock compensation project, although that project was active even back then. Rather, it was the accounting for income taxes project where property and casualty insurance companies tried to convince Congress to overrule our process. Interestingly, their chief ally in Congress on that issue was a Senator from Kansas by the name of Dole. Bankers jumped into the lobbying effort back then as well. In fact, the New York Clearing House banks sent a letter that included one of my all time favorite sentences. They said, "Some compromise, to spare the affected companies *extreme discomfort*, should be possible." Somehow I always associated those "extreme discomfort" words with products like Exlax.

Interestingly, the FEI, IMA, AICPA, AIMR and many others came to our defense back then and wrote to the SEC and Congress to discourage political intervention. That, of course, did not prevent similar initiatives in connection with OPEB, marketable securities, and especially stock compensation in later years. "*The more things change, the more they stay the same.*"

The following year, 1989, my remarks to you referred to the requests by some to speed up our process, countered by efforts by others to slow things down. I mentioned that it was never clear whether I was supposed to step on the accelerator or on the brakes. The mixed signals we received on so many of our projects was highlighted by a few companies even opposing the deferral of the effective date of Statement 96, our first standard on income taxes. This included one company that said our action was a betrayal of efforts to support our pronouncements. Notwithstanding those mixed signals, in that year we did receive some useful suggestions for improving our process such as more research before adding topics to our agenda and more field testing of proposals. What we do will never please *all* of our constituents, however. In fact, you will recall some strong letters from the FEI early this year that urged massive changes to our structure and process. They said we have to be more efficient and not take so long to issue standards and they also had several suggestions that would have the opposite effect. "*The more things change, the more they stay the same.*"

In the next year, 1990, I mentioned that I had recently spoken at a major conference on the topic of "What's right with the FASB." I also said that when I mentioned the title, "What's right with the FASB," to one of my corporate friends, he said, "Oh, I guess you gave a very short speech!" That year also was when our trustees were considering a change in the FASB's voting requirements from a simple majority of 4 of 7 votes to a super majority of at least 5. In my speech to this conference, I made a number of eloquent arguments for retaining the existing requirements. Those arguments were, of course, rejected by our trustees a few weeks later when they made the change in the voting requirements.

While this is one of the few issues that hasn't recycled during my tenure, as I mentioned already there are many who feel we take too long to issue standards. The voting requirement change in 1990 certainly seemed to be designed to slow our activity down, so perhaps this will be still another revisited area before long.

That same year was the first time I talked about international matters. I set the stage for that topic by repeating a story I'd heard recently.

Story: Man wants a divorce, being interviewed by his lawyer.

Q: Do you have grounds?
A: Oh, about an acre and a half.
Q: Well, do you have a grudge?
A: No, we just have a carport.
Q: Well does she beat you up in the morning?
A: No, we usually get up at the same time.
Q: What then is the problem; why do you want a divorce?
A: I don't know, my wife just says we can't communicate!

That story was intended to highlight my belief that there indeed had become a "failure to communicate" in the financial reporting being produced in different parts of the world—and the FASB must be prepared to play a role in addressing that problem. In the following years at this conference, the internationalization of accounting became a frequent topic in my remarks and also was covered by many other speakers. "*The more things change, the more they stay the same.*"

By the way, please don't panic and think this whole presentation is going to be a plodding walk down memory lane. Let me just quickly mention the general thrust of my subsequent talks including:

- The relationship between AcSEC and the FASB in setting standards.
- Cost-benefit considerations in FASB deliberations.
- Continuing improvements in our process coming from more active oversight by the Trustees of the Financial Accounting Foundation.
- Suggested changes in the so-called accounting model through the Jenkins Committee and similar efforts.

Of course, we were deeply involved in the stock compensation controversy for quite a while, and I devoted all of my time to that project the last two years.

Well, all of that brings me to today. It seems appropriate to spend the rest of my time doing a little crystal ball gazing and giving you some best guesses of where I see financial reporting and the FASB heading in the next several years. I won't talk about the remaining $6^1/_2$ months of my term as Jim Leisenring will do his usual excellent job of summarizing our technical projects later today. And I promise not to keep repeating the quotation that I've used four or five times already, although I will assure you that many of these issues will continue to recycle.

Most of what I'll say now is based on the FASB's initial strategic plan, adopted a little over six months ago. Some of you probably are aware of it as we've described it in our *Status Report* publication and elsewhere. To very briefly summarize, our four strategic directions are:

1. To build broader acceptance of our process and its results among our constituents.
2. To make standard setting more timely and efficient.
3. To enhance the financial reporting model as a tool for decision making in a rapidly changing economic and technological environment.
4. To promote the development and acceptance of superior international accounting standards.

Of course, there are lots of more detailed tactics behind those main points. And I must stress that this is a continuous improvement plan that will be updated on a regular basis. I have strategically scheduled the first update for the fall of 1997, just after I complete my term as chairman! These strategic directions deserve much more discussion than is possible today as they represent a sort of road map for the future of accounting standards. In particular, internationalization of accounting will continue to be a major influence on the topics we address and the conclusions we reach. I'll say more about that in a minute.

The other three strategic directions can be summarized into the following statement: "Make sure that we are working on the most important problems and make sure that we resolve them more quickly." With the former point in mind, earlier this year we asked for comments on a paper covering recommendations of the Jenkins Committee and the AIMR. Only a few more than 50 letters were received—a disappointing response given the potential importance of the topic. We had a roundtable discussion in our offices with a number of interested parties in April. And in October the AICPA sponsored a 2 day conference for about 75 individuals, including all 7 of our Board members.

While it's dangerous to generalize about such letters and meetings, my feeling is that most of our constituents aren't interested in wholesale changes to our current financial reporting system. Many people do not believe that non-financial statement information can be very useful to investors, analysts, creditors, and other users. But most of those people would strongly oppose our requiring those disclosures or making them subject to standardized formats—at least at this time. Even the major public accounting firms who directly participated in developing the Jenkins Committee recommendations generally advised us to go slow. So my prediction is that the FASB is going to be quite cautious about expanding its role beyond traditional financial statement matters. We certainly should try to be sure we're working on the items where financial information can be improved the most, but we also should concentrate on areas where our experience and processes give us a true comparative advantage.

As I mentioned a few minutes ago, internationalization of accounting is one of our primary strategic initiatives. In the past six or seven years, this topic has moved way up on our list of opportunities and challenges. As Jim Leisenring will elaborate on later, two of our major projects are joint ventures with our counterparts from other areas of the world. And several of our staff members have had significant assignments overseas in the past few years. In short, international matters have been pervasively integrated into our day-to-day activities by now. But where do we go from here?

- Will the IASC become the de facto global standard setter when the SEC considers its standards in the next couple of years?
- Will the U.S. and the FASB claim victory through an increasing flood of foreign companies that are willing to pay the price of admission to our capital markets through reconciliation to U.S. GAAP?
- Or will we continue pretty much as is, with increasing international cooperation but domestic standards that differ to one degree or another?

The honest answer is that I don't know, but I do believe the FASB must continue to be a leader by example through our emphasis on high-quality financial reporting. In this regard, I take great pride in the following words from a recent Op Ed piece by Professor Louis Lowenstein in the *New York Times*.

> A major reason that America's financial markets are the fairest and most efficient in the world is that our financial disclosure system is the most comprehensive and reliable in the world.

In an earlier article, Professor Lowenstein also included an important warning to all of us that is worth reading to you.

> Now that harmonization is on all our lips, however, there is the palpable risk that we will, under pressure from a chorus of investment bankers, issuers, not-quite-disinterested commentators and others, regard internationalization as a convenient excuse for accepting the significantly lesser standards of others who in fact have quite different histories and interests.
>
> Their histories matter, but our own is a source of remarkable strength, and it matters too.

I strongly agree with Professor Lowenstein and believe that it is imperative that the FASB continues its leadership role. In addition to the FASB's strategic planning that I've just mentioned, the Financial Accounting Foundation, our parent organization, has been developing its own plan. Related to that is a change to the FAF's membership that was accomplished this past summer. This came out of extensive discussions between the SEC and FAF. While those discussions were somewhat heated and difficult, they were all in the interests of maintaining and solidifying the FASB's important role. In effect, I believe this became a win, win, win situation because the FAF, SEC, and FASB all were pleased with the outcome. Four new trustees have been named including John Biggs, the CEO of a major pension fund, David Ruder, a former SEC chairman, Manny Johnson, a former Federal Reserve Vice Chairman, and Chuck Bowsher, who just completed his 15-year term as Comptroller General.

In my opinion, these appointments greatly strengthen the private-sector accounting standard-setting process. For one-thing, there will be more balance on the FAF between trustees who directly represent organizations with a vested interest in our activities—such as the FEI, IMA, and AICPA—and trustees at large who may be perceived as more generally representing the public interest. Also, this outcome does not result in more control of the FASB by the SEC—we clearly continue to be an independent, private-sector body. And, most important, the fact that these outstanding individuals of great reputation have agreed to join the FAF is a sign that the business community believes that maintaining the FASB is extremely important to our economy.

There is one other topic I want to mention briefly. It isn't as important as many of the matters I've discussed so far. But it's a pet topic of mine and one where I've been disappointed we haven't made more progress. It's the issue of what we call disclosure effectiveness, which is our spin on what most of you call disclosure overload. Last year we issued a prospectus and we got about 75 responses. None of these included the proverbial "silver bullet" that would clearly address and resolve the issue. In fact, we continue to receive considerably mixed messages about what the issue really is. In spite of the somewhat disappointing responses to our prospectus, we've spent considerable Board and staff time on this subject in the past year. One extremely modest step was our decision to exempt certain smaller entities from the fair value disclosures under Statement 107.

On the other hand, in an action that may benefit a wide range of companies, we recently added an agenda project to reconsider the disclosure requirements under Statement 87 (pensions) and Statement 106 (OPEB). A proposal was developed by a small group of our Advisory Council members including a preparer, a user, and auditor, and an academic. That group's proposal would actually add a couple of key pieces of information, but it also would eliminate some boilerplate requirements and suggest a standardized format. The result would be an arguably more effective footnote—that is, one that is easier to understand in perhaps 1/3 or 1/2 of the space that companies presently devote. We hope to issue a proposal early next year after we refine the details.

If this proves successful we may be able to use the same "model" to rechallenge other lengthy disclosure requirements, such as those for leases and taxes. I realize that this is a tough challenge, and we certainly don't want to significantly dilute the high-quality financial information that our capital markets thrive on. But I'm convinced that we can do better—it's a little like the "failure to communicate" story I told earlier. This is a topic that I expect to continue to push hard on in my remaining months, and I hope you'll see this as another change for the better in the years ahead for the FASB.

Thank you for indulging me a little in this commentary. And I also want to sincerely thank all of you here today and the thousands of others who have supported the FASB's process in spite of our ups and owns on specific topics over the past decade. You may recall the saying that Harry Truman made famous: "If you want a friend in Washington, DC, buy a dog." Well, that notion is true for the FASB as well, only our work must be even harder that the government in some respects. For in my time at the Board I've gone through five of man's best friends, including Debbie, Bob, Mike, and the present incumbents Millie and Murphy. They've all been great at helping me deal with job stress—they always greeted me warmly no matter how crummy others had treated me earlier in the day. So the first advice I'll give my successor is "buy a dog." But with or without a canine friend, my successor will inherit an organization that is the envy of accountants around the world. All of you should take pride in that. But you also must recognize that you have a responsibility to help my successor preserve it.

Thank you, one final time.

THE MISAPPROPRIATION THEORY:
AN EMBLEM OF CHANGE

Mark A. Segal

INTRODUCTION

Over the past three years substantial change has occurred in the legislation and approach taken by courts concerning accounting related securities litigation. Supreme Court decisions in 1994 indicated that strict statutory construction should govern the application of securities law (*Reves* and *Central Bank*). In December 1995 the Private Securities Litigation Reform Act was enacted into law in an express effort to deter and sanction abusive and frivolous securities class action lawsuits. Still questions remained as to the extent to which these developments would affect certain private actions and SEC enforcement and rule making authority, particularly those grounded upon judicial doctrines.

Utilization of a strict statutory approach would remove the courts from the ability to create a form of judicial legislation, and would instill stability, predictability and greater uniformity into the application of the

Research in Accounting Regulation, Volume 11, pages 215-221.

ISBN: 0-7623-0168-6

securities law. Implicit in this is the belief that these objectives are favored over the desirability and inherent risk of giving the judiciary flexibility to apply doctrines and implement expansive statutory interpretation further to the stated objectives of the securities law. Insight into how courts have put these recent developments into practice is evident in recent cases handed down by the Eighth and Fourth Circuits concerning what has come to be known as the misappropriation theory. The theory had been a commonly accepted basis for applying Rule 10(b)(5) liability to non-insiders. In this paper the misappropriation is explained, and these recent cases and their significance examined.

THEORIES OF 10(B)(5) LIABILITY

Under what has been labeled the "classical theory" (*SEC* v. *Chiarella* (1980), *SEC* v. *Clark* (1990), and *SEC* v. *Cherif* (1991)) Rule 10(b)(5) will be considered violated where one buys or sells securities based upon material, nonpublic information at the same time one is an insider of the corporation whose securities are traded. According to the theory, insiders possess a fiduciary duty to the shareholders of the corporation whose securities are being traded. Application of the classical theory to appropriate facts is deemed to comport with the statutory language of Section 10(b)(5). A concern has arisen over the application of Section 10(b)(5) to non-insiders who are able to trade and benefit from material, nonpublic information. For example, where an accountant rendering tax services for the CEO gains insight into an upcoming reorganization, or where a bank auditor through examination of canceled checks in a client account is able to determine corporate actions, trade based upon this information for gain. In general the accountants in these instances would not be considered fiduciaries of the parties with whom they trade. Thus, a challenge is posed in applying the statutory language of Section 10(b)(5) as the apparent wrongful act appears more related to the company rather than the third party with whom they traded. Rule 10(b) and 10(b)(5) have been applied to those facts by certain courts under what has been labeled the "misappropriation theory."

The misappropriation theory is said to have its genesis in Justice Burger's dissenting opinion in *Chiarella* (1980). The theory was expanded and gained prominence after the Second Circuit decision in *Newman* (1981), wherein the court maintained that the misappropriation of information from an employer constitutes fraud for Rule

10(b)(5) purposes such that it taints any subsequent transactions entered into for personal gain.

The misappropriation theory emphasizes the breach of a fiduciary duty to the company whose securities are traded, and considers the breach to create a general fiduciary duty applicable to subsequent dealing based upon the information. In this regard the theory provides that there is a duty to abstain from dealing in the securities or disclose such information to other parties with whom one deals. As expressed in *Clark* (1991) the elements of the theory are:

1. Misappropriation of material nonpublic information
2. By breaching a duty arising out of a relationship of trust and confidence and
3. uses that information in a securities transaction,
4. Regardless of whether duties are owed to the shareholders of the traded stock.

The theory has been accepted in District Courts [*Willis* (1990), *Peters* (1990), *Eliot* (1989)], and recognized in the Second [*Libera* (1993), *Materia* (1984), and *Newman* (1981)], Seventh [*Maio* (1995) and *Cherif* (1991)], Ninth [*Clark* (1991], and arguably the Third Circuit [*Rothberg* (1985)]. The Supreme Court has not however explicitly accepted nor rejected the theory. In *Carpenter* (1987) the Supreme Court was evenly divided regarding the misappropriation theory in affirming a securities law conviction. The two most recent Circuit Court decisions regarding the misappropriation theory however raise questions about its continued viability and that of related SEC enforcement tools.

O'HAGAN

The Eighth Circuit case of *United States of America* v. *O'Hagan* (1996), concerned an appeal of District Court convictions for securities law violations under Rule 10(b), 10(b)(5) and Rule 14(e) and 14(e)(3). The facts involved use of material nonpublic information by a partner (O'Hagan) in a law firm to purchase call options in a company (Pillsbury) which he knew was a takeover target of a client corporation (GrandMet, LLC). The takeover eventually took place at which time the value of the target company stock underwent substantial increase. O'Hagan then exercised his options and sold his entire interest in Pillsbury. The sale resulted in a profit of more than 4 million dollars.

The District Court found O'Hagan guilty under the misappropriation theory. The government did not allege violation of Rule 10(b)(5) under the classical theory due to O'Hagan not being an insider of the corporation in whose stock he traded. The 8th Circuit rejected the misappropriation theory.

According to the court, Rule 10(b) requires material misrepresentation or nondisclosure where there exists a duty to disclose. In this instance there was no misrepresentation (deception). In addition, there was no duty to disclose. In order for there to be a duty to disclose the court noted there must be a fiduciary type relationship. No such relationship was considered held between the defendant and party with whom the business was transacted. While a fiduciary obligation was violated to the client company and possibly the law firm it did not exist with the third party to the transaction. The court found the mere touching of the transaction indirectly by this type breach was inadequate to support a Rule 10(b)(5) violation under the circumstances. The possession of nonpublic information does not create by itself a duty to disclose. Imposing this type of broad requirement would inhibit market analysis and negatively impact the health of the market. It would also be inconsistent with the narrow reading given the statute by the Supreme Court (see *Central Bank*). In addition, the misappropriation theory was found wanting in that it did not require a showing of deception and did not entail manipulation as prescribed by Section 10(b).

The Court also addressed whether fraud convictions under Section 14 (e) and Rule 14(e)-3 should be vacated due to the SEC improperly defining fraud without requiring there to be a breach of a fiduciary duty. Section 14(e) of the Securities Exchange act and Rule 14e-3 were established as part of the Williams act and intended to protect investors from fraud and having to deal without adequate information where confronted by a cash tender offer for their stock. According to 14(e):

> It shall be unlawful for any person to make any untrue statement of a material fact or omit to state any material fact necessary in order to make the statements made, in the light of the circumstances under which they are made, not misleading, or to engage in any fraudulent, deceptive, or manipulative acts or practices, in connection with any tender offer...The [SEC] shall, for purposes of this subsection, by rules and regulations define, and prescribe means reasonably designed to prevent, such acts and practices as are fraudulent, deceptive, or manipulative.

In 1980 the SEC issued Rule 14e-3, which provides:

> (a) If any person has taken a substantial step or steps to commence, or has commenced, a tender offer (the "offering person"), it shall constitute a fraudulent, deceptive, or manipulative act or practice within the meaning of Section 14(e) of the Securities Exchange] Act for any other person who is in possession of material information relating to such tender offer which information he knows or has reason to know is nonpublic and which he knows or has reason to know has been acquired directly or indirectly from:
>
> 1. the offering person,
> 2. the issuer of the securities sought or to be sought by such tender offer, or
> 3. Any officer, director, partner, or employee or any other person acting on behalf of the offering person or such issuer,
>
> to purchase or sell or cause to be purchased or sold any of such securities or any securities convertible into or exchangeable for any such securities or any option or right to obtain or dispose of any of the foregoing securities, unless within a reasonable time prior to any purchase or sale such information and its sources are publicly disclosed by press release or otherwise.

The Court ruled Rule 14e-3 to be invalid due to exceeding the SEC's statutory authority. In so ruling the Court took focused on what it considered to be an attempt by the Commission to redefine the term "fraudulent" in a manner at odds with that presented in the underlying statute. In this regard the definition lacks the requirement that there be a breach of a fiduciary duty. This was determined by looking at the legislative history and following court precedent of strict statutory interpretation.

The decision and reasoning of *O'Hagan* is consistent with that of the Fourth Circuit in *U.S* v. *Bryan* (1995). In *Bryan* the misappropriation theory was rejected and a fraud conviction overturned. The case concerned an officer of the West Virginia Lottery who through his position became aware of nonpublic information regarding a lucrative contract that would be given by the lottery to a company. Based upon this information, and in alleged breach of his duty to the lottery, the officer engaged in trading resulting in substantial gain. As in *O'Hagan* the court found the language of Rule 10(b) not to support the conviction. The court based its decision in large part upon the Supreme Court acceptance of a strict statutory construction approach to securities law, and the absence of a duty to disclose between the officer and the parties with whom trading was done.

CONCLUSION

The *O'Hagan* and *Bryan* decisions reflect the attempt of courts to implement strict statutory construction and establish a pattern of reliability and predictability in the securities laws. The rejection of Rule 14e-3 in *O'Hagan* raises questions concerning other SEC interpretations and implied causes of action. The case itself may reflect courts not only rejecting traditional expansive doctrines but rejecting established theories that may arguably be supported by a reasonable interpretation of the language of the statute. This may suggest an even stronger turning away from novel arguments raised in civil and criminal actions to the detriment of those parties the securities laws were enacted to protect. The recent shift of the pendulum appears to have been desirable both for the capital markets and professionals like accountants who render services related to it. In the future however the predominant questions may be whether the pendulum has shifted so far in the other direction that the rights of injured third parties and the integrity of the markets are not adequately protected. Recently, at the request of the SEC, the Supreme Court of the United States has agreed to review *O'Hagan* and the matter of the defendant who traded stock but was held by the Eight Circuit as not having acted "in connection with" the purchase or sale of a security for Section 10(b)(5) purposes. At present, in light of strict statutory construction, the onus for appropriate action appears to have been placed in the hands of Congress—and perhaps for the sake of predictability, consistency and fairness to all parties, that is where it should be.

REFERENCES

Anonymous. 1996. SEC asks justices to restore a key enforcement tool. *Wall Street Journal*, December 3, p. B14.

United States v. *Bryan*, 58 F.3d 933 (4th Cir. 1995).

Carpenter v. *United States*, 484 U.S. 19 (1987).

Chiarella v. *United States*, 455 U.S. 222 (1980).

SEC v. *Cherif*, 933 F.2d 403 (7th Cir. 1991).

SEC v. *Clark*, 915 F.2d 439.

SEC v. *Elliot*, 711 F. Supp. 425 (N.D. III. 1989).

United States v. *O'Hagan*, 92 F.3d 612, reh. denied, (8th Cir. 1996).

United States v. *Libera*, 989 F.2d 596, cert. denied, subnorm. *Sablone* v. *United States*, 114 S.CT. 467 (1993).

SEC v. *Materia*, 745 F.2d 197 (2d Cir. 1984).

SEC v. *Maio*, 51 F.3d 623 12 (2d Cir. 1981), aff'd after remand, 722 F.2d 729 (2d Cir.), cert. denied, 464 U.S. 863 (1983).
SEC v. *Peters*, 735 F. Supp. 1505 (D. Kan. 1990).
Rothberg v. *Rosenbloom*, 771 F.2d 818 (3d Cir. 1985), rev'd after remand, 808 F.2d 252 (3d Cir. 1986), cert. denied 481 U.S. 1017 (1987).
United States v. *Willis*, 737 F. Supp. 269 (SDNY 1990).

A PERPLEXED ACCOUNTING STUDENT'S GUIDE THROUGH THE SEC MAZE

Barbara Clemenson

INTRODUCTION

When you are first introduced to the Securities and Exchange Commission (SEC) and its publications, it is easy to become perplexed and lost as you attempt to conduct research. I know. I have been thrown into the deep end and expected to swim. I managed, but it was not easy. These are the things I wish I had known before I was sent off to research. I hope they will help you better understand the SEC maze and lessen your perplexity.

After obtaining a basic understanding of the SEC, its purpose, and its requirements for public companies through secondary sources, it is helpful before conducting research to learn about the SEC's publications. Paul B. W. Miller and Jack Robertson's "A Guide to SEC Regu-

Research in Accounting Regulation, Volume 11, pages 223-230.

ISBN: 0-7623-0168-6

lations and Publications: Mastering the Maze"[1] will provide you with the basic structure you need. But how do you find the these publications, and how can you most effectively use them?

The Commission's official code (regulations) is published in the *Code of Federal Regulations*. This is an extensive, multivolume work, including an index volume, published annually by the government. It can be found in any law library. All of the SEC's codes are in "Title 17," which you will see on the spine of several of the *Code's* volumes. You may look in these volumes for SEC information. Fortunately, each volume has a table of contents which will help you locate what you need. The "Titles" are divided into sections known as "Parts," which are numbered. When you are researching the SEC in other sources, you will find references such as **17 CFR Part 210**. This refers to the specific portion of the SEC official code found in Title 17, Part 210 of the *Code of Federal Regulations.* The Parts are further divided into Subparts.

You are probably, though, using one or more SEC handbooks. The organization of these books differs from company to publisher, and it is perhaps most helpful when conducting SEC research to use two or more together. What you cannot readily find in one book's index, you might be able to locate in another. However, all of the books contain the same basic information.

SEC Forms

These are the basic forms required by the SEC. For myself, as I have learned the purpose of each form, I have written that next to the form's designation in the handbook's table of contents. This way I have a quick reference to determine which form I need.

SEC Regulations

Regulation S-X concerns the SEC's accounting rules for financial statements required by the Commission. You will see that these regulations are part of **17 CFR Part 210**; that is, they can be found in Title 17, Part 210 of the *Code of Federal Regulations.* The Regulation is broken down into "Regs." Notice that each "Reg." in Regulation S-X begins with "210." That is because this entire Regulation can be found in Part 210 of CFR Title 17. After the "210" there is a period and then another set of numbers. This last set of numbers is often referred to in the literature and by professors as "Rules." Therefore, when you read that something refers to Rule 2-01 of Regulation S-X, look for **Reg. §210.2-01**.

Regulation S-K concerns non-financial information required by the SEC; Regulation S-B, disclosures for small business issuers; and Regulation S-T, rules and regulations for electronic filings. Notice that these Regulations contain "Items." Sometimes books or professors will refer to these Items as "Rules." Do not let that confuse you. When they refer to Rule 101 of Regulation S-K, they are referring to "Item 101: Description of Business." Fortunately each Regulation is preceded by a Table of Content which assists in finding information. Therefore, if you know you are looking for financial reporting requirements, you can look in the table of content for Regulation S-X and hopefully determine where to find what you need. Regulation S-K is found in Part 229 of Title 17 of the *Code of Federal Regulations;* Regulation S-B in Part 228; and Regulation S-T in Part 232. The numbering is the same as that described above for Regulation S-X.

These forms and regulations are the SEC's minimal disclosures and rules which must be followed in complying with the Securities Acts. A quick guide to help you locate the various forms, rules and regulations within the *Code of Federal Regulations* can be found in Title 17, Part 200, Subpart N, Section 800 (**17 CFR 200.800**). Although this deals specifically with control numbers and expiration dates assigned to information collection requirements pursuant to the Paperwork Reduction Act of 1980, this several-page table also lists where each form, rule and regulation is located in **17 CRF** and is extremely helpful in quickly locating information.

The SEC publishes other official communications. Until 1982 it issued *Accounting Series Releases* (ASR) to communicate to the accounting profession its official position on SEC financial reporting matters and its enforcement actions concerning SEC registrants and their auditors. The Commission issued a total of 307 of these *Releases*. These can be found listed in any SEC Handbook.

The *Releases*, along with all official federal government documents, are published a few days after they are filed in the *Federal Register,* which is published every business day and can be located in any law library. Documents in the *Federal Register* are referenced by the volume in which they are published (one volume per year) and the page number on which they begin (with each volume having continuous pagination throughout the volume). Thus, the reference **47 FR 21030** indicates that this document is published in Volume 47 of the *Federal*

Register beginning on page 21030. Volume 47 happens to be the Volume for 1982. When you look up ASRs in the *Federal Register*, the heading will tell you they affect Title 17, Part 211: "Interpretive Releases Relating to Accounting Matters (Accounting Series Releases)." You will then see in the text a number such as **211.81**. The number after **211** is the ASR Number, in this case ASR Number 81.

If you know the year of a document but do not know its location in the *Register*, you may look it up by subject in the *Index to the Federal Register*. In earlier years you will need to use the single small volume index published by the government; however for more recent years, detailed, commercially published semi-annual volumes have been produced in both hard copy and on CD-ROM which makes searching much easier.

The *Code of Federal Regulations* is actually a special annual edition of the *Federal Register* which codifies each Federal Regulation of general applicability and legal effect first published in the *Federal Register*. Therefore information in the *Code* is referenced back to the *Register* where original documents might be found; while information published in the *Register* indicates the Title and Parts of the *Code* which are affected by the release.

The Commission realized in 1982 that it was difficult for accountants to constantly refer to their numerous *Releases*, especially since of the 307 total *Releases*, 79 were no longer relevant and 57 had been rescinded. It was even more difficult since the *Releases* dealt with both financial reporting and enforcement actions. So on April 15, 1982 the SEC decided to codify into a single document the financial reporting information in the still-relevant ASRs and provide an index to the ASRs which dealt with enforcement actions.[2] This document can be found at **47 FR 21030**: Volume 47 of the *Federal Register*, beginning on page 21030, which happens to be the issue of the *Register* published on May 17, 1982.

The Commission also decided that in the future it would no longer publish ASRs, but rather publish two types of releases: *Financial Reporting Releases* (FRRs, sometimes referred to simply as FRs), dealing with financial reporting matters; and *Accounting and Auditing Enforcement Releases* (AAERs). The SEC also publishes *Staff Accounting Bulletins*. These *Bulletins* do not reflect the official position of the Commission, but do provide guidance as to how the staff of the SEC is dealing with various matters. These are all published in the *Federal Register*. You can obtain a "table of contents" indicating their location in the *Register* from **17 CFR Part 211**: "Interpretations Relating to Financial Reporting Matters," in Title 17 of the *Code of Federal Regulations*. Photocopy these pages and keep them with you. Knowing the precise location of these documents will save you from having to cull through the *Federal Register* indexes.

As you research in the Regulations, you will find notes at the end many of the sections such as: **As last amended in Release No. FR-21, June 6, 1985, 50 F.R. 25214**. That means that the last refinement of this particular regulation can be found in *Financial Reporting Release No. 21*, located on page 25214 in Volume 50 of the *Federal Register*.

47 FR 21030 comprises both *Financial Reporting Release No. 1* and *Accounting and Auditing Enforcement Release No. 1*. FR-1, remember, is the Codification of the SEC's financial reporting policies. The SEC itself states the purpose of this codification:

> The purpose of the codification is to provide one document which is organized in a logical manner and which can be used as a reference for the Commission's current published positions on accounting and auditing.

This codification will be found in your SEC handbooks preceded by a Table of Contents which helps you locate information topically. Each section indicates the ASR or FR from which the information is garnered. If you are asked questions about specific ASRs, a list of these is typically found at the end of this codification and will reference the section within the code where information about that specific ASR may be found, provided it has not been rescinded or omitted because its material was obsolete or unnecessary. If such is the case, the list will give you that information.

47 FR 21030 also comprises *Accounting and Auditing Enforcement Release No. 1*. This release is a topical index, including short summaries of ASRs relating to SEC enforcement actions. The topics listed are:

Accounting Principles	Deferred Assets	Partner's Review
Advances	Disciplinary Actions	Payables
Advertising	Disclosure	Percentage of Completion Method
Alteration of Accounting Records	Due Process	Planning & Supervision
Analytical Review and Procedures	Errors & Irregularities	Pooling
Appraisal Surplus	Expert Witnesses	Post Audit Review

(continued)

Appraisals	Experts	
Audit	Exploration Costs	Proxy Statement
Audit Fee	Extraordinary Income	Quality Control
Audit Program	Generally Accepted Accounting Principles	Receivables
Audit Report	Inputted Interest	Regulation S-X
Audit Scope	Independence	Related Party Transactions
Bookkeeping	Insurance	Reliance on Another Auditor
Broker-Dealer	Intangible Assets	Repairs & Maintenance
Capitalization	Intercompany Transactions	Representations Made to Commission's Staff
Cash Basis Accounting	Internal Control	Reserves
Change in Accounting Principles	Inventory	Revenue
Claims	Leases	Rules of Practice Before the Commission
Collateral	Legal Opinion	Sales
Collectability	Management (Accountants as Members of)	Securities Act of 1933
Combined Financial Statements	Management Representation Letter	Securities and Exchange Act of 1934
Comfort Letter	Management Representations	Security Agreements
Commercial Paper	Manipulation (Market)	Statements on Auditing Procedures (SAP)
Computer	Matching Concept	Statements on Auditing Standards (SAS)
Concurring Partner Review	Mergers (of Accounting Firms)	Subsequent Discovery of Facts
Confirmations	Nonmonetary Transactions	Window Dressing Transactions
Consultations	Notification	Working Papers
Contingent Liability	Prior Period Adjustments	Write Downs
Correspondent Auditor	Offering Circular	

If you are questioned about SEC enforcement actions, consult this AAER to determine ASRs relevant to your research.

The *Releases* published in the *Federal Register* provide much more information than will be found in SEC handbooks, including the Commission's reasons for the *Releases* and the manner in which they decided upon their opinions. Looking them up in the *Register* will give you a deeper understanding and appreciation of the Commission's Regulations. As an example, let's look at ASR No. 81 dealing with auditor independence.

ASR No. 81, "Independence of Certifying Accountants—Compilation of Representative Administrative Rulings in Cases Involving the Independence of Accountants," was released on December 11, 1958 and published in **23 FR 9777** (Volume 23, No. 247, December 19, 1958 of the *Federal Register*). This ASR summarizes cases in the Commission's experience under the independence rule (Rule 2-01 of Regulation S-X) since the publication of ASR No. 47 on January 25, 1944.[3]

ASR No. 81 was deemed necessary to summarize previously unpublished rulings because of the growth of the accounting profession and the number of inquiries the SEC received from accountants. It "...reflects the development of policy regarding the practice of accountants before the Commission over a period of some twenty-five years." The ASR states briefly relationships in which accountants' independence is compromised and therefore they do not have the right to certify financial statements filed with the SEC, as well as relationships in which their independence is not compromised.

The ASR begins by stating that:

> The concept of independence was well developed and the value of a review by independent accountants who are in no way connected with the business was established before the passage of the first Act now administered by the Commission....

However, it continues, the original draft of the Securities Act did not require such certification. Col. A. H. Carter, President of the New York Society of CPAs, appeared before the Committee on Banking and Currency suggesting the bill be revised to include financial statement certification by independent auditors. If independent auditors did not certified the filed financial statements, then government auditors would have to do so.

ASR No. 81 further states:

> The Committee considered at length the value to investors and to the public of an audit of accountants not connected with the company or management and whether the additional expense to industry of an audit by independent accountants was justified by the expected benefits to the public. The Committee also considered the advisability and feasibility of requiring the audit to be made by accountants on the staff of the agency administering the Act.
>
> ...[I]t was deemed essential to refrain from placing upon any Federal Agency the duty of passing judgment upon the soundness of any security.

Therefore the final Securities Act required that qualified independent auditors must ascertain the fairness of presented financial statements.

The history elucidated in this ASR highlights both an important milestone in the development of government policy towards the capital market and the affect it had on the accounting profession, as well as how the profession works with and influences the government. In 1933 the government might well have taken upon itself the duty of certifying registrants' financial statements. Had this happened, the future of the profession would not have been in public accounting, but in government accounting. Auditors would have been employed by the federal government to certify financial statements. The government, also, would have developed much more direct control not only over the accounting profession, but also over the country's capital market as it would have determined which securities it deemed were sound enough to be listed on the exchanges instead of letting investors make their own decisions. But the profession appealed to the Committee drafting the law and convinced it of the importance of allowing non-government auditors to certify statements. In return for this franchise, though, the government insisted upon auditor independence: "...in no way connected with the business."

Looking at this actual ASR itself not only teaches us about auditor independence but also reveals an historic decision for both the SEC and the accounting profession as to who would certify financial statements filed with the government. It also illustrates the interaction between the government and the profession.

The SEC will only come to life for you as you learn and research for yourself. Hopefully this guide will alleviate some of your confusion as to how to find SEC information and encourage you to go beyond simply finding "quick" answers and instead look at original documents published in the *Federal Register* to understand how and why the SEC has acted as it has.

NOTES

1. Miller, P.B.W., and J. Robertson. 1989. A guide to SEC regulations and publications: Mastering the maze. In *Research in Accounting Regulation*, Vol. 3, 239-249, ed. by G.J. Previts. Greenwich, CT: JAI Press.

2. This publication is part of the Commission's continuing efforts to review the rules, regulations and releases, and to delete requirements that are no longer necessary and to simplify the remainder.

3. ASR No. 47 was an interpretive release holding that the question of independence was one of fact, to be determined in the light of all pertinent circumstances in each particular case. It also stated that it was not feasible to present in summarize form the circumstances which were determined not to compromise an accountant's independence.

PART IV

REVIEWS AND ESSAYS

Review: The Accounting Profession: Major Issues: Progress and Concerns
(Report to the Ranking Minority Member, Committee on Commerce, House of Representatives)

by United States General Accounting Office

(Washington, DC: U.S. Government Printing Office, September 1996, 2 vols.; Vol.I, 139 pp.; Vol. II, 174 pp.)

Reviewed by **E. James Burton**

On September 24, 1996, near the completion of his term as Comptroller General of the United States, Charles A. Bowsher presented a two-volume study to The Honorable John D. Dingell, Ranking Minority Member, Committee on Commerce, United States House of Representatives. The work was conducted over approximately 16 months from February, 1995, to May, 1996, (I, 36). In his letter of transmittal, Mr. Bowsher said:

> This two-volume report responds to your request concerning the status of recommendations made to the accounting profession over the past two decades by major study groups. Our objectives were to identify (1) recommendations made from 1972 through 1995 to improve accounting and auditing standards and the performance of independent audits under the federal securities laws and the actions taken on those recommendations and (2) any unresolved issues to determine their impact on the performance of independent audits, effective accounting and auditing standards setting, and efforts to expand the scope of business reporting and auditing services. (I,1)

Research in Accounting Regulation, Volume 11, pages 233-239.

ISBN: 0-7623-0168-6

OVERVIEW

Volume I is a 139 page treatise beginning with a 25 page **Executive Summary** and an 11 page **Introduction**. Included in the Introduction is a **Timeline of Major Issues Debated Over the Past Two Decades** (I,33). This timeline divides the period from 1972-1995 into 5 segments (1972-76, 1977-81, 1982-86, 1987-91, and 1992-95) and charts five (5) major issues and the various study groups that addressed these issues. These five (5) issues are:

Auditor independence
Audit quality (includes auditor's role, responsibilities, and performance)
Setting accounting standards
Setting auditing standards
Expanded reporting and auditing services

Chapters 2-6 of Volume I address these issues though not in exact correspondence. The chapters are:

Chapter 2	Auditor Independence	23 pages
Chapter 3	Auditor's Responsibilities for Fraud and Internal Control	21 pages
Chapter 4	Initiatives to Improve Audit Quality	13 pages
Chapter 5	Accounting and Auditing Standard Setting and the Financial Reporting Model	31 pages
Chapter 6	Impact of Growing Business Complexity on the Traditional Audit Function	15 pages

Each of these chapters is similarly organized with a discussion of the issue followed by **Observations** and **Comments and Our Evaluation**.

Volume II is 174 pages of **Appendixes to Major Issues: Progress and Concerns**. It contains:

	Letter of Transmittal
Appendix I	Major Studies of the Accounting Profession From 1972 Through 1995
Appendix II	Recommendations From 1972 Through 1995 and Actions Taken to Improve Auditing and Financial Reporting

Appendix III	Statements, Opinions, and Releases Referenced in Appendix II
Appendix IV	Experts Consulted in Our Review of the Accounting Profession
Appendix V	Comments From the American Institute of Certified Public Accountants
Appendix VI	Comments From the Public Oversight Board
Appendix VII	Comments From the Financial Accounting Standards Board
Appendix VIII	Comments From the Securities and Exchange Commission
Appendix IX	Major Contributors to This Report

In particular, Appendix I and Appendix II provide comprehensive historical overviews. Appendix I contains a listing of 37 studies, identifying the **Study/Date/Members** and the **Background** of each study. Appendix II is organized around the five (5) content chapters of Volume I. For each of these the Appendix contains **Recommendations, Action Taken, Recommendation made by/date**, and **Recommendation directed to**. For Auditor Independence, 100 separate recommendations are listed. For Audit Quality, 189 recommendations are detailed. For Setting Accounting Standards, 130 recommendations are shown. For Setting Auditing Standards, 30 recommendations are given. For Expanded Reporting and Auditor Services, 125 recommendations are provided.

ANALYSIS

This two-volume work is a significant addition to the literature, providing what is, arguably, the most comprehensive conjoint analysis of the major initiatives in accounting over the study period. In this respect, Mr. Bowsher and the other major contributors to the report, listed in Appendix IX, have done a splendid job. While one senses the influence of Representative John Dingell in the **Observations**, the analysis is thorough and mostly dispassionate. One criticism to be offered relates to that which might have been done which would have added further value. That is, a thorough, two-way, cross-referencing of Appendix II and Appendix III would provide considerable value in following through from **Recommendation** to **Action Taken** and to tracing the precipitating causes for various **Statements, Opinions and Releases**. These two Appendixes do not articulate as well as one might have expected from such a comprehensive work.

The "sound bites" contained in the **Executive Summary** provide insight into what the full study may mean to our ability to explain and to anticipate relationships between the federal government and the profession. In short summary, the analysis is dispassionate but the **Observations** are not. They suggest that government agencies, in particular the SEC, have but have not exercised sufficient authority to cause resolution to these major issues over the study period and these government agencies should exert more authority in the future.

The study indicates that the profession has, through many and various means, attempted to respond to issues. Progress is evident in improving financial reporting and in the auditing process for public companies. Firms auditing SEC registered companies have developed and implemented effective quality assurance programs. Yet, the issues remain and are not yet fully resolved. (I, 4)

Changes in the nature, scope, and complexity of business transactions are not well handled by traditional models. Auditors are being forced to adapt to more timely, relevant data than historically. The report suggests that the auditor's ability to accomplish this difficult task is directly linked to the ability to review and report on internal control structure. Yet, there is an ongoing concern about the coupling of such assurances with the increasing volume of other consulting services and the issue of independence. Changes in the auditor/client relationship are indicated—reporting directly to a board of directors or to an independent audit committee are suggested. (I, 5-6).

The study also suggests that the current financial reporting model is passé and that some change is necessary to adapt it to future needs. Information technology makes data access readily available to investors on a timely basis and the profession must be responsive. Since it is not feasible to review data on a continuous basis as investors access it, some form of assurance on the generation of the data is warranted. (I,6)

Bowsher praises the SEC for increasing public representation in the FASB process and suggests that this "leadership" should be extended in a cooperative venture with the profession to address the other issues of the study. (I, 6) The GAO seems to advocate that pressures be brought to bear on the SEC to move resolution of the issues as quickly as possible.

In the section of the **Executive Summary** labeled **Recommendations**, the report says:

> Although GAO is not making recommendations in this report, GAO believes the SEC, given its responsibilities under federal securities laws, is in a pivotal position to assume a leadership role in working with not only the accounting profession, but also the stock exchanges, public companies, and users of financial reporting to resolve these issues. (I, 18)

The section entitled **Principal Findings** contains a number of statements which seem to contradict the idea that "GAO is not making recommendations." Consider the following:

> GAO believes measures that would limit auditor services or mandate changing auditors at set intervals are outweighed by the value of continuity in conducting audits and the value of traditional consulting services. *However*, GAO also believes that questions of auditor independence will continue as long as the existing auditor/client relationship continues. (emphasis added) (I, 8)

> GAO supports a recent proposal by the AICPA's Public Oversight Board to bring the independent auditor into a more direct working relationship with the board of directors. (I, 8)

> As an alternative to voluntary action, the SEC, which has the responsibility and authority under federal security laws to ensure that accountants who audit companies registered with the SEC are independent, could more clearly define the roles of boards of directors and audit committees as they relate to the independent auditor. (I, 9)

The GAO also suggests that the SEC, working with stock exchanges, could make the changes without legislation using listing requirements as the vehicle. It seems apparent that the GAO is recommending major changes in the auditor/client relationship and attempting to show the SEC that it has the authority and responsibility to make those changes happen and that "GAO does not believe that many businesses will likely voluntarily change the auditor/client relationship." (I, 11)

The report also links the auditor's ability to assess internal controls with the responsibility for preventing and detecting fraud. It suggests that, "The scope of audit work required by existing standards is too limited to address..." the expectations of the public concerning fraud and risk management controls. (I, 10)

> GAO believes that auditor reporting on the effectiveness of internal controls is fundamental in successfully addressing the public expectation gap for fraud. GAO's work on internal controls and compliance with laws and regulations as a part of its financial statement audits of federal entities shows that auditors have the capacity to examine the adequacy of controls to prevent and detect fraud in financial reporting and in the acquisition, use, and disposition of assets. (I, 10)

The report applies subtle pressure with the statement:

> GAO has expressed concern that weak controls, given the large volume of derivatives activity among major brokers and dealers, pose a *systemic risk to the stability of the entire financial system.* (emphasis added) (I, 11)

It is interesting to note that GAO uses itself as the standard to indicate the ability to prevent and detect fraud. Virtual daily reports of fraud in Medicare, Medicaid, student loans, defense contracts, etc. do not seem to validate GAO's assertions. Additionally, the relationship between GAO and its "clients" is not the same as the relationship its seeks to change. Nonetheless, "GAO expects that audits will be expanded to include internal control reporting, either because of market demand or some systemic crisis." (I, 12)

GAO indicates that it analyzed 724 peer review reports during 1992-1994. While only a small portion (10%) were modified, GAO expresses concern about the frequency with which certain weaknesses in reports were found. The report advocates closer audit supervision and suggests that the AICPA enhanced requirements are, at least, a partial remedy for this. (I, 13)

The report suggests that the standard-setting process is flawed because of the limited involvement of users, the timeliness of issuing standards, and the pressures brought by certain interest groups. While they agree that the AICPA and FASB have attempted to deal with these problems, it is clear that the result is not considered satisfactory. The report praises the SEC for the authority it has exerted to strengthen the process, reinforces the idea that the SEC has "ultimate authority" for the process, and says that, "…it is important that the SEC monitor the operation of the standard-setting process to ensure FASB's ability to objectively set standards." (I, 14-15) GAO does suggest that changes to the manner of operation of the FASB must be balanced with a concern that standard setting continue to be independent since independence is viewed as essential to ultimate acceptance of the process.

GAO recognizes there are realistic difficulties in implementing changes in the financial reporting model—"…cost of preparing and auditing expanded disclosures, disclosure overload, and litigation risk." (I, 16). In a conciliatory statement, the report says:

> GAO believes it will take a concerted effort by the AICPA, FASB, the SEC, and other interested parties to achieve a comprehensive reporting model that meets the needs of today's financial statement users. (I, 18)

This is immediately followed by a statement which appears to be anything but conciliatory:

> How the accounting profession handles this issue will affect the nature and extent of its future role in providing business information to users. *Absent strong leadership from the SEC, obstacles to implementing a comprehensive model will be even more difficult to overcome.* (emphasis added) (I, 18)

CONCLUSION

This two-volume study is a significant addition to the literature. It pulls much needed information together in a comprehensive, readable format and should stimulate productive conversation about substantive issues. It is not, however, without bias.

One can expect Representative Dingell to use this report as continuing leverage to press the SEC to take a more aggressive role in the standard setting process, to change the current financial reporting model, to make auditors more responsible for assessing and reporting on internal controls and for detecting and preventing fraud, and to change the auditor/client relationship.

Although the Private Securities Litigation Reform Act of 1995 might be viewed as providing some protection from "unknowingly" committed acts, the suggestions contained in this report bode ill for the accounting profession. It appears that the GAO is suggesting more government involvement based at least partially on a model (the GAO) that is not congruent to the situation and, even if it were, does not show promise of better results than have been attained.

Performance Results in Value Added Reporting

by Ahmed Riahi-Belkaoui

(Westport, CT: Quorum Books, 1996, 171 pp.)

Reviewed by **Ronald L. Campbell**

Globalization has caused accounting standards-setters to give more consideration to accounting issues, policies and procedures affecting disclosure. Currently one major concern is whether there should be common accounting practices among U.S. firms and all multi-national firms. More importantly, a concern of accounting standards-setters continues to be the kinds of accounting information to disclose and the placement and format of these disclosures. Ahmed Riahi-Belkaoui's book entitled *Performance Results in Value Added Reporting* presents very pertinent theories and research methodologies that directly address these present day accounting disclosure issues.

Belkaoui epitomizes the role of accounting research in this book by reporting on his identification and investigation of accounting information that is useful and should be reported to a firm's stakeholders. Research methodologies that have been applied in his research are timely and appropriately used to investigate (1) the information content of accounting numbers derived from alternative accounting systems, and (2) the relationships of these accounting numbers to profitability, performance, and the price of the firm. All accounting data and sample firms are derived from the Compustat files and all security returns retrieved from the CRSP files. Regression analysis is the primary method of statistical testing, along with other statistical methods such as

Research in Accounting Regulation, Volume 11, pages 241-252.

ISBN: 0-7623-0168-6

correlation analysis, analysis of variance, and analysis of covariance. Belkaoui adequately tests for heteroskedasticity, unwanted correlation among regression variables, and provides for precision in estimation by including methods to reduce estimation error.

Belkaoui's 171 page book is an eight chapter discussion that advocates the need for an increase in Value Added (VA) reporting by U.S. firms. Specifically, he reports on his research methodologies that investigate and his research findings that provide evidence supporting VA Reporting. The overall research question is whether U.S. firms should be required to disclose accounting information that makes possible the computation of VA measures. VA is defined as a firm's total return to be ultimately distributed to providers of capital, employees, government and stockholders. Generally each chapter forms a strong link in the chain supporting VA reporting. Belkaoui's overall conclusion is that VA-based accounting measures provide information beyond that provided by conventional accounting-based measures. The overall implication for accounting policy-makers is that U.S. firms should be required to join many other multinational firms in disclosing accounting numbers that facilitate the computation of VA measures.

The discussion that follows is a chapter-by-chapter recapitulation of the book's contents, statistical methodologies, and findings. A conclusion ends this review.

Chapter 1. Value Added Reporting Under Price Change Models

Belkaoui defines VA reporting as the disclosure of a firm's wealth increase resulting from the productive use of the firm's resources prior to the allocation of that wealth to shareholders, bondholders, employees, and government. The underlying argument in chapter one is that an accounting-based profit measure is limited as a measure of a firm's change in wealth. Improved reporting, especially for U.S. firms, calls for the integration of VA reporting with the accounting for price level changes.

Six price level change models are tested to compare the VA statement against the conventional income statement. These models include: (1) historical cost, (2) replacement cost, (3) net realizable value, (4) historical cost with price level adjustment (PLA); (5) replacement cost with PLA, and (6) net realizable value with PLA.

A fictional example it used to test the performance of each model under the VA format and the conventional income statement format. The final analysis shows that under both formats the net realizable value model did not include any timing error or measurement error. The PLA did eliminate the measurement error from all models, while timing error remains in certain models. Belkaoui does not include the detail computations for either the timing or measurement errors. The model comparison shows the integration of VA disclosure with price level change models as a more accurate measure of change in wealth. Students and users of financial data should be aware of these models, their strengths, and limitations.

Chapter 2. Information Content of Value Added Data

Chapter two poses further argument that U.S. firms be required to disclose VA data. The research question is whether net value added (NVA), NVA/P_{BEG}, is appropriate for analyzing the association between VA and returns. Moreover, does the disclosure of nonearnings VA data provide any incremental information content when released concurrently with earnings? The relationship between NVA and returns is modeled as either

$$R_{jt} = a_{t0} + a_{t1}(NVA_{jt} - NVA_{t\text{-}1}) / P_{jt\text{-}1} + \ldots + a_{t5}(NVAt_{jt\text{-}4} - NVA_{jt\text{-}5}) / P_{jt\text{-}1} + \boldsymbol{E}, \qquad \text{[A]}$$

or

$$R_{jt} = a_{t0} + a_{t1}(NVA_{jt}) / P_{jt\text{-}1} + \ldots + a_{t5}(NVAt_{jt\text{-}4}) / P_{jt\text{-}1} + \boldsymbol{E}, \qquad \text{[B]}$$

where model A models price as a reflection of the past time-series changes in NVA and model B assumes that price is a reflection of the past time-series levels of NVA.

The results of regression models for pooled cross-sectional and time-series samples over a 10-year period are presented and supported by a test for heteroskedasticity. The models' R^2's are interpreted to indicate that levels of NVA and changes in NVA play a role in security pricing, even though levels model (B) performed better than the change model (A). The reader should note that one-half of the coefficients are not significant for the time-series levels model and the changes model's results were only slightly better while the coefficients for the pooled sample models are all significant at .01 level.

Corroborative finding are reported in the second section of the chapter. The information content of nonearnings measures of NVA is indicated when a statistically significant relationship is found between disclosed earnings and nonearnings measures of NVA and annual stock returns. This relationship is modeled as

$$(AP_{jt} + D_{jt}) \,/\, P_{jt\text{-}1} = a_0 + a_1 ECW_{jt} - a_2 NECW_{jt} + e_{jt}, \qquad \text{[C]}$$

where P is the security market price, D is the dividend, ECW is the earnings component of wealth, and $NECW$ is the nonearnings component of wealth.

The F-statistic is used to report significant results which support the information content of nonearnings NVA measures. The coefficients for all years are significant at the .05 level. Consistent with past research, the analyses are extended to include inflationary and growth effects. Grouping the firms into three portfolios based on inflation rate and GNP growth did not alter the signs of the earnings and nonearnings components of NVA. Overall, the market appears to view the returns to equity holders positively and the returns to other stakeholders negatively, as hypothesized. Additional evidence is provided that supports the relevance of VA data. Belkaoui calls for further research in this area.

Chapter 3. Explaining Market Returns: Value Added versus Earnings and Cash Flow

Further evidence on the superiority of VA data to accounting earnings and cash flow measures is presented in chapter three; essentially a continuation of chapter two. One research question is whether information "beyond the bottom line" (i.e., VA information), is relevant in explaining the behavior of security prices. A second question is whether the quality of the VA-based measure is determinable by the ability of that measure to aid in the prediction of securities' behaviors.

The traditional earnings valuation linear model tested is

$$(\Delta P_{jt} + D_{jt}) \,/\, P_{jt\text{-}1} = p(\Delta A_{jt} / P_{jt\text{-}1}) + U_{jt}, \qquad \text{[D]}$$

where P is the security price, D is the dividend, and A is the accounting earnings theorized to be most associated with security returns. The superiority (information content) of VA is tested using the linear model

$$(\Delta P_{jt} + D_{jt}) \,/\, P_{jt\text{-}1} = p(\Delta NVA / NVA_{jt\text{-}1}) + W_{jt}, \qquad \text{[E]}$$

where NVA is net value added. Pooled cross-sectional and time-series regressions show that security price changes are associated with both changes in earnings and with VA data. Models based on VA measurement, however, revealed more explanatory power than earning-based models. A model combining earnings and VA is specified as

$$R_{jt} = a_{t0} + a_{t1}RNVA + a_{t2}RE + \varepsilon_{jt}. \qquad [F]$$

The results are consistent with those for the individual models, but reveal more explanatory power.

Part two of chapter three is an investigation of the information content of VA versus earnings versus cash flow-based numbers. The return valuation model tested is

$$(\Delta P_{jt} + D_{jt}) / P_{jt-1} = a_0 + a_1(\Delta AR_{1,jt} / AR_{1,jt-1}) + a_2(\Delta AR_{1,jt} / AR_{1,jt-1}) + a_3(\Delta AR_{2jt} / AR_{2jt-1}) + a_4(\Delta AR_{2jt-1} / AR_{2,jt-2}) + e_{jt}. \qquad [G]$$

The potential impact of earlier years is included in this one-lag model where P is security price, D is dividend, and AR represents two measures of accounting returns derived from cash flow accounting and/or accrual accounting, and/or VA. Results show that while all three variables are significant in explaining security returns, VA shows greater relative information content than accrual accounting returns or cash flowing accounting returns.

The third segment of chapter three addresses the usefulness of cash flow accounting, accrual accounting, and VA reporting. The usefulness of indicators derived from each of these reporting systems is evaluated by observing their variability and persistency (i.e., median rank correlation between the indicator in the year of formation and the same number in the subsequent years). The indicators are rate of return measured as: (1) cash flow per share divided by stock price, (2) earnings per share divided by stock price, and (3) NVA per share divided by stock price, alternative measures of rate of return.

Computation of the statistical properties of these three indicators first reveals that the variability of the VA indicator, measured by the coefficient of variation, is extremely lower than that of the two remaining indicators. The author provides a theoretical discussion to explain the results. Briefly, the VA return is not plagued by intervening variables (e.g., classification decisions) that are variable in nature.

The median rank correlation for each indicator revealed a long-term persistency in the VA return while the persistency for the accrual and cash flow indicators are low. The theoretical explanation given for the variability difference is the same given for the persistency difference.

The final segment of chapter three is an investigation of the nonlinear specification relating unexpected earnings to market-adjusted returns. Belkaoui's research extends the literature by incorporating raw returns (rather than expected returns) and including NVA-based variables. His primary objective is to test whether more comprehensive disclosure of VA variables provides information relevant to security pricing. A secondary objective is to investigate nonlinearities previously detected by Beneish et al. (1993) and Freeman et al. (1982). The two linear models tested are

$$(P_{jt} + d_{jt}) / P_{jt\text{-}1} = a_{1jt} + a_{2jt}(A_{jt}/A_{jt\text{-}1}) + a_{3jt}SIZE_{jt} + a_{4jt}LEV_{jt} + a_{5jt}MB_{jt} + e_{3jt}, \quad [H]$$

and

$$(P_{jt} + d_{jt}) / P_{jt\text{-}1} = a_{1jt} + a_{2jt}(NVA_{jt}/NVA_{jt\text{-}1}) + a_{3jt}SIZE_{jt} + a_{4jt}LEV_{jt} + a_{5jt}MB_{jt} + e_{3jt}, \quad [I]$$

where *A* represents the accounting returns, *NVA* is net value added-based returns, *SIZE* is the natural log of assess, *LEV* is the long-term debt over total assets, and *MB* is the ratio of market to book value. The nonlinear models are

$$(P_{jt} + d_{jt}) / P_{jt\text{-}1} = b_{1jt} + b_{2jt}(A_{jt}/A_{jt\text{-}1}) + b_{3jt}D(A_{jt}/A_{jt\text{-}1})^2 + b_{4jt}SIZE_{jt} + b_{5jt}LEV_{jt} + b_{6jt}MB_{jt} + e_{4jt}, \quad [J]$$

and

$$(P_{jt} + d_{jt}) / P_{jt\text{-}1} = b'_{1jt} + b'_{2jt}(NVA_{jt}/NVA_{jt\text{-}1}) + b'_{3jt}D(NVA_{jt}/NVA_{jt\text{-}1})^2 + b'_{4jt}SIZE_{jt} + b'_{5jt}LEV_{jt} + b'_{6jt}MB_{jt} + e_{5jt}. \quad [K]$$

Cross-sectional and pooled cross-sectional regression results show that in the linear model the NVA to returns relationship is slightly stronger than the earnings-return relationship. Generally, the nonlinear models including the NVA-based earnings variable, rather than accounting earnings, have greater explanatory power. Overall, the nonlinear models have more explanatory power than the linear models (based on the adjusted R^2).

Chapter 4. Productivity, Profit, and Firm Value

The first three chapters provide strong evidence supporting the relevance of VA data in understanding security price changes. Moreover,

NVA data is shown to have more information content than traditional accounting-based or cash flow-based numbers. Belkaoui turns the focus in chapter four to productivity (a nonearnings variable) and its relevance in the prediction of future profitability and firm value. He uses Ohlson's valuation models to show the association between productivity and firm value. Productivity is the ratio NVA divided by total assets or sales.

Regression models to evaluate the prediction of future profitability are

$$ROE_{it+1} = B_0 + B_1 ROE_{it} + e_{it}, \qquad [L]$$

and

$$ROE_{it+1} = B_0 + B_1 ROE_{it} + B_2(NVA/TA_{it}) + e_{it}, \qquad [M]$$

where *ROE* is net income divided by book value of common equity and *NVA/TA* is the measure of productivity. Regression models to evaluate the relationship of productivity to firm value are

$$(1) \quad MV_{it} = Y_0 + Y_1 BV_{it} + e_{it}, \qquad [N]$$

$$(2) \quad MV_{it} = Y_0 + (Y_1 + Y_2 ROE_{it})\, BV_{it} + e_{it}, \qquad [O]$$

and

$$(3) \quad MV_{it} = Y_0 + (Y_1 + Y_2 ROE_{it} + Y_3[NVA_{it}/TA])\, BV_{it} + e_{it}, \qquad [P]$$

where *BV* is book value, *ROE* is net income divided by book value of common equity, and *NVA/TA* is defined to be productivity.

Models L and M show that productivity does not provide incremental information about future ROE above that provided current ROE information. The Pearson and Spearman Correlation Coefficient shows a positive correlation between current and future ROE. Models N, O, and P show that information about market value is provided by book value, ROE, and productivity, where the explanatory power is greatest for productivity (as included in model P). Thus, productivity is useful in understanding the role of accounting variables in predicting profitability and determining firm value.

Chapter 5. Performance Plan Adoption and Performance

Belkaoui introduces research on performance plans, determinants of plan adoption, and stock market reaction to plan adoptions in chapter five. The research contributions are: (1) the focus on ex post determinants of plan adoption, rather than ex ante determinants reported in prior research, (2) examination of profit performance rather than market performance, and (3) distinguishing between owner-controlled and manager controlled firms following plan adoption. The hypothesis supported by Belkaoui's longitudinal study is that following the adoption of performance plans, profit performance will increase in owner-controlled firms and decrease in manager-controlled firms. No hypotheses about VA data is noted in this chapter.

The framework for the research includes the Contingency Theory of Ownership Structure. Belkaoui borrows this theory whereby the affect of ownership structure on profit performance following performance plan adoption is dependent on whether the firm is owner controlled or manager controlled. The convergence-of-interest hypothesis and the entrenchment hypothesis are offered as two competing hypotheses depicting the relationship between a firm's performance and management's stock holdings.

Analysis of Covariance is performed to test for relationships and interactions. Other tests focus on the variable means and standard deviations by ownership structure before and after plan adoption. The overall results are a verification of the contention that performance plans are effective in aligning the interests of owners and managers The names of the firms included in the sample are listed in the chapter appendix.

Chapter 6. The Systematic Risk and Value Added Variables

Chapter six continues from chapter four's discussion on the usefulness of VA data. Belkaoui's objective is to test the incremental ability of VA measures to explain cross-sectional variations in firm risk (market betas) beyond the ability of earning-based and cash flow-based accounting numbers. The research question is whether market risk is captured in the value added measure beyond the component of risk captured by earnings or cash flow.

The research results show that generally VA does have incremental power. The regression analyses performed include three alternative measures of accounting beta (accounting-based, cash flow-based, and VA-based) as the independent variables and market risk as the dependent variable. The equation to compute market beta is the conventional market model:

$$R_{it} = a_i + \beta_i R_{mt} + u_{it}, \qquad [Q]$$

where R_{it} is the security i rate of return in period t, β is market beta, R_m is the market portfolio of return. Monthly returns over a 20-year period were used. For the same 20-year period, the estimates of accounting betas were based on the following regression:

$$r_{it} = a_i + b_i r_{mt} + e_{it}, \qquad [R]$$

where r_{it} is an accounting return variable, b_i is the accounting beta, and r_{mt} is the market index for accounting returns (i.e., an average of the sample accounting returns r_{it}). Beklaoui addresses Beta estimation error by implementing two approaches: (1) Vasicek's Bayesian technique, and (2) four-security portfolio analysis. Accounting return variables used were based on earnings, cash flow, and VA measures.

Results from seven regression models were tested where the dependent variable is the market risk and the independent variable(s) is (are) one, two or all three of the accounting beta measures. VA market betas showed the highest explanatory power; even models where VA betas were included with other betas showed an increase in overall explanatory power. A portfolio analysis, however, had greater explanatory power for earnings beta than VA. The VA variable still had significant explanatory power and added power in models with cash flow beta.

Correlation results based on Pearson's product movement correlation are consistent with the regression analysis. Belkaoui indicates that possible research limitations may be related to (1) sample size, and (2) the stability of findings over time.

Chapter 7. Takeover and Value Added Variables

VA-based data is characterized in chapter seven as a firm's ability to efficiently generate wealth. This ability and efficiency is measured by VA divided by total assets. The first research hypothesis is that the VA to total assets ratio is below the industry average for firms that experience takeover or merger. This hypothesis is tested by comparing the mean and median ratios of targeted firms with their industry ratios prior to the takeover.

Next, Belkaoui evaluates the relationship between a firm's wealth distribution potential and its cumulative abnormal returns. This measure of wealth distribution potential is defined as the difference between (1) the market ratio of VA to total assets, and (2) the firm's actual VA to total assets ratio (DVA). The second research hypothesis is that DVA is positively related to the cumulative abnormal returns of merged or takeover firms during the period from takeover announcement to actual takeover.

The full regression model to test the relationship between DVA and cumulative abnormal returns and including control variables is

$$CAR = b_0 + b_1 DVA + b_2 CASH + b_3 HF + b_4 BIDS + b_5 AFT80 + b_6 SIZE, \quad [S]$$

where *CAR* is the cumulative abnormal return of the target firm; *CASH* is an indicator variable where 1 is a primarily cash takeover and 0 otherwise; *HF* is an indicator variable where management reaction to the takeover equals 1 if management's reaction is hostile and 0 otherwise; *BIDS* is an indicator of the number of bidders equal to 1 if more than one bidder and 0 otherwise; *AFT80* is an indicator variable equal to 1 if the merger was before 1980 and equal to 0 if the merger was during or after 1980; and *SIZE* is the natural log of the firm's total assets at the beginning of the year prior to the year of the takeover announcement.

Two-tailed sign tests are performed to evaluate the first hypothesis. The comparison shows that the target firms have VA ratios significantly lower than non-target firms in their industries in the year prior to the year when the takeover is completed. Additionally, the signs of the DVA are (1) more positive than negative three years prior to the takeover completion (using the 4-digit SIC code), (2) more negative two years prior to the takeover completion, and (3) even more negative one year prior to takeover completion. The results are virtually the same using the 3-digit and 2-digit SIC code. Significant DVA are only reported under the 2-digit SIC for two years prior and one year prior to takeover completion.

Regression analysis is performed to test the relationship between cumulative abnormal returns and DVA (including the control variables). The cumulative abnormal returns are predicted by the market model and are the model's prediction errors for each day in the cumulation period cumulated to form CAR. The analysis excluding the control variables indicates no relationship between CAR and DVA. The coefficient for DVA is significant and positive when the control variables are included in the model. Coefficients for (1) CASH and BIDS are significantly and positive, (2) AFT80 are negative and significant at .10, and (3) not significant for HF and SIZE.

The research findings contribute to existing evidence that merger firms (target firms) are undervalued and substandard performers as indicated by other accounting and market-based variables. In addition, VA is useful as a measure of a firm's wealth distribution potential (i.e., DVA) whereby the greater the DVA the abnormal return of the firm increases (i.e., more wealth to distribute). Abnormal returns are even higher when there are multiple bidders for the target firm and the takeover is for cash.

Chapter 8. The Effects of Ownership Structure on Earning and Value added Performance

Ownership structure is revisited in chapter eight. Belkaoui's overall premise is that ownership structure has significant implications for a firm's efficiency and strategic development. The conceptual framework in this chapter is taken from the research of Morck, Schleifer, and Vishny and includes two measures of ownership structure and variables for diversification. Ownership structure is measured as either (1) management stockholding or (2) stock concentration. Related diversification and unrelated diversification are measured by the number of 4-digit SIC industries within a firm's 2-digit SIC and the number of two-digit SIC industries outside the primary 2-digit industry, respectively. Three research hypothesis are: (1) there is a positive (negative) association between a firm's performance and management stockholding held at a lower (higher) range; (2) there is a negative (positive) relationship between firm's performance and stock concentration at a lower (higher) range; and (3) there is a positive association between performance and diversification (where the relationship will be lower for unrelated diversification than for related diversification).

Piecewise regression analysis is performed where the dependent variable is either the log of net profit (a normalized measure) or market capitalization (number of common shares times year-end common share price). Independent variables are one of the two alternative ownership structure measures, the diversification measures, and total assets (a control variable). Turning points to determine low and higher range are 0-5% (low range) and 5-25% (higher range). The results show a nonmonotonic relationship between performance and ownership structure and a positive relationship between performance and diversification. The convergence-of-interest and the entrenchment hypotheses are supported.

Belkaoui's research premise in the second section of chapter eight is that VA measures of performance (i.e., total return) provide a better indicator of ownership structure effects on performance than accounting return-based performance measures. Three research hypotheses are: (1)

there is a negative (positive) association between a firm's NVA-based performance and management stockholding held at a lower (higher) range; (2) there is a negative (positive) relationship between firm's NVA-based performance and stock concentration at a lower (higher) range; and (3) there is a positive (negative) association between NVA-based performance and the sum of stock concentration and management stockholding at higher (lower).

The piecewise linear regression models utilize a turning point of 10% and the dependent variable is NVA divided by total assets. The results do not contradict other research supporting the entrenchment hypothesis. The 10% turning point used is in conformance with the results based on the 25% turning point. Fundamentally, NVA is negatively (positively) related to the three measures of ownership structure at lower (higher) levels. Belkaoui asserts the need, as implied by this study, to focus on VA-based performance rather than profit-based performance to better understand the diverse interests of shareholders and managers.

CONCLUSION

This text by Ahmed Riahi-Belkaoui is recommended for use in a doctoral research methods seminar and/or financial accounting seminar. The level of reading and research rigor is appropriate for doctoral students and would be an appropriate inclusion on the reading list in other related seminars. It is a very valuable source of information for individuals interested in and currently researching in the area of accounting disclosure and performance plans. The references at the end of each chapter are quite comprehensive and could prove most valuable to researchers. The book might also be used as supplemental reading in a masters level course (e.g., special topics) on financial accounting and disclosure. There is sufficient narrative such that master's level students could obtain a clear introduction to financial accounting reporting and disclosure without being bombarded by statistical models and analyses, and theorization.

WILLIAM VICKREY:
ECONOMIC TRANSACTIONS AND THE REAL WORLD

Thomas R. Robinson

William Vickrey was awarded the Nobel Prize in Economics on October 8, 1996 and passed away several days later at the age of 82. Given his long and productive career, it is perhaps appropriate that he died en route to an academic conference (Taxation, Resources, Economics and Development). Vickrey was born in British Columbia in 1914 and immigrated to the United States at an early age. He received a Bachelor of Science degree from Yale University in 1935, a Master's degree from Columbia University in 1937 and a Doctorate from Columbia University in 1947. Vickrey was Professor Emeritus at Columbia University and continued to make contributions to both academe and practice up to and even after his death (several essays have been published posthumously).

Research in Accounting Regulation, Volume 11, pages 253-256.

ISBN: 0-7623-0168-6

THE NOBEL PRIZE

These contributions to scholarly thought and their applications to the real world were acknowledged by The Royal Swedish Academy of Sciences in the awarding of the Bank of Sweden Prize in Economic Sciences in Memory of Alfred Nobel, 1996:

> William Vickrey has above all contributed to enhancing our knowledge about the efficient use of resources in the public sector. Notwithstanding his numerous and far-reaching practical applications, it is the depth of his theoretical endeavors which gives lasting value to his scientific lifework. Vickrey has a characteristic style of writing; almost in passing, he interposes deep insights in seemingly routine economic arguments. This has sometimes inferred that his theoretical contributions did not become apparent until long after they were written.

The award was presented for Professor Vickrey's contributions to economic theories of incentives under asymmetric information. The award was shared with Professor James Mirrlees of the University of Cambridge. While theoretical and analytical, this research has practical implications in a wide variety of settings including lending, insurance and even the sale of used cars. The Royal Swedish Academy of Sciences highlighted Professor Vickrey's development of the second-price auction. Vickrey presented this auction in a 1961 paper and it is commonly referred to as the Vickrey auction. In a second-price auction, bidders enter sealed bids with the winner (highest bidder) paying the second highest bid price. This type of auction is expected to result in bidding which represents an individuals true willingness to pay. Vickrey has made numerous similar contributions in the areas of equitable tax systems and the pricing of public services.

The announcement of The Royal Swedish Academy of Sciences, which discusses these other contributions and contains a bibliography of some of Professor Vickrey's notable publications can be found on the Internet at "http://www.nobel.se/".

PARTING SHOTS

"At last I have my bully pulpit," Vickrey is quoted in *The New York Times Magazine* (December 29, 1996, p. 16). The award gave Vickrey the opportunity to publicly expound on his somewhat controversial ideas on the U.S. economy and a balanced budget. Vickrey's ideas to increase the federal budget deficit to reduce unemployment caused Newt Gingrich to label him a socialist (Reuter Information Service, October 11, 1996, 3:01 PM). While he was not around long enough to use this "bully pulpit" personally, several of his writings have been published and disseminated after his death. Several reports which Vickrey submitted prior to his death regarding topics such as the U. S. corporate tax system, state and local taxation and unemployment have been published in Tax Notes Today (*Tax Analysts*, November 4, 1996).

Another work "Fifteen Fatal Fallacies of Financial Fundamentalism: A Disquisition of Demand Side Economics," is being disseminated through the Internet [http://www.columbia.edu/cu/economics] and was partially abstracted in *The New York Times Magazine* (December 29, 1996, p. 16). This document presents Vickrey's analysis of the impacts of deficits and balanced budgets on unemployment and inflation. According to Vickrey, a stable unemployment rate of 5 to 6% is detrimental in terms of domestic production, poverty, and crime, among other issues. Vickrey points out that an overall rate at this level results in a much higher unemployment rate among disadvantaged groups. This essay will review a few of the more interesting fallacies, the remainder of which can be examined on the Internet.

Fallacy 1. Deficits are considered to represent sinful profligate spending at the expense of future generations who will be left with a smaller endowment of invested capital.

Vickrey asserts that deficit spending increases the disposable income of individuals which when expended on goods and services enables producers to invest in additional capacity. Vickrey makes a good point that if corporations were not permitted to borrow we would have "no corporate bonds, no mortgages, no bank loans and many fewer automobiles, telephones, and houses."

Fallacy 6. It is thought necessary to keep unemployment at a "non-inflation-accelerating" level (NIARU) in the range of 4% to 6% if inflation is to be kept from increasing unacceptably.

Vickrey considers this level of unemployment "intolerable" since the portion of those unemployed is disproportionately those in disadvantaged groups. Vickrey argues a much lower unemployment rate is attainable without serious inflation problems.

Fallacy 11. It is claimed that exemption of capital gains from income tax will promote investment and growth.

Vickrey argues that differential treatment of different types of income is not appropriate and can result in undesirable consequences. His proposals would instead reduce or eliminate the corporate level tax and assess the individual tax on a cumulative basis.

Some of Vikrey's ideas are controversial and go against conventional wisdom. However, in discussing Vickrey's 1969 analysis of road congestion The Royal Swedish Academy of Sciences notes, "As usual, Vickrey was ahead of his time. His model was rediscovered by road engineers and economists in the early 1980s."

DOTTING THE "I"s IN ACCOUNTANCY

Gary John Previts

This volume contains papers and studies which address the state of the accountancy profession, litigation, standard setting, and insider trading.

Considering Denny Beresford's remarks causes one to recognize that one of the "I"s of Accountancy is the

"I"nternational

aspect of setting standards for financial accounting and reporting.

Jim Burton's review of the special GAO report on the accounting profession refers to the issues and relative significance of auditor

"I"ndependence

and in his paper on misappropriation theory Mark Segal touches upon the matter of

"I"nsider "I"nformation....

Research in Accounting Regulation, Volume 11, pages 257-259.

ISBN: 0-7623-0168-6

These are a few of the "I"s in Accountancy that continue to require attention and which seem to defy resolution in any sense of that word.

The "I"nternational issue as it relates to Standards is now being weighed carefully by the Securities and Exchange Commission. If the SEC accepts and endorses the standards of the IASC will US companies feel they are no longer obliged to follow US GAAP as set by the FASB? What are the views of the financial analyst community with regard to the issue of who shall be recognized as the agency to set standards? How will enforcement be made effective?

And while it appears that both the preparer and auditor community are supportive, the user/analyst community has been less transparent and, as has been consistent with the past, difficult to assess with regard to a single position. Moving forward without clear expressions from the user's of financial information seems inconsistent with the norms espoused in contemporary disclosure models. Or could it be that there are sufficient other sources of information that the analysts are indifferent? Is silence to be taken as consent, or indifference?

"I"ndependence

is another "I" and is once again a watchword in profession. A special working group of the AICPA, chaired by Vincent O'Reilly, a senior partner of Coopers & Lybrand, has worked during the past two years to identify principles which can be stated so as to guide auditors in the coming expanded scope of service environment. Made even more important, if that is possible, by the study of the Public Oversight Board's Kirk panel in 1994 and that group's identification of the audit committee's role and charter as key factors in audit effectiveness. Independent auditor services are a declining percent of the total service base of the entire profession, not just large firms. The O'Reilly SEC Practice Section Task Force on Auditors' Independence and Non-Audit Services has worked to provide guidance on managing dependencies by identifying or reaffirming what it terms "underlying principles" which include recognizing that, for example, working in the equivalent capacity of management is not permissible, and assuming the role of a promoter or advocate of investment in a client is not permissible. The groups work is not complete as of this writing, and there are, as in any such important endeavor, critics who will find fault with what the group may finally propose. What is perhaps most important in our system and tradition of professional self-responsibility and self-determination, is that the profession has taken action and not limited itself to "reaction."

Less conspicuous among the "I"s in Accountancy is the issue of

"I"nsider "I"nformation

as it relates to insider trading and the decision of the United States Supreme Court to review the Eighth Circuit's decision of the O'Hagan case which involved an attorney from Minnesota who illegally used money from two client accounts. O'Hagan purchased large amounts of another client' stock and short term options prior to that client's acquisition.

O'Hagan was convicted of "theft by temporary control" and was imprisoned for a time. He also faced conviction in federal court for trading on the then-secret takeover plans. But this conviction was reversed on appeal, and now raises the issue of what manner of acquiring and type of non public information is within and without the law. In December the SEC asked the Supreme Court to consider the case and now the Court has decided to do so. The legal issue is whether or not O'Hagan "acted in connection with" the purchase or sale of a security for Section 10[b] purposes. How the Supreme Court decides to establish the proper construction of the "in connection with" clause in the context of misappropriation of information will likely affect how lower courts apply the clause in other Section 10[b] cases.

So we await the "dotting" of these "I"s in the practice of Accountancy...with an awareness that they will not long remain...since each generation of accountants finds it necessary in the changing environment of its practice to revisit these and many other matters.